RAYMOND L. DITMARS

His Exciting Career with
Reptiles, Animals and Insects

By L. N. WOOD

JULIAN MESSNER, INC.

NEW YORK

PUBLISHED BY JULIAN MESSNER, INC.

8 WEST 40TH STREET

ELEVENTH PRINTING, 1960

Jacket design by Helene Carter

ONE

NOBODY KNOWS QUITE when Ray Ditmars took a fancy to reptiles and all living creatures, but it was early in his life. He was not much more than eight when he entered the living room of his Grandmother Knaus's big house in Hartford, one day, clearly pleased and with bulging pockets.

"What *has* he in his pockets?" the old lady demanded of nobody in particular, and apprehensively tucked her feet into her chair. It was a question frequently asked, and it had a variety of answers, all of them disquieting to his elders.

"Nothing, Grandmother, just some little toads." Ray quickly unloaded them onto the floor. "I thought they'd like it here. This nice green carpet is so like grass."

"Never mind *what* they like—get your little playmates out of my parlor!" Grandmother commanded, rocking excitedly.

It was not the first time, and it was far, far from the last, that family protests interfered with his simple pleasures.

Wondering, helplessly, where Ray got his strange taste in pets, each of his parents could say, and very likely did, "He certainly didn't get it from *my* side of the family!" There is no record to suggest that either the Ditmars or the Knaus family had any more traffic with reptilians than they could help.

The first Van Ditmarsen (as the name was in its original form) reached America from Holland in time to obtain one of the early land grants on Long Island. His descendants became people of substance and property. By the time of the Revolution the name had contracted to Ditmars, and the patrimony had expanded to make young Johannes, head of the family,

3

one of the wealthiest men on the island. Himself a Whig, he suffered from the embarrassment of having a Tory for a guardian, so was involved in difficulties with both sides. He remained loyal to the Revolutionary cause, however, even when, according to tradition, zealous but ill-informed patriots tried to burn his barn. He fought as a militiaman and, when his poor health prevented further soldiering, contributed much money and food to the American troops. In the more peaceful times that followed, he married and had children, and they in turn had children; and, in multiplying, the family scattered, so that in the course of generations the various branches lost track of each other.

Our next concern is with John Van Harlingen Ditmars, eventually the grandfather of Raymond, who, toward the second quarter of the last century, settled on a plantation near Pensacola. There he farmed, and established three factories, one to make coaches, another mattresses, and the third those tall white columns with which prosperous planters of the pre-Civil War South enhanced the dignity of their mansions.

The labor of slaves was the only kind readily obtainable in the South of those days, but John Ditmars could not reconcile himself to the institution of slavery. Refusing to own slaves himself, he hired them from near-by owners, selecting ones whose masters had a reputation for harshness, taking entire families—parents, children and old folk—to spare them the pain of separation, and treating them with unusual care and kindness.

John Ditmars was prosperous and happy. Then the Civil War intervened to destroy beyond any hope of repair the pattern of his pleasant life.

Like many of his classmates, his oldest son, John Van Harlingen, Jr., in his final year at Oglethorpe University in Georgia, immediately joined the Confederate Army. The two younger boys went with the Union troops. The elder Ditmars, sadly torn, remained faithful to the adopted state which had

4

given him wealth and success; he joined the Rebels. The choice cost him his fortune.

The war was a four years' horror, but to John, Jr., a young man of romantic disposition, it was not without compensations. He went through much of it with the Army of Northern Virginia, and contracted an abiding case of hero-worship for Robert E. Lee, the Confederacy's greatest man.

"When I have a son," he promised himself, "I'm going to name him for General Lee."

There was not only the rather rarefied satisfaction of being near Lee, but there were less austere ones, too. The entertainments behind the lines, though poorly victualed, were gay; and the girls smiled kindly on the slender, fair, blue-eyed young soldier. To the tune of *The Railroad Truck Step, The Geranium Waltz, The Flirt Polka,* he danced with them most of the night, and dreamed of them the rest of it. He lost his heart repeatedly, and always recovered it with reasonable promptness. When he finally lost it for good, it was, remarkably, to a Yankee girl.

But before that happened, he had to get through with the war. Wounded at Gettysburg and captured, he spent a few months in a Baltimore prison, then was exchanged. Rejoining the Confederate Army, he fought through the last desperate phase of the war, and was, ironically, captured again on April 9, 1865, the very day of Lee's surrender, near Appomattox Court House. After two months of suffering and illness as a prisoner at City Point, he was released to visit some of his father's family in Philadelphia.

It was while he was with his relatives that he met Mary Knaus, a pretty Hartford girl, slim, with dark eyes and black hair, who was paying a timely visit to Philadelphia cousins. John fell in love again, this time for keeps.

The Knaus family, Pennsylvanians, with a good lacing of Puritan and Quaker blood, were as long established in this country as the Ditmars. Business had taken Mary's father,

5

Samuel, from his own state to Hartford, where he was inspector of firearms at the Colt arms factory. Mary was immediately taken with the handsome young southerner whose resilience of spirit had survived wounds, illness and a lost cause. When he wrote her a poem, she found herself hoping that he was expressing something more than conventional gallantry. She need not have worried.

When the war was well over, John Ditmars, like thousands of other young southerners, had to decide what to do with his life. Looking around, he saw little of promise in the general ruin; and the girl he loved was in Hartford. So he went north. In Newark, where he was visiting some of the numerous Ditmars clan, he learned of a good opportunity in the furniture business, and settled there. Two years later, on May 29, 1867, John Ditmars and Mary Knaus were married in the South Congregational Church of Hartford.

Thus the Ditmars and the Knauses—with not a snake-lover on record among them—came together, and the stage was set for the appearance of Ray Ditmars.

Raymond Lee (the Lee for the venerated general) Ditmars was born on June 22, 1876, in Newark. His sister, Ella, who had preceded him into the world by a few years, had been born in the boardinghouse where her parents lived then. In the years between her birth and Ray's, John Ditmars had prospered, and he now owned his own home on High Street. A two-story frame house with a big attic, it stood on a high embankment at an intersection, surrounded by a wide lawn and covered with grapevines that clambered up its walls on trellises.

It was there that Ray spent the first four or five years of his life, years of which, naturally, he retained only scattered impressions. He could remember being trotted on his father's knee to the tune of *Dixie;* seeing his mother take his father's old gray uniform out of the trunk in the attic and brush it, to make sure the moths hadn't got into it; hearing John Ditmars tell glowing tales of the invincible Stonewall, the sublime Lee.

In the big yard Ella played feminine games with little girls her own age; Ray amused himself, often grubbily, at the foot of one of the big trees or in the pleasing privacy of a clump of bushes. It was useless for his mother and sister to admonish him to keep clean; he was already fascinated by the little creatures that lived in and close to the earth.

He watched the industrious ants toss up their tiny pyramids. He caught grasshoppers and was amazed—the first time—at their "tobacco juice." Toads, caterpillars and the occasional box turtles in the low bushes at the back of the yard delighted him.

It was about this time that his mother, the victim of one or two horrid surprises, began turning out Ray's pockets when she put him to bed, disposing with little exclamations of disgust of the animal life she found in them. It was about this time, too, that the question he was to hear for so many years gained currency:

"What *has* he in his pockets?"

TWO

WHEN RAY WAS about six, his family moved to New York. Manhattan, in the early eighteen-eighties, had a population of well over a million. Its houses, packed tightly side by side, stood flush with the pavements. There were no lawns, and city urchins played their games, not under shade trees and beside flower and vegetable gardens, but in the streets, and scrambled impudently, at the last possible moment, from the path of passing wagons and carriages.

There were the familiar horsecars in the streets, of course, but there was also a means of transportation which was new and startling to Ray. This was the "elevated," a train that ran on tracks supported high in the air by strong pillars, and showered cinders and hot ashes from its coal-fed engine over unwary earth-crawlers. Most of the streets in this astonishing city were still lighted with gas; but for a few prophetic blocks Broadway, anticipating its title of "The Great White Way," was dazzlingly illuminated by electric lights.

The Ditmars, however, lived away from this bustle, in a four-story apartment house on Pleasant Avenue, a quiet, tree-lined street in Harlem. From its windows they could look out on the East River, which, Ray was puzzled to hear, was not a river at all; and on Randall's Island, with its House of Refuge and other city institutions standing among the trees.

As Ray got older, John Ditmars would sometimes take his children on jaunts around the city. They would go to Coney Island, with its wonderful beach and carnival atmosphere; or to the Battery, where, through Castle Clinton, hundreds of thousands of European immigrants poured yearly into the promised land. They admired the famous buildings—the City

Hall, the Grand Central Station, St. Patrick's Cathedral; marveled at the almost completed Brooklyn Bridge, the longest suspension bridge ever built up to that time; and stared with a sort of incredulous respect at the huge forearm of the Statue of Liberty, on view in Madison Square.

What Ray liked best, however, was to go to Central Park, that extraordinary landscape achievement devised by the genius of Frederick Law Olmsted. With his mother or Ella or some like-minded school friend, he would hurry over to the park in the afternoons as soon as school was out to visit the menagerie or play in the woods. In the almost undisturbed wildness of its northern end, Ray could imagine himself an Indian scout, a hunter, or a soldier of the War of 1812, of which a relic, the old blockhouse, crowned the rough hill that was the topmost point in the park.

He was a curious kind of hunter, however, for a young boy: he was less concerned with imaginary exploits involving dangerous wild beasts than with observing beetles, butterflies, frogs, garter snakes, turtles, all the various forms of timid life which actually abounded right at hand, and which a less observing boy would have dismissed contemptuously as too tame.

Lying flat on the ground, Ray would happily watch an ant hill; or he would prowl along the edges of the north lake catching tadpoles and frogs, popping them into a can to examine at leisure at home. He explored the hillsides sloping up to the little blockhouse in all seasons, finding cocoons, garter snakes sheltered in rocky ledges, beetles, June bugs, crickets. When he got home he would go to his room and eagerly examine his finds, or, halfheartedly, open his schoolbooks and start his lessons.

His mother, looking him over, decided that perhaps she had something to worry about.

"He's so thin, John, and such a quiet boy," she said one evening after he had gone to his room to puzzle his head vainly over an arithmetic assignment. She hitched her rocking chair nearer to the gas lamp to get better light on her embroidery. "Half the time I can't tell whether he's in the house or out of it."

"Except at mealtime," John Ditmars reminded her. "He's brisk enough then."

"Or until you go into the bathroom and find some kind of *thing* scrambling around in the tub," Ella added plaintively.

"I don't think you need worry, Mary," John said reassuringly. "He's a skinny youngster because he's growing fast; and his hobby may be queer, but it's innocent and healthful. And you may have noticed," he added, "that he's got a normally well-developed capacity for mischief."

"Yes, he has," Mary said, brightening momentarily. Then she added severely, "Sometimes I simply don't know what to say to him."

"Oh, that Quaker sternness!" her husband twitted her. "Just because he shook a little girl until her pigtails rattled, and gave her a caterpillar. It was simply a demonstration of affection—he told me so himself. It was his *best* caterpillar."

In spite of herself, Mary's severity dissolved into a smile. "I hope his future wife will appreciate demonstrations like that," she remarked.

John Ditmars got to his feet and knocked out his pipe, moving a little stiffly on his wounded leg. He took down his fiddle and began to tune it.

"A little music?" he suggested, drawing the bow across the strings.

Mary Ditmars sat down at the piano, drawing her gray skirt (she loved gray and usually wore some shade of it) toward her to make room for Ella. In a few minutes the little group was absorbed in the music, too absorbed at first to notice Ray at the door, his blond hair all endwise from mathematical effort. He stood there a moment watching the pleasant domestic scene. His parents were smiling as they played, Ella singing earnestly—it looked worth a chance. He entered the room unobtrusively and slipped onto the piano bench on his mother's other side. She welcomed him with a little nod, signaling him to turn the page. He settled down happily. This was much nicer than working over those old lessons.

No one could pretend that Ray was a good student. At the public school he attended for a while he made such erratic progress that his parents were depressed. Maybe, they thought, he would do better at a private school. When he was about twelve, they selected Miss Ransom's School for Boys, on West One Hundred and Twenty-sixth Street. It was a new school, a better school, but, so far as Ray was concerned, it was still school. He cared much more for the butterfly collection he was starting than for English grammar; and far more for the friendly horses in Quinn's livery stable on One Hundred and Twenty-fifth Street than for his history lesson. His preference was quite clear. Why spend an afternoon over columns of balky figures when he could visit the fire house at One Hundred and Nineteenth Street and reverently examine the beautiful engine, pet the handsome dapple-grays that whirled it clamoring through the streets, and hobnob with Jake, the company's Dalmatian mascot?

Ray thought that the best thing about school was vacation time, and the next best thing to that, the lunch hour. It was a lunch-hour episode that relieved him, finally, of Miss Ransom's educational guidance.

The baseball game in the lot beside the Ransom School was a regular lunch-time occurrence in good weather. On this day, the pitch came straight for the plate, and Ray was ready for it. He swung hard. Ball and bat met squarely, with a solidly satisfying *sock*. Ray dropped the bat and sprinted. His team uttered yells of encouragement, yells that suddenly froze and died. The ball was heading straight for one of the school building's wide glass windows. No last-minute miracle intervened, either. The shivering jingle of smashed glass paused for a moment in the air, then dropped into complete quiet. The boys looked at one another apprehensively.

The principal, severe behind a tall pompadour and a starched shirtwaist, appeared at the broken window and surveyed them through it. Ray raised his hand and stepped forward.

So far as Miss Ransom was concerned, it was The Last Straw. He was a nice boy, he wasn't stupid; but he would *not* work. For almost two years he had been drawing pictures of turtles and butterflies in study hours; now he had begun smashing windows in lunch hours. She acquainted Mr. Ditmars with her views, and he, poor man, had to look around for another school for his son. It was really rather discouraging.

"We'll see how you get on at a military academy, Ray," he said, almost threateningly.

"With uniforms and a band?" Ray exclaimed happily. "Oh, Pop!"

THREE

THE BARNARD MILITARY ACADEMY, lodged in a building ornamented with two wise owls on West One Hundred and
Twenty-sixth Street, was operated by Mr. William Livingston
Hazen. About a hundred and thirty boys, most of them from
upper Manhattan, attended it. Ray liked his new school: there
were military drill, gymnastics, a brass band and uniforms.

The uniform, he decided as he admired himself in front of
his mother's long glass, was quite a smart-looking affair. It
consisted of a gray jacket, frogged and brass-buttoned, gray
pants and a long blue overcoat and cape. It was agreeably
reminiscent of West Point. Altogether, he thought compla-
cently, there was something about a soldier.

But even a uniform and the hope of rising above his lowly
rank of corporal could not make Ray a student. Mr. Hazen
could understand his being lazy but what he couldn't understand was Ray's seeming stupidity, because the boy *wasn't*
stupid. He was intelligent; he had an inquiring, interested
mind. Only it plainly wasn't interested in mathematics. Mr.
Hazen scowled at the sheet of figures. It was Ray's arithmetic
homework, and the schoolmaster had already spent some
minutes vainly trying to see how Ray could have figured
correctly clear to the end, and then reached a completely
improbable answer.

"Raymond," he said finally, "come up here, please."

Ray left his seat, uncomfortably aware of everyone in the
room watching his lonely progress to the headmaster's desk.

"Yes, sir?"

"Let's go through this problem, Raymond. Do each step

13

of it aloud. I want to see how in the world you got this answer."

Ray began to figure in an embarrassed mumble. Mr. Hazen listened, nodded occasionally, and his frown of bewilderment got deeper and deeper. Reaching the end at last, Ray stopped and looked uncomfortably at the master's face.

"But that's the right answer," Mr. Hazen said blankly.

Ray looked blank, too. "Is it really, sir?"

"Yes, really." Mr. Hazen's tone was dry. "Why didn't you get it the first time? Obviously there's nothing you don't understand about the problem."

"It just didn't look right, sir. It looked too small, so I added a bit on to it."

"At random?" demanded the incredulous schoolmaster.

"Well—ah, I guess so," Ray admitted.

"Don't do it again." Mr. Hazen felt the inadequacy of this command, but he was quite unable, for the moment, to think of anything else to say.

When he realized that his intuitions served no useful purpose in mathematical calculation, Ray began to do better in his arithmetic. His other lessons had improved considerably under the direction of Mr. Hazen and his well-selected staff, who could make even grammar and Latin interesting. Composition and history were subjects he enjoyed and he excelled in them. Now there were days when he actually liked school.

The day he liked it best, however—all his new enjoyment of it notwithstanding—was the day it caught fire.

The big fire engine with its brass-banded boiler and black stack, that he had so often and so reverently admired on his visits to the fire house, came clanging through the streets at a fast gallop, the gray horses snorting excitedly and the firemen clinging tensely to it. They sprang off almost before it stopped, and in no time at all had the hose in action. The boys who were still in the building pitched everything loose they could lay hands on out the windows—books, erasers, chairs—then retreated in good order to the street. There they collected the salvage, stacked it carefully out of the way, and crowded around to enjoy the fire. Ray was thrilled. There was nothing he liked better than a good fire, and this one was a dandy.

What a wonderful life, being a fireman, he thought. You could tend that beautiful engine and the splendid horses every day of your life, and you could go to *all* the fires—not just the ones that happened after school hours—riding proudly and dangerously on the speeding engine. Being a fireman meant you were brave, you took danger lightly, you had an exciting life.

"Maybe someday I'll be a fireman myself," he reflected.

"Hello, Ray," a young fireman friend called, seeing him in the crowd around the engine. "Looks like you'd get a holiday for a while."

Ray grinned. "Maybe I'll be over to see you tomorrow," he answered.

What a wonderful prospect! In the morning he'd go to the fire house and chat with the boys about the school fire. He'd drop in at Quinn's livery stable, too. Then, if his mother would fix him a couple of sandwiches, he could go to the park and have a picnic on the blockhouse hill and look over the butterfly situation. And in the evening there wouldn't be any lessons to do! Not only a fire, but a holiday too!

Mr. Hazen, with a nonchalance that seemed practically criminal to Ray, had disappeared before the fire was under control, but now he was back. He clapped his hands sharply to get the attention of his pupils.

"Company, fall in!" he ordered.

They formed ranks in the street and stood at attention, every face struggling, with no particular success, to present a grave expression suitable to the sad destruction of the school building.

"The Reverend Mr. Jenks," Mr. Hazen announced, "has been kind enough to offer us the use of the parish house of his church until our building is again ready for use. This makes it possible for us to miss not even one day of school." He glanced slowly, expressionlessly, up and down the thunderstruck ranks. "And I know how you will all appreciate it. This afternoon we will make the parish house ready, and school will meet there tomorrow morning at the usual hour. Company dismissed."

It was one of the most unpleasant shocks of Raymond Ditmars' whole life.

It was during the summer of 1888, as nearly as Ray could remember afterward, that it happened, the insignificant occurrence that helped determine the course of his life. It was the kind of thing that might, for as long as the brief memory lasted, distinguish one summer day from the vacation days before and after it in the mind of the usual twelve-year-old boy, but on Ray it had a lasting effect. It happened in the salt marsh near Gravesend Bay not far from Brooklyn's rural outskirts where the Ditmars family were spending the summer.

Wandering through the marsh one day, Ray noticed a spot where the cattails had toppled over to form a sort of tangled mat. Pushing through the waist-high growth, he saw two garter snakes slip from it into the safety of the surrounding cattails. It was not the first time he had seen a snake, but these slender little creatures, that, with flowing grace, glided beyond the range of his intrusion, filled him with a sudden curiosity and wonder.

The following day he was back again at the matted place in the marsh, and so were the snakes. He looked at them for a long time, getting cramped in his effort to make no noise that would alarm them. He came again the next day, and the next, until his vigil developed into a routine. It seemed to him, finally, that they must have become used to him, for they no longer glided away when he was there. It occurred to him that the harmless reptiles would make interesting pets.

16

He made the suggestion, not without misgivings, to his mother. She was even more horrified than he had feared.

"Snakes!" she almost shrieked. "Ray, are you out of your mind?"

"But, Mama, they're perfectly harmless."

"Snakes, ugh!" she shuddered, not bothering to answer that protest, to which, Ray thought, no good answer existed.

He felt a certain resentment, not so much on his own account, but on behalf of the snakes. They were pretty, inoffensive little things; why should they be hated, sight unseen?

"Look, Mama," he tried to explain, "they can't hurt anybody. I'd make a cage for them, anyway, so they couldn't get out. You'd like them if you saw them; I know you would. They're so glossy and have such pretty markings, and they move so smoothly, almost pour along, and it's so curious the way they flicker their tongues."

"Raymond," his mother gasped imploringly.

"Raymond!" his father said quietly. "That's enough. You can't have snakes for pets. Your Mama doesn't like them. And neither," he finished with emphasis, "do I."

"Where in the world did the boy get such an idea?" he wondered out loud, as the door closed on his disappointed son.

"What's wrong with snakes?" Ray grumbled to himself, on the other side of the door. "What's *wrong* with them? You'd think I'd asked to keep a couple of man-eating tigers, the way they acted."

He set off to view his snakes, and forgot his disappointment in plotting a campaign to overcome, if not his parents' aversion to snakes, at least their refusal to let him keep some. He had his work cut out for him.

Vacationing on Long Island was not the usual custom of the Ditmars family. In the summer, while John Ditmars stayed in the city, attending to his prosperous business, Ray escorted his mother and Ella—so he liked to think—to Hartford, where

17

they spent the summer visiting Grandmother and Grandfather Knaus, or his uncles, John and Jacob Knaus.

Ray enjoyed his Hartford summers. Samuel Knaus, inspector of fire arms at the Colt factory, often took his grandson to the proving grounds, and let him handle and fire the lighter weapons, explaining their workings to him.

Even when the weather was bad Ray had a good time. During heavy storms, when lightning split the leaden sky, and the thunder rolled and crashed like a thousand drums, and rain whipped down in wind-driven torrents, he would stand at the window and watch the display with a kind of inner excitement that left him a little depressed as it receded. When there was simply rain, nothing spectacular or thrilling to watch, he would twist himself comfortably into a big chair in the green-carpeted parlor—the same parlor into which he had some years before introduced his toads—and read. He liked best stories of exploration and adventure, those with plenty of lore about volcanoes, wild animals and tropical countries. Paul du Chaillu, whose remarkable account of his own experiences in *Explorations and Adventures in Equatorial Africa* had been first ridiculed and distrusted, later fully confirmed, was one of his favorite writers. A remark du Chaillu made in one of his books stuck in Ray's mind:

"The abundant results of the sale of my *Adventures in Equatorial Africa*," the explorer had written, "and the proceeds arising from the disposal of my gorillas, and my collection of beasts, birds, insects, and shells, alone enabled me to undertake this new expedition, for not one dollar has ever been given by any scientific society to help me in my travels or explorations; but I was very happy in expending a part of my means in the interest of science and for the enlargement of our knowledge of unknown countries."

That, it seemed to Ray, was precisely the right spirit for a scientific explorer. The only thing wrong with the books of the

18

intrepid "Chally," he thought, was the lamentable scarcity of snakes. There were lots of gorillas, pygmies, man-eating ants and other tropical wonders, but not enough snakes. Snakes were by now Ray's paramount interest. He thought they were fascinating, and he wanted other people to appreciate them, too. It was the beginning of a lifelong crusade.

Sometimes he brought them home with him and there were occasional "incidents" when he frightened Grandmother.

"But Grandmother," he would protest, "what harm can a nonpoisonous snake do?"

"Snakes, ugh!" Grandmother repeated his mother's unspecified but unanswerable complaint. "Anyway, they're no earthly use."

"They're not only pretty and interesting, but they're *very* useful," he insisted. "They eat mice and rats that destroy grain and young poultry."

"Those slimy things!" Grandmother abandoned the utility angle to enlarge on her prejudice.

"They are *not* slimy," Ray corrected her firmly. "They're dry to the touch."

"You don't mean to say you *touch* them?"

"How can I get a good look at them unless I handle them? Of course I do."

"Ray! Someday you'll get hold of something poisonous, and you'll get bitten. John and Mary oughtn't to allow this nonsense another minute!"

Ray smiled. "They don't like it much, but they know I won't get hurt. The only poisonous snakes in this part of the country are rattlers and copperheads, and they're easy to recognize. I've seen some handsome rattlers around here," he added.

His grandmother noted with uneasiness the speculative look that came into the light blue eyes when he spoke of rattlers.

19

"You wouldn't want to catch one of *those* frightful things, would you, Ray?"

"Well," he said, and let the answer dangle. There was nothing on earth he wanted so much. What a row there'd be if he mentioned it, though! Well, maybe next summer, or the one after. . . .

FOUR

RAY LOVED ENGINES, both fire and locomotive. As soon as the new catalogues were published by the fire-engine manufacturers, the Chief would give Ray the old ones. He would study them with the same interest that he devoted to "Chally's" African adventures.

In school one day Mr. Hazen, correcting papers on his platform at the front of the room, noticed Ray's deep concentration. He supposed that it was schoolwork that was responsible for his absorption. Leaving his platform, the master strolled down the aisle, to see what Ray was working on so hard, a word of encouragement ready for utterance on his tongue.

Suddenly realizing his approach, Ray looked up, surprise and guilt on his face, and moved to cover his paper with his arms.

"Give it to me, Raymond," Mr. Hazen ordered.

Mr. Hazen never had to speak twice. Ray handed him the paper. The schoolmaster glanced at it quickly.

"You may return for Detention Class today, Raymond." Attendance at Detention Class was the usual punishment for unpreparedness and minor misdeeds.

"Yes, sir," Ray agreed meekly.

Back at his desk, Mr. Hazen looked at the drawing more closely, while Ray watched him anxiously out of the corner of his eye. It was a picture of a locomotive, drawn in minute, accurate detail and carefully shaded. The schoolmaster looked at it reflectively for a full minute, then laid it in his drawer. Ray let out the breath he had been holding. At least Mr. Hazen wasn't going to destroy it—it had been half an afternoon's work!

Ray meant to ask for its return but couldn't find an appropriate time, and eventually forgot it. Forty years later, he received a note from his old schoolmaster.

"Dear Raymond," Mr. Hazen had written, "in looking through some old papers recently, I came across this, and thought you might like to have it. I thought it an excellent drawing at the time, and I still do."

Enclosed was the sketch of the locomotive that had captured his fourteen-year-old fancy.

Ray kept quiet about another hobby he was developing. His father was already uneasy about the dispersal of his interests—butterflies and bugs, snakes and engines—so there was no point to disturbing him with the news that he thought he was becoming a weather fan.

He was fourteen or fifteen when the idea came to him of observing the weather—seriously, so as to be able to predict and understand it. He was coming home from school at the time, walking down Seventh Avenue, and he noticed that, although the morning had been clear, there was now a film of cloud, shot through with faint streaks of gray, obscuring the sun. The streaks seemed to be drawn out of the southwest, and the edge of the advancing cloud sheet was low against the northwestern horizon.

He had noticed that kind of hazy, streaked cloud before. As he remembered, when it approached from the southwest in the winter, northeast wind and snow usually followed. He didn't know the name of the cloud or the storm tracks, but he recognized them and knew that they meant something.

"Snow before morning," he predicted to himself.

Arriving home, he hurried up to his room and looked out at the weather vane on Quinn's livery stable. The gilded horse atop the flagpole was still pointing northwest. He sat down to do his homework, looking up every once in a while to keep track of the weather vane. By the time darkness shut down it had moved around toward the north.

At dinner that night Ray was preoccupied and when the meal was finished he hurried over to the stable. What was the weather vane doing now? he kept wondering. Had it veered back to the clear weather point of northwest, as he had sometimes seen it do, or had his prediction been right? A strengthening wind whirled the dust of the streets in his face, and, deflected by the walls of buildings, sprang at him from all angles.

Arriving at the stable, he stared upward. The gilded horse was pointing directly into the northeast.

When he awoke next morning, he lay in bed listening. The sounds from the street, the rattle of wagon wheels, footfalls, the clop-clop of horses' hoofs, all had a curious character—a muffled quality. He jumped out of bed and went to the window, to look out on a world transfigured by falling snow.

"I have to learn more about this," he thought as he scrambled into his clothes. "Maybe I can find out at the museum."

The American Museum of Natural History had been founded some twenty years earlier to satisfy just such curiosity as Ray's. Through its exhibits, library and lectures, it advanced the knowledge of the natural sciences among all who had the interest to learn. The museum stood on the west side of Central Park at Seventy-seventh Street, and was open every day, free to all comers.

Ray had spent many a rainy Saturday afternoon roaming through its halls, looking at the forestry exhibit, gaping at the great model of a sulphur-bottom whale suspended from the ceiling, and raptly studying the exhibits of stuffed and pickled reptiles. This omniscient institution had, he knew, the answer to almost any natural history question you could ask, so it did not surprise him to find that two lectures on the weather were to be given there soon.

23

The first one had the somewhat untempting title of "Cloud Formations and Their Significance"; but it sounded wonderful to Ray. It was just what he wanted to know. He sat, strictly attentive, while the elderly speaker, a dry, gray man who looked as though he had long been preserved from the weather under a bell jar, talked to the sparse audience.

The particular kind of cloud he had seen, Ray learned, was called a cirrus. When it had the appearance of a hazy veil, it was called a cirro-nebulus; and a cirro-nebulus was an ominous thing, meaning the approach of a severe storm, or even a cyclone. A magic lantern, set up in the back of the room, projected images of cloud formations on the screen one after another, while the speaker explained them and Ray earnestly scribbled notes until his hand felt as stiff as the hard auditorium seat.

He could hardly wait for the second lecture, "Storm Tracks in the Western Hemisphere," scheduled for the next week. He went to school, visited the fire house, played the piano, much as usual, and, to the detriment of his studies, hung out the window ogling the weather vane on the livery stable and scanning the sky. When the day came, he was almost the first one in the auditorium.

The second lecture seemed even more interesting to Ray, because the speaker told how the weather came into being.

As he explained it, the weather was produced by a series of great inverted waves of atmospheric pressure, and the valleys between them. The crests of these waves pointed toward the earth from above, and during most of each year they rolled across the United States like the swells of an enormous sea, moving from west to east. The atmospheric waves, perhaps a thousand miles in breadth, with the valleys between equally wide, proceeded majestically, invisibly, some thousand miles a day; and their passage was indicated by high pressure areas as the crest rolled along, low pressure or storm areas as the atmospheric valleys passed overhead.

24

"By observing the barometer in his home," the lecturer explained blandly, "with a diligent and critical interest, the amateur weather-watcher can learn to anticipate the approach of high and low areas."

"Barometer?" the amateur weather-watcher who had only Quinn's gilded horse for a guide said to himself. "I'll have to get hold of one some way or other."

After the lecture, the speaker gathered up his notes and started for the door. Ray, trotting to keep up with his long stride, was at his heels.

"I attended your first lecture, sir," he panted.

"Indeed? You are interested in the weather, young man?"

"Yes, sir!"

The lecturer regarded him with kindly interest. "If you're really interested, the thing for you to do is to study the points of cirrus clouds in winter. In summer they don't usually mean much—just drifts off thunderheads and unassociated with a storm sheet."

Ray had an important question. "Are there any small barometers?" he asked hopefully.

"A fair aneroid will cost you about twenty-five dollars. And you ought to subscribe to the *Monthly Weather Review*, too."

Dashed, Ray watched him put on his hat, and helped him into his coat. Twenty-five dollars! It might as well be twenty-five thousand. It would take him a lifetime to save that much out of his thirty-five cents a day lunch money.

As he walked slowly home up the arc-lit avenue, past the silent darkness of the park, he speculated on how to get a barometer. Perhaps his father would give him one for Christmas if he asked for it, and then his mother might subscribe to the *Monthly Weather Review* for him. For a moment, it looked like a good solution, then he reluctantly dismissed it. He knew too well how John Ditmars felt about his varied interests.

FIVE

In 1889 the Ditmars family left Pleasant Avenue and moved into an apartment hotel on Seventh Avenue near One Hundred and Sixteenth Street. So far as Ray was concerned, it was a step in the right direction. He had loved a good horse ever since he first began hanging around the fire house, and the wide, tree-lined street, flanked by vacant lots, a number of houses, and a few hotels, was one of the favorite avenues for the sporting young men of the city to exercise their horses. Better than that, though, the Seventh Avenue home was nearer the park, nearer the museum, and nearer the cars and ferries that got him to the fields and woods in upper Manhattan and the Bronx, and the wilderness of the Palisades on Saturdays and Sundays.

His parents, beginning to realize that their son was a confirmed nature-lover, were giving ground slowly. The first crumbling of their opposition came when he was about fifteen. They finally allowed him to keep a pair of garter snakes. Their permission had not been won, however, without a shrewd campaign. He had picked his time cannily.

The move to Seventh Avenue had, of course, been attended by all the commotion and turmoil usually associated with a major crisis. A more fundamental change, however, was Ella's no longer being with them. In a semi-joyous, semi-tearful (on Mary's part) atmosphere of good wishes, good advice, music and flowers, she had married James Rutherford Mathews and now had her own home.

In the midst of all these changes, while his parents were still attuned to novelties, Ray had pressed the cause of snakes for pets. There had been machinations, pleas, promises on his

26

part; warnings, threats, provisos on theirs. Finally he had wrung permission from his parents to keep two *small* garter snakes. He caught a pair of them on the Palisades, carried them home in a bag in his pocket, built them a neat wooden case with a finely screened front, and installed them in his room. He was walking on air. That was more than his parents were doing.

"Maybe when he has to feed them and take care of them all the time, he'll get snakes out of his system," John Ditmars remarked to his wife, without much conviction.

"You're sure they're harmless?" she insisted. Admitting a pair of reptiles to her well-run household did not greatly appeal to her, but to see Ray so happy went a long way to offset her misgivings.

"Absolutely. They're definitely not poisonous. Ray tells me, though, that even a nonvenomous snake can inflict a painful wound if it bites you, so it's only good sense to handle them gently."

Mary Ditmars sniffed. "You don't have to worry about *my* handling them gently, or any other way," she said.

As he grew older, Ray spent more of his time on the business of acquiring an education. In later years some of his classmates were even able to recall that he was studious. That his application to his work was not without success a certificate stating that "Cadet Raymond L. Ditmars has attained the first degree of excellence in scholarship for 1891 and 1892" still exists to testify. The school records show, too, that he won a prize for excellence in English composition.

What Ray enjoyed most in the way of physical training was gymnastics, which were taught by a severe German whose rigid discipline caused some of the boys to dislike him. He and Ray, however, were good friends, and the instructor was almost as proud and pleased as the pupil on the day that Ray was awarded a gold medal for his work in the gymnasium.

Ray's favorite diversion when he was about fifteen, however, was an organization which he had founded, The Harlem
Zoological Society. Its members—Charlie Caldwell, the insect
member, Ward Crampton, the bird member, Emelius W.
Scherr, and the rest of them—all wore a small silver pin,
marked with HZS in blue letters, which, they hoped, aroused
a certain amount of longing and envy among their non-
zoological friends. Ray, the snake member, according to the
recollection of one of these elite, held most of the offices in
the society, and was the chief speaker. His virtual monopoly
of all the most interesting functions aroused no resentment
among his friends. Ray, they were all agreed, knew more
natural history than any of them, and the club had been his
idea.

The club met sometimes in a schoolroom—Mr. Hazen
thought it a fine idea and encouraged it—and sometimes in
one of the boys' homes. They would plan their field trips (on
which occasions Ray would offer authoritative weather pre-
dictions which proved, sometimes, embarrassingly inac-
curate), talk over their observations, and demonstrate their
finds. Insects, butterflies, turtles and Ray's precious garter
snakes would be passed carefully from hand to hand, while
the club's expert on whatever creature was under examination would discuss it.

They were all very serious about their investigations and
sometimes, with innocent boldness, took their problems to
the top men in their professions, Doctor Hornaday, the
eminent zoologist, and Doctor Beutenmüller, the insect specialist at the American Museum of Natural History. The two
scientists listened to them patiently, and with unfailing kindliness answered their questions.

One thrilling and unforgettable evening, Doctor Hornaday
was their guest speaker and gave them a talk on "The Buffalo."
Then he listened, with a courteous gravity that became
slightly glassy-eyed only toward the end, while fourteen-year-

old Ward Crampton read an hour-long paper on "The Habits of the Common Birds of New York."

It was an occasion of the deepest concern when Ray's garter snakes first shed their skins. Ray had learned from inquiries at the Central Park menagerie and the museum that, when a reptile is getting ready to shed, the cap-like covering of the eyes, which is also cast, becomes opaque, like a smoke-filled bubble, a week or ten days in advance. Then, a couple of days before the casting, the eyes clear because a watery film forms under the skin and loosens it. From then on the snake should have no difficulty. He should slide readily out of his old skin and emerge, iridescent, in a gleaming new one. If for any reason he is unable to cast, the watery film dries up and the old skin, hardening, tightens on him and may cause his death.

One of Ray's little reptiles had shed and lay, glossy and smug, under a small chunk of log with which Ray had equipped the case. The other snake had not succeeded in getting started, and, seeing that its skin looked dry and hard, Ray had several times gently dipped it in its shallow water pan in an effort to soften it.

After school a half dozen anxious members of the zoological society came to Ray's room to observe the progress of his specimen.

"I'm afraid he's stuck," Ray uttered the verdict after lifting his little serpent out and examining it. "If he could only get started, the rest ought to be easy. Maybe I can help him along a little." He rummaged a moment in his desk and came up with the flat-tipped tweezers he used in handling the dried insects and butterflies of his collection. Feeling around the snake's upper jaw with gentle fingers, he touched a gossamer-thin covering that seemed to be coming loose, and grasped it with the tweezers. He didn't know whether being artificially peeled would be harmful to the snake, but he didn't see how a little assistance could injure it.

Pulling gingerly on the fragile skin he found that it came away fairly easily. He drew it slowly over the head, disclosing the gleaming new skin beneath. With growing confidence, he repeated the operation on the lower jaw. Soon the garter snake was emerging from its skin, slipping out of it across Ray's lap as he carefully, almost holding his breath, pulled back the old skin. It was just an experiment. He had nothing but common sense and his little experience to guide him, but it was working. He was excited by its success, but knew better than to betray the fact by any sound or sudden move that would alarm his pet. Stiff with concentration, he manipulated the tweezers, while the other boys watched tensely. When the little snake, disengaging its tail from its old garment with a brisk wiggle, finally emerged in its glowing new skin, the boys sighed with relief.

"Whew! I hope he feels better now. I certainly do."

"How did you know what to do, Ray?"

"Oh, it was easy," nonchalantly answered the snake member, rubbing beads of perspiration off his forehead with his sleeve. "The skin was supposed to come off, so it just seemed practical to give nature a little help in getting it going. In this sort of thing," he generalized, "you have to use your judgment and feel your way." He held the snake up. "Doesn't he look pretty, with his yellow stripes so clear?"

The boys gazed with respect at this example of Ray's successful intervention in nature's mismanagement, and the snake, from the vantage point of Ray's wrist, gazed back at them expressionlessly, flickering its little forked tongue.

SIX

RAY WAS SPEAKING only the simple truth when he told his friends that he was having to feel his way along. In those days there were no books available to the amateur snake-fancier telling him the habitat, habits and temperament of the various reptiles. All he could learn from books were facts about their scientific classification. For clues to the care and treatment of his pets, Ray had to rely on his own judgment, and the kind of intuition developed, he always insisted, by one who has a strong and sympathetic interest in a subject.

Now that he had breached his parents' opposition to reptiles, Ray felt it was time to follow through by expanding his collection. He prepared the ground by making calculated but casual references to the harmlessness of the entire garter snake group, with an eye to introducing one of the garter snakes' larger relatives.

The relative he had in mind was a water snake in the window of Mr. Otto Eggling's bird and pet store. It had been on display about a month, and nearly every day after school he hurried down to the shop to look at it, consumed with anxiety all the way lest some other ambitious herpetologist had snapped it up. It was priced at the astronomical figure of three dollars, but Ray felt he *had* to have it.

Grimly throttling down his appetite, Ray for a couple of weeks had been having only a glass of milk and a coffee roll for lunch, thus saving twenty-five of his thirty-five cents lunch money. When he had accumulated the three dollars, his next problem was to sell the idea of another snake to his family. He decided not to refer to the fact that the prospective acquisition was some four feet long, an inch and a half thick and ugly in disposition. Instead, he emphasized its nonvenomous character and relationship to the garter snakes.

First he approached his mother, and outlined the situation to her. She listened sympathetically, if without enthusiasm.

"This new snake you're talking about is like your garter snakes?" she wanted to know. "I thought water snakes were poisonous."

"Not this kind. It's the cotton-mouth, the water moccasin, that's venomous, Mama. This one of Mr. Eggling's is just a harmless water snake, a relative of these little fellows. A bit larger, to be sure," common honesty compelled him to add, "but harmless."

"They are pretty little things," she conceded, as she watched her son lift them out of their case. "Oh, no, thank you, dear," she exclaimed hastily when he offered one to her. "I don't think I care to hold it. But I suppose it will be all right," she went on, "if your father agrees. I hope you appreciate"—with a touch of severity—"how indulgent he is to you, Ray. You know how he feels about snakes."

Bending over the case to replace the reptiles, Ray concealed a quick smile. Almost his father's very words! "I hope you appreciate what a concession Mama's made to let you keep these things," he had said. "She can't abide snakes, but she wants you to be happy."

"I certainly do, Mama," he said warmly, "and you, too."

"Well, you talk it over with Pop, and if he agrees I shan't object."

Talking it over with Pop, Ray feared, would prove a tougher matter. His father, however, had already reconciled himself to yielding, but he wanted iron-clad guarantees of the innocence of the new snake. To convince him, Ray invoked the support of the printed word.

John Ditmars, pursing his lips and twisting his blond mustache, scanned the scientific list that his son offered him and assured himself that the genus *Thamnophis* (garter snakes) was comfortably close in relationship to the genus *Natrix* (water snakes). Not that he couldn't take Ray's word for it, but there was something about seeing it in black and white.

"I guess the creature's harmless, all right," he admitted.

He still was not enthusiastic, and he looked at his son dubiously. He did wish all this zeal for snakes were directed toward something *sensible*. Well, the boy was still young. "You can have it, Ray," he decided, and added plaintively. "I never thought I'd see the day when I had to share my home with a bunch of serpents!"

Almost furtively Ray hastened through the side streets of Harlem at dusk, lugging a small burlap bag.

He had just paid Mr. Eggling three dollars in small change, and in return he had assumed ownership of the big water snake. Immediately his purchase had made trouble—it had shown fight when he tried to take possession of it. Mr. Eggling, equal to the emergency, had placed a burlap bag over the terrarium in which the snake lay and, inverting the bowl, had tumbled snake, moss and pebbles into the bag. The process, although it had ruffled the snake's feelings, secured for Ray background accessories for the container he had built for his new pet.

His mother and father, he knew, had gone over to the Hudson, where battleships from various nations were staging an illumination, and he wanted to get the snake home and established in his room in their absence. He was not relishing the prospect of the meeting between this outsized reptile and his parents.

He let himself into the dark apartment, and listened a moment. Yes, they were gone. Darkness and silence from the kitchen indicated that the maid, too, had finished her evening's work and departed. Ray turned on the kitchen light, brought the case from his room and placed it, with its glass front slid open, on the floor. He picked Mr. Eggling's firmly tied knot and with one hand upended the bag, while with a broom handle in the other he prepared to guide the reptile, as it emerged, into the open cage.

The snake, however, had other ideas. It surged suddenly, wrathfully, out of the bag and coiled on the floor, alert and angry. Ray was transfixed with horror. It was not that he was afraid of it, but he had a vision of his father's reaction to it. The scientific list might truly describe it as an "innocuous Colubrine snake," but, flattened on the kitchen floor, it looked twice as big as it had in the shop window. He could hardly hope that its family resemblance to his little garter snakes would present itself to the startled paternal eye. Maybe, it occurred to him too late, he should have laid less emphasis on that resemblance and more on the discrepancy in size.

The snake, thoroughly shaken up and resentful, launched a vicious swipe at Ray's foot, and started to pour across the floor, making a slithery noise on the well-waxed oilcloth. In those days vertical water pipes passed through generous floor openings. As the snake headed for the pipes, Ray, with a gasp of alarm, headed it off with the broom, and swept it hastily toward its cage, where it indignantly took refuge.

He quickly shut the glass front, and sat down with thumping heart to recover himself.

Breakfast the next morning was almost over before the subject he was dreading was brought up.

"How is your new snake, dear?" Mary Ditmars asked brightly.

John looked up from the morning paper and observed with a jocularity that his son found appalling:

"I suppose you'll introduce us to it after breakfast? We want to welcome the new member of the family."

"Well," Ray temporized, "I really don't think you'd better see it just yet. It's pretty nervous still, and it oughtn't to be disturbed for a while."

34

"Moving upset it? It must be a sensitive little thing."

Ray wondered how long his father's good humor would last, once he laid eyes on the "sensitive little thing."

"Yes, sir," he said weakly. A glance at the clock on the mantel suggested a way out. "I'll be late if I don't hurry!" he exclaimed. He swallowed his milk in a quick gulp and bolted out of the room.

Before leaving for school, he turned the front of the case to the wall, then worried all through the day for fear someone would move it for a look. When he got home in the afternoon, he was relieved to find it untouched. He turned it around to gaze long and happily at his acquisition.

It wasn't a particularly pretty snake, and no one but an enthusiast could have loved it. It was the dingy, lusterless brown of the full-grown, common water snake. Its scales were rough, its body was thick, its head flat and its disposition choleric. Ruddy brown blotches marked its back, and bright-red ones its yellow abdomen. Ray was enraptured with it. For several days he kept the cage turned to the wall, discouraged visitors, and gazed at it himself, tirelessly and lovingly.

The snake, meanwhile, had to eat. It was rather a problem. Ray could, of course, divert some of his allowance from his own lunches to provisions for the snake, but he had had enough of short rations. He decided instead to go to the north lake in the park and catch a frog. A certain risk was involved, but no expense. With a watchful eye out for inopportune policemen, Ray prowled around the edge of the little lake, spotted a big green-headed frog, and pounced on it with practiced agility. Wrapping it in his handkerchief, he stuck it in his pocket and carried it home. The greed with which the snake devoured it and darted its head back and forth searching for more prey made his heart sink—he had been lucky in avoiding a policeman once, but, to judge from the snake's appetite, he was going to have to be lucky rather often.

He need not, however, have worried about overstraining his good luck. It was already used up, as events quickly demonstrated.

His snake, he realized, could not be left indefinitely in a case faced against the wall. It occurred to him that he might rig a sort of sun-porch extension to the cage and place it on the fire escape outside the window. Then he would invite his parents to see his new pet. It was his hope that, viewed through the window and at the far end of the fire escape, its formidable size and ugliness would be minimized. It was not a bad idea, but it failed to take the neighbors into account.

In a busy afternoon's work he completed the extension of the case, and then set it out on the fire escape. The water snake had been enjoying its luxurious new quarters only a day or so when the lightning struck.

It was late afternoon. Ray was home from school, Mary Ditmars from paying calls, John from the office, and they were all together in the parlor. The doorbell rang, and in a few moments the maid appeared to say that Patrolman Mulcahey wanted to speak to Mr. Ditmars.

John Ditmars looked surprised. "Show him in, Jane," he requested.

Patrolman Mulcahey, large, ruddy and ceremonious, entered. Grasped conspicuously in one massive paw was an official-looking envelope.

"John Van H. Ditmars? Mr. Ditmars, sir?" he demanded formally.

"Yes, officer. What can I do for you?"

"I have a complaint to deliver, sir," announced the law in awful tones. Ray turned cold with a horrid premonition.

Mr. Ditmars took the envelope, ripped it open and read the document aloud. It was a combination complaint from the police and health departments to the effect that John Van

Harlingen Ditmars was harboring on his premises a dangerous reptile, to the peril of his neighbors and to the detriment of their peace of mind. Several of them, the health department implied, had been so shocked by the sinister spectacle of the serpent sunning itself that their health had been impaired, and any improvement in it would be contingent on the removal of the snake from the neighborhood.

There was stark silence for a moment, then everyone began to talk at once.

"What is the meaning . . ." demanded John, with heat.

"But, Pop! Officer! It's harmless!" Ray protested shrilly.

"Now, John! Hush, Ray! Really, officer! Such busybodies! What do you mean . . ."

"Lady, all I'm doing is my duty. . . ."

It took some minutes for the commotion to subside. The bewildered Mr. Mulcahey was bundled out. Ray's mother retired to her room to bathe her forehead with cologne, and John Ditmars, followed by his quaking son, marched to Ray's room to inspect, at last, the water snake.

When he saw it he exploded. Ray could never remember, and never wanted to, precisely what he said. The sense of it was clear, though: he was to get these snakes out of the house, and it wouldn't be a bad thing if he got snakes out of his head, too.

"Not the garter snakes, too, Pop?" Ray wailed.

"The garter snakes, too!" his father decreed in a tone that brooked no protest. "You'll take them all back to Mr. Eggling tomorrow, young man!"

Dinner that evening was not a happy meal. Afterward, Ray shut himself in his room. He was a big boy now, almost sixteen, but that night be cried himself to sleep.

His father had to be obeyed, of course, but, Ray decided, there was no need to be too literal about it. So he took the garter snakes, not to Mr. Eggling's, but to the wooded northern end of Central Park, where he liberated them by a ledge of rock and watched glumly while his little pets, with never a token of regret, slipped into a cleft in the rock and out of his life. Then he went home again, fought his cross-grained water snake into a pillow slip, placed that in a small satchel and trailed over to Eggling's.

Sadly he explained the situation to Mr. Eggling. The German, a kind old man, was sincerely distressed by his young client's misery. Perhaps, he suggested, starting a frog collection would alleviate it. Ray's response was tepid—frogs, after snakes, seemed pretty tame. Mr. Eggling coaxed and encouraged, and walked him along a line of terraria containing fine specimens of bullfrogs, European pond frogs, pickerel and leopard frogs, whose merits he extolled feelingly. In the end, with limited enthusiasm, Ray helped him select and pack a small collection which he carried home. He felt that the whole business was a humiliating comedown.

Ray looked sadly at the frogs, and decided that he could never love them; but at least he could enjoy building a house for them.

It was a fine structure when he finished it, four feet long, with screened windows and divided inside by partitions that did not quite reach the top, so that the flies he intended feeding them could circulate from one apartment to another. The next job was to find some flies, live ones.

For a quarter he bought a small flytrap at a hardware store, and, using it as a model, made a two-foot one of wood and screening. Ray carried his trap, baited with a scrap of beef, to Quinn's livery stable. The stableman listened to his story, and expansively invited him to help himself to all the flies he wanted. Ray placed the trap on a window sill near the stalls.

The next day, on his way home from school, he was delighted to find it swarming. Big and little flies, bluebottles, ordinary stable flies, even some horseflies, buzzed and droned around in it. Ray asked for a newspaper, and wrapped it around the trap.

"Thanks a lot, Sam," he said. "This ought to take care of my frogs for a few days."

"Don't mention it, Ray." The stableman grinned at him. "Come again any time, and we'll have plenty more for you." A funny young fellow, he thought, as he watched the tall, slim boy, paper-covered bundle under his arm, walk down the street. A good thing his pa had made him get rid of his snakes—they might have scared somebody half to death. With frogs, now, he couldn't get into any trouble. So Sam the stableman thought.

It was almost time for dinner when Ray got home, but looking at the clock, he decided that he would have time to feed the frogs. Setting the trap of loudly buzzing flies on the floor, he started to unwrap it. He pulled off one layer of paper, and reached around the trap to loosen another, when his finger caught in its door, and jerked it wide open.

The swarm of flies, suddenly released, cascaded into his face and soared into the air. Thunderstruck, Ray could not move for a moment; then he sprang to the door, but he was too late. Attracted by the lights in the hall, the legion of insects had already poured out of his room and were distributing themselves throughout the house.

Ray sped to the dining room, hoping to shut them out of that room, but again, it was too late. They were in it, and in every room, buzzing, booming, blundering against walls and ceilings and into his hair as he entered. Even Quinn's had never sounded like this. Desperately he looked around him. He had to do something, *something*, before his father got home.

It was at that point that the front door opened and John Ditmars came in. Ray heard him call a cheerful hello to his wife, heard his exclamation of annoyance as a fly bumbled against his face, heard the *swish*! as he swung his hat at one.

"Pshaw!" John Ditmars exclaimed testily. "*Shoo!*" Then

39

with rising irritation, "Where in the world did all these flies . . ."—a sudden, ominous silence—"RAYMOND!"

"Yes, Pop," Ray answered wearily, and went to meet his irate parent.

Dinner, for the second time that week, was an unhappy occasion. John Ditmars, to Ray's alarm, was speechless. Mary, on the other hand, was highly vocal. All of them fought with the repulsive intruders over every mouthful of food.

After dinner, Ray was sternly ordered to produce some flypaper, fast. He bought a large quantity at the hardware store—the same one at which he had purchased the flytrap—festooned it from the gas fixtures, and laid it on all adequate flat surfaces where, immediately, both his parents unwarily entangled themselves in it. Ray went to bed to escape further attention.

Breakfast the next morning was an oppressive affair, well attended by flies. Having pulled the sheets over his head, Ray had slept soundly. His father and mother, however, he was given to understand, had had a very *poor* night's rest, interrupted and finally shattered by the loathsome buzzing and crawling of the flies that had chosen to retire with them.

John Ditmars patted his light mustache with his napkin, flicked it angrily at a groggy bluebottle, and fixed Ray with a cold blue gaze. The ax fell.

"You are to dispose of those frogs at once, Raymond," he commanded. "This is the end of your collections—all of them."

Ray looked despairingly at his mother—she was always on his side. But this time the gentle dark eyes were stern.

"Very well, Pop," he sighed. It had been a catastrophic week, and he was exhausted by his misfortunes. There was nothing left for him but resignation.

Snakeless, frogless, totally petless, the future stretched bleakly before him. His career as a naturalist seemed to have run into a dead end. He was terribly depressed, so much so

40

that Mary Ditmars couldn't bear it. First she, then John, relented. Ray was permitted to have pets again—but no snakes. He consoled himself with some small lizards that fed on mealworms—which were safely confined to a tin can—and a vegetarian land crab.

There was nothing, however, to prevent Ray from catching snakes during his vacations.

Bolder now, and with more confidence in his ability to handle the creatures, he was anxious to try his luck with a rattler. While he was spending some time with an uncle near Waterbury, an old Connecticut farmer told him about a den of rattlesnakes. To find them he scrambled up a mountainside, covered with scrub oaks and broken by rocky outcroppings. The snakes, intricately coiled together on a ledge, looked like carelessly piled, mottled velvet. His grandmother's shuddering question came back to him: "You wouldn't want to catch one of those frightful things, would you?" Now was his chance.

With a stick forked at the end, he deftly pressed a small rattler's head against the ground and quickly seized it by the neck, just behind the head, so that it would have no room to turn and strike him. The mouth, fitted with needle-like fangs, gaped impotently and Ray, with a shiver of respect, looked closely, and for the first time, at the rattler's lethal equipment.

The fangs, which in rattlers and viperine snakes are situated in the front part of the upper jaw, are canaliculated teeth, much like a hypodermic needle, rigidly attached to a movable bone. When the reptile's mouth is closed, these fangs fold back against the roof; when the jaws are open they rotate forward. Each fang connects, at its base, with a poison gland situated in the head. As the wickedly incurved fangs are struck into the prey the poison is ejected through a small elongated opening on the front face of the fang near the tip. Most of this Ray learned later, through further observation and experi-

4 ₃

ment, but he could easily see the tiny openings, about the size of the eye of a darning needle, through which the poisonous fluid was shot into the victim's body. With awe he gazed at the forbidding apparatus. It occurred to him, as he cautiously released the snake, that he was separated from the nearest habitation by several miles of scrub oak and rocky field.

There were plenty of rattlers in the Connecticut hills, and, far beyond the reach of anxious relatives, he handled and examined them with fascinated curiosity for the rest of the summer. He took no chances, ran no risks; his respect for their dangerous potentialities was too keen for that. The horrible consequences of a bite—either a painful death, or an illness almost as terrible—were never absent from his mind. Doctor Calmette, of the Pasteur Institute, was only at the beginning of his antivenin research, and the practical use of the product was still several years in the future. To avoid a bite the most painstaking precautions were necessary, and Ray never neglected them.

SEVEN

SHOULD HE PREPARE for West Point, as his father expected, or should he do something else with his life? He was seventeen, and it was high time he decided. The question was ideally answered, so far as Ray was concerned, the day that Dr. William Beutenmüller offered him a job at the American Museum of Natural History.

In later years Ray attributed this remarkable piece of good fortune to that tendency his father so deplored of pursuing a number of interests at a time. In his enthusiasm for engines, horses, the weather, and, above all, snakes, he had never lost his zeal for his earlier interest, butterflies. His specimens, which he had been collecting for several years, were neatly mounted in picture frames. He had no idea, when he went to call on Doctor Beutenmüller that spring afternoon with several specimens of a puzzling little moth, that he was approaching a turning point in his life.

Doctor Beutenmüller was, as usual, busy, but he looked at his familiar visitor with a sort of impatient kindliness.

"Well, what is it this time, Raymond?"

"Some *Utetheisa bella*, sir. I can find only one species listed for this part of the country, but in the specimens I've caught the lower wing varies in color all the way from faint pink to almost red. Do you think they're all the same species?"

Ray unwrapped his frame and presented it to the entomologist. In it were several specimens of *Utetheisa*. It was a beautiful little creature, with a wing spread of about an inch. The upper wings were snowy white, speckled with minute black dots. The lower wings in the several specimens

43

ranged from pink to red, just as he had said. The curator lifted out a red one and looked at it with interest.

"Yes, it does seem a bit dark, but there's bound to be some variation. As a matter of fact, I'm not very familiar with this species. They're rather rare hereabouts—I've seen only a few."

"Rare? I have at least twenty in my collection. I've caught them on the Palisades."

The scientist lifted heavy brows in polite skepticism. "Twenty? Of *Utetheisa*?"

"Yes, sir. All mounted to show the color variation."

Doctor Beutenmüller picked up his pen and glanced at the letter he had been writing.

"Bring them in sometime."

Ray realized that he was dismissed.

He was back the very next day with his entire collection of *Utetheisa*. This time there could be no doubt of the scientist's interest. He spent a quarter of an hour examining them with a glass.

"Who mounted these?" he finally asked. "It's a good job."

"Thank you, sir. I did," Ray told him, "with a very fine needle so as not to tear the wings."

Doctor Beutenmüller stared absently at the moths for a long minute, then spun around in his chair to face his caller.

"We need somebody here to mount a large series of moths and butterflies we've just acquired. There's a chance for advancement in the museum, too. How would you like the job?"

How would he like the job! For a moment Ray was too overcome to answer. When he recovered his wits, he managed to say that he'd like it fine, and that he would ask his parents.

To his dismay, both his mother and his father were cool to the idea of his taking the job. Mounting butterflies at the museum might be pleasant work for a couple of months in the summer, but what promise, what prospect, did it offer for a career? Nobody, John Ditmars insisted for the hundredth

44

time, had ever made a success of life just by chasing butterflies and snakes.

"And I thought you'd almost decided to go to West Point, too, Ray," his father reminded him.

"Think how expensive the preparation will be for you, Pop, and how long it will take me. Besides," he glanced quickly at his mother, "a military life would take me away from home for long periods at a stretch. Why, I'd get to see you only once in every three or four years."

Mary looked at him with a startled, stricken expression. Ray decided it would be heartless to pursue that line of argument any further.

"We'll think it over, dear," she promised him.

The school term ended, and the question was still not settled. Ray did not dare imagine how he would feel should his parents decide against letting him take the job. Then, quite without meaning to, he touched off the train of thought that turned the decision in his favor.

One night shortly after the close of school Mary Ditmars came into her husband's study, where he was enjoying a last pipe before going to bed.

"What's the trouble, Mary?" he asked her in surprise. He had not been married to her for more than twenty years without being able to tell when she was upset.

"Raymond!" she exclaimed, and sat down, nervously fingering a fold of her gray dress.

"Well?"

"He's in his room, drawing pictures of moths—with his *left hand.*"

"What's wrong with that?" John was bewildered.

"You've heard him speak of that German drillmaster he admires so much? Well, he noticed that the boys were approaching the overhead apparatus in the gym with their right hands. He said it was bad, that a soldier ought to be able to do with his left hand everything that he can do with his right, in case—in case—" she faltered, unable to formulate the sickening eventuality.

John looked at her with surprise, noticed tears in her dark eyes.

"I see," he said slowly.

The following morning Ray took his seat at breakfast, wondering how much longer he would have to wait for his parents to make up their minds about the museum job. He was completely taken aback when his mother announced to him, without preamble:

"Ray, your father and I have decided that you may accept Doctor Beutenmüller's offer."

It was only considerably later that he realized that the possibility of his returning maimed from the wars, suggested indirectly by the German drillmaster, had been the deciding factor.

So far as Doctor Beutenmüller was concerned, he had merely engaged a new assistant; but Ray felt he was taking the first step toward that dazzling goal, a scientific career. The first day was bewildering, and somewhat disappointing. There was little to do, beyond placing defunct butterflies in a softening box with pads of wet cloth, so they could be handled the next day without crumbling. When he had done that, Ray had to figure out something else to do. The entomologist, muttering to himself, was peering at specimens through a magnifying glass and jotting down notes. Ray, thoroughly in awe of his chief, decided that it would be unwise to disturb him, and that he might as well busy himself dusting the glass-topped drawers of insects that were ranged on a steel balcony around the big room. So all morning he dusted, although it was not his idea of the proper work for an incipient scientist, and the drawers didn't need it.

After lunch his chief noticed him long enough to exclaim gruffly:

"Don't bother to dust any more, Raymond. That's not your job."

Ray spent the rest of the afternoon wandering around the two big rooms, joined by an arched doorway, straightening books and stacking pamphlets. By the end of the day he was depressed.

His discouragement was of short duration. He quickly came to find that working with Beutenmüller was an education in itself. The entomologist often called his young assistant in to demonstrate methods of work which he thought Ray, as a prospective scientist, ought to understand.

"Come in here, Raymond," he shouted, and Ray left the tray on which he was mounting butterflies and hurried to his side.

"Look at these *Noctuidae*," he commanded, gesturing toward a group of moths. "Look at the tibial joints. What do you see?"

The little moths looked almost alike, although a slight difference of wing pattern showed here and there. Ray examined their legs through a magnifying glass.

"I see that the specimens having long tibial joints have hair the entire length of the joint, those with short joints are haired only on the basal part, and those with medium joints have hair on both segments."

"Right. And that solves a scientific problem in the analysis and separation of this large group. It's of more than academic importance because of the damage done by the larvae. Hold the office down. I'm going to the printer's."

Like a well-ordered tornado, the chief rushed from the room, slamming the door behind him. When he was in the midst of a piece of work, nothing could stop him. He plunged into a problem, worried it until it was whipped, wrote up his findings, and dashed over to the printing house that did the museum's work with a draft of his article. He played with as much enjoyment as he worked. There was nothing he liked better than to watch a ball game from a good seat in the grand-stand. Sometimes, as Ray soon realized, his excursions to "the printer's" were comparable to the attendance at a "grand-mother's funeral" pled by less imaginative persons.

In his absences from the office, Ray explored his new sur-roundings. Although he had long been familiar with the museum, this was his first opportunity to investigate the en-tomology department in detail and from the inside. In the cases were gorgeous bird-winged butterflies from New Guinea with green-marked wings and bodies like red velvet, dazzling morphos from tropical America with glowing blue wings, huge moths from Malaysia with bodies the size of a small mouse, a whole wonderland of extraordinary, unimaginable creatures.

He became acquainted, too, with other members of the museum's staff. Dr. Joel A. Allen was curator of mammalogy, the later celebrated Frank M. Chapman of birds. Dr. Edmund Otis Hovey, geologist, mineralogist and climatologist, was astonished and pleased to find in a boy Ray's age a fellow weather enthusiast. Dr. Louis K. Gratacap, curator of precious stones and later Ray's good friend, one day caught him poking happily among dusty jars of pickled snakes. Knowing his busi-ness was mounting butterflies, he twitted him good-humoredly and walked back to Ray's office with him discussing snakes as seriously as though the entomologist's young assistant had been a man of his own age and scientific standing.

The friendship that came to mean most to Ray was the one that sprang up between him and Professor Henry Fairfield Osborn. Walking down a corridor one morning, he came face to face with Doctor Osborn, whom he knew only by sight.

"Good morning, sir," he said, and was surprised when Osborn stopped.

"Good morning, young man. You must be Doctor Beuten-müller's new assistant, Mr. Ditmars, aren't you?"

Flushing with pleasure at being known by name to so eminent a man, Ray admitted his identity.

"And how are you enjoying your work?" Osborn asked.

"Very much, Doctor Osborn, thanks. I've never lost my interest in butterflies."

"Although you've developed new ones?"

"Yes. Snakes, principally."

"Now, that's a good field," Doctor Osborn encouraged him.

With some surprise, Ray found himself telling this sympathetic scientist about his enthusiasm. Five minutes later, as he hurried off on his delayed errand, he reflected with a little glow what a friendly man Doctor Osborn was to spend his time chatting with one of the least of the museum's employees. From then on he was devoted to the older man who, on his side, always gave him unfailing friendship and encouragement.

Association with such men as Chapman and Gratacap, Beutenmüller, Osborn and the rest, was good training for Ray, and he realized it. At his work he learned responsibility and system. From them he learned respect for thoroughness, accuracy, authenticity. He was absorbing the atmosphere of science with every breath.

EIGHT

THE CHIEF WAS in another of his effervescent and harmless rages. Working over a tray of moistened insects, Ray could hear him in his office pacing the floor and roaring plaintively about the injustices to which he was always being subjected.

"And just when I'm over my head in this revision of *Noctuidae*, too," he thundered.

"But you've known for weeks that Jesup's been planning this course of popular lectures. I have to talk about gems," Ray heard Doctor Gratacap say pacifically. Mr. Morris K. Jesup was the president of the museum, an august personage whom Ray regarded with great reverence.

"Popularizing! Bah!" Ray judged from the entomologist's tone, which had subsided to a shout, that he was slightly soothed by the reflection that the other curators were in the same boat. "Schoolteachers!" he rumbled. Then, "Raymond!"

Entering the office, Ray exchanged a quick grin with Gratacap, who was slumped in an easy chair patiently drumming on its arms with his fingers.

"Yes, Doctor Beutenmüller?"

"This is going to be your problem, too," the chief said grimly. "It's your job to dig up the slides to illustrate these wretched lectures."

Ray searched industriously among the lantern slides in Professor Bickmore's department of illustrative records, and came up with an appropriate collection for the first lecture, which was on methods of collecting and studying insects. The second lecture, which was to be about moths and butterflies, was a harder problem, because of the lack of illustrative material.

"I want life histories!" demanded Doctor Beutenmüller, going through the slides Ray had presented to him for his next lecture with ferocious dissatisfaction.

"There's only one life history in the files, and that's the cecropia moth," Ray said. He hesitated. "I think I have an idea, though," he ventured.

Beutenmüller looked at his assistant, noticing, with a little surge of friendliness, how young and eager he looked.

"Well, don't you *know?*" he asked with gruff good humor.

"How about explaining a typical life history before the slides come on, then show them with a sort of running fire of description? You wouldn't have to write a thing—I'd work it up for you and you can keep right on at *Noctuidae*."

"That's not a bad idea. We'll see how it works out."

With the feeling that a great responsibility rested on him, Ray toiled over a commentary on *attacus yama maia,* a large moth indigenous to the mountains of southern Japan. In its caterpillar phase, the insect chooses a big leaf which it covers and binds to the bough with a strong network of silk. After bending the leaf around to form an oval chamber with an escapement valve at the top and an outlet at the bottom through which any rain admitted at the upper end can leak, the caterpillar sheds its skin. In its pupa form, the creature sleeps until its hour of emergence. Then it blindly squeezes through the escapement, and emerges as a moth with gorgeous wings, extremely sensitive antennae, large compound eyes—and no mouth parts. It flies off to mate, breed, and die battered by the vigorous island winds, in less than a month of leaving the cocoon. The pathos of this life-cycle, which spanned so short a time, impressed Ray, and he dwelt on it touchingly.

Reading his commentary, Doctor Beutenmüller growled:

"Cut out all that sentimentality! 'Youth to death in a few brief months' indeed! I'll thank you to remember that, even if I am delivering popular lectures, I'm not a sob sister! Otherwise it'll do," he added.

Ray smothered a grin. His little flight of pathos had embarrassed the crusty scientist; but he could congratulate himself that in its essentials his article was satisfactory. The lecture, a few days later, was a great success.

When Doctor Beutenmüller asked him to prepare a similar commentary ("Remember, no sob stuff!") for the next lecture, Ray was elated. He was only too glad to extend the sphere of his usefulness, for mounting butterflies day after day was a monotonous business, and one only occasionally relieved by the almost equally uninteresting operation of fumigating all the cases against the depredations of a minute beetle, dreadfully destructive to butterfly collections, which sometimes attacked the exhibits.

He could, however, count on livelier relief from time to time. There was the morning in early June when Doctor Beutenmüller, who kept a sort of calendar of events important in the insect world, suddenly remembered that the seventeen-year locusts had already emerged. Ray, who had been yawning and repining over a tray of butterflies, and gazing longingly out the window at the beckoning sunshine, was brought sharply to his feet by his chief's explosive shout. Almost before he could gather together his faculties and his collecting equipment, Ray found himself on the elevated, bound for the ferry and the New Jersey Palisades, beside a chief who was wrathfully lamenting the inopportune emergence of the insects just as he was immersed in a learned monograph on an entirely different subject, and the careless inaccuracy of the popular mind that insisted on referring to them as seventeen-year locusts when they were not locusts at all, but cicadas. Ray did his best to look sympathetic.

Every day for more than a week, Doctor Beutenmüller and Ray visited either New Jersey, where the creatures had been regularly recorded at seventeen-year intervals ever since 1775, or orchards on Long Island where, because the egg-laying operation of the female injures trees, they were an acute problem to fruit growers. For an exhibit the entomologist was planning to illustrate the cicada's life cycle, they collected the wingless insects as they emerged from the earth, the shells they cast on reaching the surface, and the final winged version. Ray had wangled permission from his chief to keep a few harmless snakes caged in his workroom, so he particularly rejoiced at the opportunity to turn over rocks and poke into rotten logs where he might find for his collection a garter snake, a salamander, or some other creature more to his liking than cicadas.

Assorting and synthesizing all the knowledge he had accumulated on rattlesnakes during the several summers he had been catching and handling them in Connecticut, Ray composed his first scientific paper. He wrote it out in longhand, then typed it. The title, "Rattlesnakes of Connecticut," centered clear and bold at the top of the first page, gave him quite a glow of scientific achievement. Standing before his mother's long mirror, in which he had so often inspected himself as a cadet, he read it aloud, critically appraising his platform manner. He hoped to deliver it at the bimonthly meeting of the Linnaean Society, to be held the next evening at the museum. How he would get a paper on snakes onto a program dealing with birds he didn't quite know, but, he reflected, the two forms of life were rather closely related to each other. Maybe he could introduce it during the general discussion period.

Uncomfortably aware of the noise his heels made on the tiled floor of the museum's hall, Ray diffidently approached the library where the members of the Linnaean Society were assembling. A bit overawed, he lingered outside the door. Approaching down the hall and moving with a diffidence much like his own, he saw a skinny, pleasant-faced youth about his own age, carrying a bundle which Ray immediately diagnosed as a stuffed bird. It was Will Beebe. The boys nodded to each other.

"Isn't it about to begin?" Beebe asked. "Let's go in."

"All right," Ray agreed, and followed him in, feeling considerably better for his company. The two boys slipped modestly into seats in the back row, beside an elderly gentleman with sideburns, whom young Beebe immediately engaged in a conversation. Before the meeting began he unwrapped his bird and offered it to the older man for examination. Ray admired his self-confidence.

The meeting was called to order. The minutes of the previous one were read, several motions made and passed, and the main speaker of the evening was introduced. His paper, which was about birds, was long and not, to Ray, unduly interesting, but it was received with dignified enthusiasm by the audience. The general discussion period began.

At a little nod of encouragement from the man beside him, Will Beebe stood up and read a short note on his stuffed bird, which he passed around. There was a general buzz of comment to which Ray could not listen. He was completely preoccupied with his stage-fright. The thought of reading his modest little paper—on snakes!—to all these eminent birdfanciers was making him so weak he could hardly swallow.

"Now!" he urged himself desperately, and started to rise to address the chair.

"Adjourned!" boomed the chairman unexpectedly.

Ray's next effort to address a scientific society, however, came out better.

The New York Entomological Society, of which Doctor Beutenmüller was secretary and Ray a member, was going on one of its field trips.

Doctor Beutenmüller had decided to collect only beetles

and had packed his vest pockets with test tubes, so Ray had nothing to carry except a couple of cloth bags in which, he hoped, he could carry captured snakes. The day, spent in the country around Lakehurst, New Jersey, was a great success. Although he was disappointed not to find any reptiles, Ray caught frogs for the snakes he kept at the museum, and some beetles for his chief. Best of all, he had an opportunity to talk with several of the most eminent entomologists in the country about their specialties. To Christian Groth, a New York jeweler who was also president of the society, Ray recounted his abortive effort to read a paper on snakes to the Linnaean Society. Groth, a warmhearted and kindly man, was sympathetically interested.

"The next time you have a paper on snakes to read, Raymond," he told him, "present it to your own society. Don't toss your pearls in front of a lot of bird lovers." His eyes twinkled.

"Oh, thank you! I'm working on one now. It's about the snakes in Central Park, and I think I can have it ready in time for the next meeting."

"Fine. You can read it during the general discussion."

It was with very different feelings that Ray approached the library along the red-tiled corridor to attend the Entomological Society's meeting. He walked into the room confidently, receiving a friendly nod from Doctor Beutenmüller and a smile from Mr. Groth. Two members he had talked with on the field trip shook hands with him cordially. As he subsided into a seat—in the third, not the back, row—he had a gratifying sense of really belonging.

Beetles occupied most of the meeting. Inwardly fidgeting with impatience, Ray listened respectfully. After a learned and interminable paper on tiger beetles, insects in which Ray took absolutely no interest, the general discussion period was reached. There was a short pause. Apparently nobody had anything to discuss. Taking his courage in his hands, Ray stood up.

"Mr. Ditmars," the chair acknowledged him.

"Mr. Chairman," he began feebly, then added in a firmer tone, "and gentlemen."

The hand that held the paper entitled "The Serpents of Central Park" trembled. The voice that uttered it trembled too, at first. There was a rustle of surprise as the assembled entomologists realized that this whiskerless boy was addressing them on snakes, not bugs. The surprise settled into attention as Ray launched into the body of his paper. He described the ledges of the northwest corner of the park, and the harmless brown snakes and garter snakes that had their hibernating dens among them. He mentioned, too, that albino snakes were to be found there with unusual frequency, a fact that he attributed to the park's being an area where the character of the soil and the feeding habits of its wild denizens had been changed by the encroachment of the city. To illustrate his lecture, he had specimens of Central Park snakes, several of them albinos, in glass-fronted cases which one of the museum's handymen wheeled in on a hand truck.

As the members, at the close of his paper, crowded around his exhibits with every evidence of sincere interest, Ray almost burst with joy. He had made his first contribution to a critical scientific group, and they had approved it!

When Doctor Beutenmüller, the next morning, congratulated him, Ray flushed with pleasure. The scientist's next remark left him wordless with rapture.

"If you'll extend your article to cover the serpents of New York State, and incorporate the material you read us last night, I'll publish it in our journal. Point out how to tell the difference between dangerous and harmless snakes. Entomologists are always poking under stones and logs, and that angle of it ought to interest them."

When the next issue of the New York Entomological Society's journal came out, Ray's article was in it.

"I guess this is serious," John Ditmars said with resigna-

56

tion, looking over the author's reprint that Ray, with some ceremony, had presented to him.

"Yes, I guess there can't be any doubt about it," his wife agreed with a sigh.

To their son, carefully compiling a list of the persons to whom he intended to send autographed copies, it was certainly serious. It was the most momentous thing that had ever happened to him. He had become—in a small way to be sure, but officially—a scientist.

NINE

THE WEATHER, meanwhile, had been continuing as usual, and so had Ray's interest in it. He had a barometer, now, too. By exercising an uncongenial thrift he had saved enough money from his tiny salary to buy it.

"Storms and snakes," growled Doctor Beutenmüller, not unkindly. "It's a wonder you've got any space left in your head for your work."

Ray turned from the window and reluctantly sat down at his tray.

"I think we're in for a hurricane," he said. "The glass was awfully low this morning, and the sky looks like it."

"Fiddlesticks! You fuss like an old granny over the weather. It's hot and we'll probably have a thunderstorm. Finish that batch of bugs today, like a good chap, and we'll spend tomorrow on the Palisades. I want to check up on that report that the summer brood of *Orgyia* is full of parasites."

It was August 23, 1893. The paper that morning had said that a hurricane was approaching the coast and was heading for New York. Ray, whose family was living in Brooklyn now, had consulted his barometer before catching the ferry, and had found that it read 29.80. Maybe the paper was right, he thought with elation.

After lunch he stopped to look at Professor Hovey's office barometer. It was still 29.80. The southern sky was hazy with a white cirro-nebulus, through which lead-covered cumuli thrust their threatening heads.

"I shouldn't count on a hurricane, Ray," Professor Hovey warned. "These storms usually turn out to sea. Just a stiff northeaster's more likely."

"But they usually curve off an air-pressure gradient of 30 or more. We're well under that now."

"We'll see," the climatologist said. "You'd better scamper now. There'll really be a hurricane if your chief finds you're in here gossiping with me about the weather."

Standing at the rail of the ferry on his way home that evening, Ray watched the canopy of clouds, dark and wind-torn, sweep swiftly in from the east, bringing with it a misty rain squall. Jamming his hat down tight against the gusty wind and turning up his coat collar, he sprinted home, in haste not so much to keep dry as to see his barometer. It had fallen to 29.70.

By the time dinner was over it was 29.60. Outside, the leaves were rustling in the light northeast wind. The sound was strangely threatening, like a soft, angry whisper. The storm had not recurved, and Ray was sure it would strike the coast about New York with terrific violence. He waited for it expectantly.

It built up deliberately. By eight o'clock rain squalls, whipped by savage gusts of wind, slashed through the thickening darkness. The glass continued to fall, the wind to rise. Around midnight Ray and his father closed all the shutters on the north and east sides of the house, and got well drenched doing it. Under the ferocity of the ever-increasing wind, the rain, driven almost horizontally, was forced in around the window casings as a fine spray.

Through the torrent of driving rain the arc light outside the house gleamed waveringly. The wind roared ceaselessly, deeply, producing a numbness of hearing, through which the various tones given off by the straining house penetrated. The entire family, restless and half-alarmed, prowled from room to room, watching the spectacle from the unshuttered south windows, straining anxiously to hear the creaking of the joints of the trembling house, and hearing the rain fall with the thunder of cataracts on the roof. No one went to bed. No one dared to, with the house staggering on its foundations under the fury of wind and rain.

At dawn, after the barometer had dropped to 29.20, calm fell abruptly. The silence now was as incredible as the unremitting roar earlier. Ray had the queer feeling that a whisper could be heard the length of the city. They were in the vortex. He heard a whimper at the basement door, and opened it. Crouched shivering at the top of the cellar stairs was his fox terrier, and there was water three feet deep in the basement. Scooping the little dog up in his arms, he carried it, still trembling, to his room, to find that the swaying and shaking of the house during the night had jiggled his bed from one side of the room clear to the opposite wall.

The blow following the passage of the vortex, when the wind came out of the southwest, was no longer of hurricane force, but it was still a stiff gale. Pale and heavy-eyed, but buoyed up by the excitement of the most thrilling experience of his life, Ray at his usual hour picked his way through the wreckage of fallen trees, overturned wagons and broken chimney pots to the pier. The harbor was running in great, muddy swells, so rough and heavy that no horses were being taken aboard the ferry which, although it was broad-beamed and blunt, was pitching like a yacht. With his legs braced wide against the roll of the boat, Ray clung to the rail and watched the ragged, reddish clouds, driven by the southwest wind, hasten across the clearing sky. Suddenly he grinned.

"I wonder what Doctor Beutenmüller's going to have to say this morning," he thought.

What Doctor Beutenmüller said was, "All right, all right, so it *was* a hurricane! And you're a good weather prophet, my boy," he added handsomely.

"All I did was read the barometer," Ray said deprecatingly. "Wasn't it terrific! I can hardly wait for another."

Doctor Beutenmüller grunted doubtfully, and Ray got the impression that his impatience was not shared.

While he was waiting for another hurricane Ray was not, of course, idle. (It was just as well, since he had to wait more than forty years.) There were enough snakes, insects, and engines to fill his time twice over. Engines, for instance, were always on his mind. When Doctor Beutenmüller wanted pictures demonstrating the differences between the various species of local grasshoppers to illustrate a paper he was preparing, he got the idea of having Ray prepare them, since his assistant had told him he could draw.

"Bring in a sample," he ordered. "Something with lots of details."

Ray brought in a beautifully drawn sketch of an Amoskeag fire engine, complete even to the rivets. Beutenmüller, after one glance, roared that he had wanted a sample drawing of a *grasshopper's* details, not just *any* details. Ray turned red and stammered, and Gratacap, who witnessed the incident, laughed until he had to wipe his streaming eyes.

Ray's love of engines was no laughing matter to his father, though. When he found him one day poring over some illustrated catalogues of fire-fighting equipment, John Ditmars felt his spirits incautiously rising. Maybe Ray would be diverted from his preoccupation with snakes and bugs and apply himself to something useful.

"Perhaps you can get a job in one of the companies that designs this equipment," John Ditmars suggested. "With buildings getting higher and cities bigger all the time, there should be a good future there for a bright young man."

Ray answered vehemently, "But I don't want a job where they make fire engines, Pop. I just *like* them. I want a job with snakes!"

The disappointment John felt was familiar, but no less keen for that.

"Snakes, butterflies, engines, horses, the weather!" he said bitterly. "You have too many interests, Ray, and not, I'm afraid, enough concentration to get anywhere with any of them." He opened the door. "Except maybe snakes," he added gloomily, and shut it behind him.

Much as he respected his father, Ray couldn't believe that he was right in this case. It seemed to him sensible and right to have a number of interests. He could understand his father's point of view, but not share it. To his relief, he found support for his opinion in his friend, Doctor John B. Smith.

Doctor Smith was a government entomologist of wide reputation whom Ray often met at the scientific meetings he was attending with increasing frequency. A number of times he had helped the scientist arrange his exhibits and they had gradually become good friends. Ray was elated when Doctor Smith invited him on a bug-hunting expedition to Florida. His parents gave him permission to go. They no longer had any hope that the drawbacks of a naturalist's life would deter Ray from following it, and they thought he might as well make his first long field trip under good auspices.

The Clyde Line's ship *Arapahoe* took the professor, his excited young assistant, and a trunk full of equipment down the coast. Having arrived, they worked through the Indian River country, and then into the cypress swamps, searching, for the most part, for butterfly and moth larvae. Ray, accustomed to the sea of dead cattails in the New Jersey swamps, felt as though he had entered a new world in the vast, ghostly Everglades, where the interlacing foliage of the trees laid down a perpetual shade, and the reddish wet soil, in which the strange-shaped cypress knees and buttressed trunks were rooted, absorbed the filtered sunlight to make a deeper shade.

Ray was impressed by his elderly friend's versatility. While catching his insects, the entomologist would remark on the names and properties of the surrounding vegetation, and Ray realized that he was also a skilled botanist. As they scrambled over a railroad track after a rare tiger beetle, the doctor would launch into a discussion of the effect of temperature on the rails, or of the transmission of the railroad's electrical signals.

One day at lunch—which consisted of bread spread with canned tomatoes, fare easy to carry and thirst-quenching—the professor talked with obvious authority about the character of the Everglades soil; the evolution of steam engines; the application of steam power to fighting craft in the Civil War; and, finding that Ray was a weather fan, discussed cloud formations and their meanings.

The professor was a distinguished man in his field, yet his interest was distributed over a wide range of unrelated subjects. It became evident to Ray that exclusive concentration on one thing was not necessary to success.

TEN

IN ONE RESPECT his Florida trip had been a disappointment to Ray: he had not captured a magnificent diamond-back rattler he had come upon in the Everglades, because he had no place to keep it. The snake, coiled on an open patch of ground not thirty feet from the spot where Ray and the professor were having one of their learned luncheons, had watched them closely, following every motion with its gleaming, cat-pupiled eyes. With regret and longing Ray had finally watched the six-foot, dull-green body, with its pattern of diamond markings, uncoil and glide into the bushes. He wanted a rattler terribly.

In the end, it was his long-suffering chief, Doctor Beutenmüller, who made it possible for him to have one. Although the museum at that time had no reptile department, and no room for one, Beutenmüller yielded to Ray's pleading and told him he could add a couple of venomous snakes to the little collection in his workroom. When Ray came back from Connecticut one fall day with a handsome timber rattler he had captured, his chief was disagreeably surprised, but he stuck to his bargain.

"Where do you propose to keep the thing?" he asked.

" 'Chips' has built me a box with a sliding glass panel, and I thought it could sit on the end of my worktable."

Beutenmüller was still doubtful. "Well, if you want to work with a lethal snake glaring at you, it's your own affair, I suppose," he said.

Ray went downstairs to find the carpenter, "Chips" Coggeswell, and reappeared shortly with the snake's new home. He placed it on the end of his table, and, under Beutenmüller's anxious eye, maneuvered the reptile into the box with a staff. His chief watched with a sort of fascinated distaste, but all he said was "Whew!"

Ray had always believed that, when one captured a wild thing, every effort should be made to avoid shocking or frightening it, because it might be so affected as never to recover. He had used great care and gentleness in securing his dangerous specimen. As a result, the snake was unalarmed and manageable, and, established in its cage, quickly became accustomed to it, and fed regularly.

It proved quite an attraction, and Ray was frequently interrupted, to Doctor Beutenmüller's annoyance, by members of the museum's staff who dropped in to see the snake.

"How about stirring him up, Ray, and making him rattle?" they would sometimes suggest.

"It isn't good for him to get scared or angry," Ray would explain. "He might injure his nose if he struck the glass, or he might quit eating. Wild creatures in captivity are likely to be sensitive."

But when the august Morris K. Jesup came in with a retinue of staff members and wanted to see the snake at closer range, Ray felt he had to accommodate him. With a long staff he lifted the rattler out of its cage and placed it on the table, well away from the tray of butterflies on which he was working. The snake drew itself into a loose coil and, without alarm, lifted its rattle but made no sound.

"A fine creature," the president approved. "Why doesn't it rattle?"

"It's not scared, sir. It's used to handling."

Mr. Jesup looked at it thoughtfully. "Perhaps if I poked it . . ." he said, and before Ray could stop him he gave the rattler a smart dig with his cane. He was instantly rewarded with the sharp buzz of the rattle.

The snake, however, made no effort to strike. Instead, it turned and swiftly glided up the table. Ray darted around

65

to head it off, but not quickly enough. It plowed rapidly into and through the tray of butterflies, scattering tattered bits of wings on all sides, and took refuge in its cage where it coiled for a strike, rattling threateningly. Ray hastily slid the glass panel shut; then, apprehensively, looked at the wrecked tray.

Valuable specimens, days of laborious work, were in ruins! He was very young, and the situation, to him, was tragic. To Mr. Jesup, urbane man of affairs, it appeared merely that a tray of butterflies had been spoiled.

"You have replacement specimens, of course," he reminded Ray. "You know, that's the very first time I've ever heard a rattler," he added genially.

Later, understandably distressed by the loss of rare specimens, Doctor Beutenmüller scolded Ray. The chief gave him to understand that his venomous reptile had outstayed its welcome in the entomology department. Ray listened respectfully, and gloomily, thinking that, if anyone ever encouraged him to keep a snake, he'd probably faint.

When Doctor Beutenmüller had finished, Ray removed his rattler and his other specimens upstairs to the taxidermist's storeroom. He wanted to study living creatures, but the likelihood of his doing so seemed to be receding momentarily. Deprived of all but the very minimum of opportunity to observe his snakes, he was surrounded, as far as his imagination could reach, by dead bugs. There seemed to him to be a depressing symbolism in the fact that, to get at his reptiles, he had to scramble over the dusty, dismantled skeleton of a long-dead elephant.

Even so, there was considerable consolation to be had from visits to the Central Park menagerie. His favorite haunt was the lions' house, where the menagerie's small collection of serpents was kept. After a hasty lunch he would start from the museum at Seventy-seventh Street and, alternately running and walking, reach the menagerie on the opposite side of the park at Sixty-fourth Street in time to spend about twenty minutes with the snakes and monkeys before starting back across the park to his job.

It was on such a flying visit that he observed that one of the boas couldn't get out of its scarf skin. Its ten-foot-long body looked cracked and wrinkled, and under the old epidermal layer the new skin, beautifully patterned, showed dimly. It was plain to Ray that the snake was past the point when it could shed unaided.

Ray sought out the keeper, Hugh Downey. He wanted to make a suggestion, and he thought it had better be advanced tactfully. So far, the longest observation he had succeeded in eliciting from Downey had been an indifferent "Hello."

"That's a handsome boa you've got there, Mr. Downey," he began.

Downey took his pipe out of his mouth and looked at him. "Umh," he answered noncommittally.

"I've got a few snakes myself," Ray went on. "Nothing that large, of course."

"Have you? What kind?"

"A few of the nonvenomous local snakes, and a good-sized rattler I caught in Connecticut. I keep them at the Museum of Natural History where I work."

"A rattler? Had its fangs drawn?"

"Oh no. He's pretty tame and I'm careful, so we get on together. By the way, that boa seems to be having trouble shedding."

"Yep."

"I wonder if you've had the experience with large snakes that I've had with small ones?" Ray asked, phrasing his suggestion as a respectful inquiry. "I've found that, when one can't shed, you can cover it with a damp cloth for a day to soften the old outer skin, and then loosen it around its mouth and help it out. Can you do that with the big fellows."

"I don't see why you couldn't, except I haven't got a blanket and the stable wouldn't lend me one to use on the snakes."

"If you'd like to try it on the boa, I could get you something from the museum," Ray offered.

"Sure," agreed Mr. Downey, without any inkling that he was making Ray the happiest boy in the city.

The following day Ray appeared at the lions' house with a big piece of coarse burlap, the kind expeditions use for shipping fossils. Together he and Downey folded it into a large square and wet it down with the hose.

"Better leave this to me," the keeper said, starting into the snakes' cage. Several boas were festooned around an upright tree trunk, some water moccasins were distributed over the floor, and the patient in its uncomfortable old skin was in the farthest corner. Downey looked doubtfully at the venomous moccasins and added, "I'll sling it over him from here."

Ray was horrified. "Oh, please don't, Mr. Downey!" he begged. "That will scare him and he'll come right out from under. It ought to be done gently."

Downey heeded his warning. He got Ray a pole with a cross-piece at one end, and let him ease the moccasins out of the way. Together then, they laid the wet burlap over the boa, and Ray tucked it around carefully, with the thrilling consciousness that an audience of snakes, some of them capable of cracking his ribs, were looking on with disturbed and attentive interest.

He could hardly keep his mind on his work the rest of the afternoon, and the next morning time seemed barely to poke past.

When, after bolting a cup of coffee and a doughnut, he got to the menagerie, he was considerably dashed to find Mr. Downey nonchalantly eating steak sandwiches as though this day were just like any other. With a deliberation that made Ray frantic—he had, after all, only an hour—the keeper finished his lunch, lit a bad-smelling pipe, and sauntered to the snakes' cage. The moccasins were still grouped against the wall out of the way, and the boa was still tucked under its pad.

With a scraper the keeper slid the seventy-five-pound reptile toward the door, and Ray, all anxiety, removed the burlap. Accustomed to his harmless water and garter snakes, and one rattler, he found this creature colossal.

"I'll hang onto it by the neck, and you scrape," suggested the keeper.

Ray, who was anticipating an operation of some delicacy, shuddered.

"He seems so gentle that I don't think he'll need holding," he countered tactfully. Kneeling beside the snake, he lifted its head, as big as his two hands, off its coil. It looked huge, and it was not without a shade of apprehension that he began feeling around its strong jaws for the loose edge of the old skin with the spatulate-tipped tweezers he had brought from the museum. Hugh Downey, steadily smoking, watched without making any move to participate in the operation. Ray suddenly realized that the whole matter rested entirely in his hands. He was impressed, and slightly scared.

With the scarf skin, thin as gossamer, firmly grasped in the tweezers, he drew it back. Working around to the other side of the jaw, Ray loosened it there and began cautiously rolling it back from the big head, disclosing the beautiful pinkish tan beneath. The serpent lay quiet as he repeated the operation on the lower jaw and turned the old epidermal layer back from the neck. Then it began to crawl slowly across his lap, while he held the under and upper flaps, leaving its old skin turned inside out in his grip as it moved. The operation was precisely what it had been on his first little garter snake, only on a much larger scale. Through a haze of mephitic tobacco smoke, Mr. Downey nodded approvingly.

The process continued with painstaking slowness. Ray was so absorbed that he lost track of time. Finally, with a last wiggle, the boa disengaged the end of its tail from the old integument and glided away, beautiful in gleaming new skin, and again comfortable. The clock said quarter to two.

Ray, seeing it, was panic-stricken. He would be a whole hour late! How to explain it to Doctor Beutenmüller, who disliked snakes, and hated unpunctuality? With all his earlier elation reduced to miserable apprehension, Ray ran all the way to the museum and panted up to his office. Propped against his inkwell was a note in the familiar writing.

"Going from lunch to the printer's. Won't be back today."

Ray collapsed into his chair, and pushed the hair back from his wet forehead.

"Thank heaven for baseball!" he said feelingly.

ELEVEN

AT LAST IT had happened! Parental objections to his snake collecting had finally, without reservation, been withdrawn. It was 1896, and the family was moving to the Bronx.

"Ray, you can have the top floor all to yourself and your snakes," his father told him. "Mama and I give up. Since you're so infatuated with the creatures, maybe you can make something of your hobby."

"Oh, Pop! Oh, Pop!" Ray exclaimed. He couldn't think of anything else to say. Then a thought hit him. "Any kind?" he demanded incredulously.

"Any kind," his father assured him. "No strings attached."

As soon as they were settled in the brownstone house at 1666 Bathgate Avenue, Ray explored the neighborhood grocery stores and came home laden with stout wooden boxes. He took them up to the top floor, and his parents heard pounding and planing until late at night. At the museum, the good-natured Mr. Coggeswell knocked apart packing cases, cut the boards to Ray's specifications and planed their surfaces smooth, so that Ray could assemble the larger cages at home. In the evenings he reeled homeward under these piles of lumber, sometimes having a spirited engagement with the elevated guard before he was admitted to the train.

While he was building his cages Ray kept the door locked. He didn't want anyone to see the snake room until it was ready for occupancy; it was to be a surprise for his parents. They had to form a notion of his progress by the sound of his carpentry. When he had put together the six large and twenty smaller cages, he painted them with walnut stain, sandpapered them inside to mirror smoothness, treated the floors and walls with wax to render them non-absorbent, and sat back to wait for his bimonthly pay check so that he could buy the sliding glass panels that were to form the front of the cases. This final purchase left him destitute, but he didn't care. He had some of the finest snake cages he had ever seen. There was not a thing in them, to be sure, but to his delighted eye, they were glowing with promise.

When he ushered his parents in on a tour of inspection and proudly indicated his handiwork, they were fully as surprised as he had hoped, but considerably less pleased. The big tier of cases, with their glass fronts polished until they gleamed, carried suggestions more alarming than gratifying to them. They stared wordlessly. The next day, when Ray came home from the museum with all his specimens that had been lodged behind the elephant's bones in the taxidermist's storeroom, he found that his father had had a carpenter install wire screening on all the windows.

How did a snake collector collect snakes? That was Ray's next problem.

Local reptiles, of course, were easy enough to obtain; you caught them yourself on week ends and vacations. Tropical snakes were a different matter. Purchasing them was the obvious method. In Ray's case, however obvious it might be, it wasn't practicable: his minute salary was not geared to such expenditures. Perhaps, he reflected, he could get a raise.

Encouraged by the good wishes of Doctor Beutenmüller, who was delighted to get the live specimens out of the museum, Ray presented himself, rather nervously, before Mr. Jesup. The president of the museum remembered him well.

"Good afternoon, young man. How is the rattler?"

"Very well, thank you, sir. It's at home now. I'm starting a snake collection there, and it's my first venomous specimen."

Mr. Jesup expressed interest and asked several questions. His cordiality encouraged Ray to come to the point.

"I need more money to purchase specimens and to advance my studies," he explained, "and I wondered if I could be given, not a raise for my work in the entomology department, but an additional salary for arranging the museum's collection of pickled snakes. It has been neglected so long that it needs attention badly." As he listened to his case with a critical ear, it seemed to him so reasonable as to be irresistible. He misjudged Mr. Jesup's power of resistance.

Ever urbane and friendly, Mr. Jesup answered, "Raymond, so young a man as you should be well content with his salary, and, far more valuable than that, with the opportunity to learn the ethics and methods of science. I am truly alarmed at your intention of collecting poisonous snakes. In your own interests, I am happy that the expense will be an obstacle."

Astounded by the rejection of so well put a plea, Ray nevertheless had to believe his ears. He was not getting any raise. It occurred to him, though, that he didn't have to keep his job forever. Meanwhile, he would increase his collection as best he could.

His first addition to it was a windfall, a six-foot Florida diamond-back rattler. A New York doctor, C. Stover Allen, had been conducting a series of experiments with snake venom. As he finished with his water moccasins, he gave them to the Central Park menagerie, and it was there, one day, that Ray met him. Learning that Ray was collecting snakes, Doctor Allen told him that he could have his rattler. All he had to do was take it away.

Equipped with a large Gladstone bag, Ray turned up at the doctor's house on the appointed day to claim his snake. Doctor Allen escorted him into the cellar where it was lodged, not very comfortably, in a coal bin closed across the top with wire netting. The reptile, coiled for action in a corner, rattled sharply.

Used as he was to snakes, Ray found that he was a little awed by the size of this one. Its head was impressively broad and its body thick—about ten inches around. Furthermore, there was evidently nothing pacific about its disposition; its rattle continued to buzz warningly. Boldly, however, Ray entered the bin.

Gripping a long pole in one hand and keeping an eye on the coiled rattler, Ray placed the Gladstone bag on the floor and propped it open. Then he moved slowly toward the snake. It struck at him savagely, with such force that it was carried, sliding, over the smooth cement floor several inches beyond its normal reach. Ray slipped the pole under the loop of its neck, and gently eased it toward the bag.

His heart was pounding so that he could feel it in his ears, and he was conscious of being thrilled and not afraid. Carefully he lifted the forward end of the angry rattler and laid it across the edge of the open bag. It began to glide in, and Ray lightly touched the end of its whirring tail with his pole to speed it. When it had withdrawn completely into the bag, Ray, still using the pole, knocked the props from under the lid, and the top fell shut.

"Well done, young man!" exclaimed the doctor.

"Thank you, Doctor. When he's calmed down and gets accustomed to his new surroundings, he'll be all right, I think. It's a fine specimen. I'm very grateful to you."

"A bit scrawny from his long fast. I haven't been able to induce him to eat. If you can get him to feed properly, you'll have a nice specimen."

Carrying his innocent-looking bag with its lethal contents into the elevated, Ray entertained himself on the ride home with plots to tempt the appetite of his acquisition, and with thoughts of the reactions of the stout woman next to him, should she learn she was sharing her seat with a rattlesnake.

A vacation trip a little later netted Ray some timber rattlers, copperheads, milk snakes, black snakes and two or three other local serpents; and Doctor Allen gave him the name of

74

a man in Florida from whom, for a very modest price, he was able to buy a batch of water moccasins, and several king snakes, coachwhips, indigo snakes and harmless water snakes. The snake cages were slowly filling up.

He could capture snakes himself, he could rely on an occasional gift, and he could rarely afford to make a purchase, but it was a slow way, Ray thought, to gather together a collection, and unsatisfactory in that it got him only North American reptiles. Then, unexpectedly, a source of tropical snakes was disclosed. The captain of a freighter just in from a South American port sent a young boa constrictor that had been found in his cargo of fruit to the museum.

"We've already got a couple of these things pickled," growled Doctor Beutenmüller, eying it with disfavor. "No doubt it was kind of the man, but what am I supposed to do with it? How'd you like it for your collection, Raymond?"

"I'd like it fine! Thank you, sir!" He looked questioningly at his chief. "Do you suppose I could have the afternoon off, Doctor Beutenmüller?"

"I suppose so. And I know what you're going to do with it, too —you're going to comb the harbor for boats on tropical runs."

"That's right," Ray agreed with a smile. "This sort of thing must happen rather often, and when it does I'd like to have the snake."

On the water front, later that day, Ray learned that most immigrant reptiles were killed on discovery. When he explained what he wanted, his enthusiasm was so contagious and his manner so friendly that everyone he spoke to felt it would be a pleasure to do the young fellow with the queer hobby a favor. As a result, he received a number of promises to rescue and save reptilian stowaways, promises that, in the course of time, produced for his collection some pretty and unusual nonvenomous snakes.

Ray was learning that, to a herpetologist of ingenuity, small funds need not be a barrier to a good collection.

TWELVE

"THIS IS your department, Raymond."

Doctor Beutenmüller tossed him a letter that had been sent up from the secretary's office. Ray picked it up. It was from Trinidad, from R. R. Mole, editor of a Port-of-Spain newspaper. Mr. Mole stated that he was an enthusiastic herpetologist and had a collection of specimens indigenous to Trinidad. He was anxious to obtain some North American snakes for study, and he wondered if the museum could put him in touch with a collector who would exchange a series of North American reptiles for tropical ones.

For Ray, opportunity was not merely knocking at the door. It was assaulting it with a ramrod.

The discussion in the snake room that night was portentous. Mr. Ditmars was grave, Ray jubilant. They sat on either side of the teakwood table, gift of a friendly Chinese who had heard of and come to visit Ray's collection.

Mr. Ditmars sighed. "I hope that you will never for an instant be careless with these creatures," he said earnestly.

"Don't worry. I don't want to get bitten any more than you want me to. What do you think of this to open the exchange?" Ray pushed his list across the table.

His father scanned it. A pair each of timber rattlers, copperheads, water moccasins, king snakes, coachwhips, and milk snakes; one indigo snake, one chicken snake, one mountain black snake; four each of black racers and spreading adders; six each of striped snakes, nonvenomous water snakes and ringneck snakes; a dozen brown snakes.

"What will you get in return for a shipment like this?" John Ditmars inquired.

76

"Well, I can hope for a coral snake and a fer-de-lance—they're not too uncommon—and some very pretty nonvenomous specimens. And if my luck's too good to be true—a bushmaster. It's the most formidable of all the South American vipers, and it's a real prize."

John Ditmars' only answer was another deep sigh.

Ray had a busy time preparing his shipment of snakes for Trinidad. He packed them all into a crate with two trays divided into compartments. Each reptile was in a bag in a properly identified compartment. He wrote Mr. Mole a detailed letter, which he sent off by an earlier boat, about the shipment, dispatched the crate, and settled down to wait for the exchange.

Three months passed. Ray did not become impatient, because he knew from his own experience the difficulties and delays of collecting snakes. Finally one evening, on returning from the museum, he found a letter with a Trinidad stamp waiting for him on the Chinese table.

Eagerly he tore it open and skimmed through it. His shipment, Mr. Mole reported enthusiastically, had arrived in perfect condition. In return, he was sending a pair of fer-de-lances, four coral snakes, some rat snakes, a pair of emerald tree snakes, a tree boa, two boa constrictors—and a handsome young bushmaster! He had delayed the shipment in order to procure the bushmaster, and he advised extreme caution in handling the creature. The shipment, he concluded, was on the *Irawaddy*.

And the *Irawaddy* was even then in port! Excitement kept Ray awake most of the night.

In the morning he hurried to the pier to pilot his snakes through customs and onto an express wagon. They were in a large crate, and when he indicated its contents, everyone from customs officers to truck drivers showed a disposition to treat it with respectful caution. The next day it was deposited in the hall outside the snake room by a pair of panting expressmen who could not get rid of their burden fast enough.

His mother insisted that Ray eat dinner before opening the crate. To please her, he made the effort, but it was not a very successful one. As a matter of fact, they all merely made the gesture of eating that night. They were too excited. Ray, however, was the only one whose excitement was pleasurable. His mother, frankly anxious, insisted on witnessing the unpacking. Ray, who wanted any mistakes he might make to be known only to himself, firmly refused on the grounds—those well-tried grounds!—of wanting to surprise the family. He had his way.

With hammer and crowbar he went to work on the crate. His first anxiety was that some of the snakes might have died on the voyage. As the edge of the cover came away, an anxious sniff assured him that there had been no mortalities. Being temperamental creatures, snakes drink at irregular intervals and only when they feel like it. A snake can go for weeks without food, but if the packing for a long shipment occurs during a period when it is not drinking, it may be in bad shape from thirst, or even dead, on arrival.

On prying off the lid Ray found the case was divided, as his own had been, into two trays. The top one was sectioned into straw-cushioned compartments, containing burlap bags labeled with the name of the snake within. Lifting each bag carefully, he carried them all into the snake room, and returned to inspect the bottom tray. The boa constrictors, reported by Mr. Mole to be six and ten feet long, and the bushmaster had it to themselves.

When he raised the empty tray and looked into the bottom of the crate, he had a jolt—the boas were not in bags, but intertwined, loose, on the bottom. The larger one reared its huge head to stare at him. In the same instant Ray saw the bushmaster, in a bag in the other compartment, stir. He hastily replaced the tray.

To keep the boas from striking at him as he removed the

bushmaster, he dropped his bathrobe over them as he took off the top tray. Then he reached in and fished out the bushmaster's bag. It was disappointingly light, he thought. He put the bag on the floor and began to release his other snakes into their cages.

The nonvenomous reptiles, transferred to their new homes, made straight for their water pans and drank thirstily. The coral snakes, brilliantly marked with bright red rings, wide purple-black bands and narrow rings of yellowish white, seemed gentle, too, and though venomous, gave him no trouble. He was thrilled by the fer-de-lance. Relatively slender, it snapped the front of its body into a loop like an S laid flat, and its glittering eyes stared at Ray out of a triangular-shaped head, while its tongue flickered rapidly. Lifting it on a long piece of telegraph wire, he slipped it into its cage and, still with the wire, slid the door shut. What a creature! he thought.

"How are you getting on? Everything all right?" John Ditmars' voice boomed suddenly from the foot of the stairs.

"Fine," Ray shouted back. "Just a little longer. Wait till I call you." Now for the bushmaster, he thought. He had never seen one and he knew little about them, except that, equipped with huge fangs and a large supply of poison, they were regarded as especially dangerous.

He selected a long staff with a piece of heavy wire, bent into a crook, affixed to the end, from an array that he kept in corners of the room. Placing the bushmaster's bag in one of the big cages, he cut the draw strings and, stepping back, raised the end of the bag with his staff to tip the snake toward the opening mouth. Slowly it began to emerge. Ray was fascinated by its startling color, dusty pink with big jet-black markings. The snake's progress was slow. Only one section, somewhere along the middle of its length, showed. Overcome by curiosity and impatience, Ray stepped closer, and reaching down with his bare hand whisked the bag off the rare reptile.

Its appearance was even more astonishing than he had expected. The coloration was bold. The skin was rough as a pineapple, due to the raised center of each scale. It was a moderately slender snake, far longer than he had judged from the weight of the bag, and gracefully tapering to the long thin spine of its tail. The head was large, the snout blunt; and the reddish eyes, set above pinkish jowls—were coming closer to him! Ray sprang back.

His first look took no more than a couple of seconds and terminated instantly as he realized that the reptile, forming a striking loop with the whole front half of its body, was deliberately pouring itself toward him. Backing inadvertently into one of the chairs, Ray thrust his crook against the snake, by now well out of its cage.

He saw at once, with alarm, that the reptile had a dextrous way of flowing over the outthrust staff. Faster than he could push it away, it gained ground. There was nothing for him to do but continue to back up. He knew that bushmasters were highly venomous, but no one had told him that they were aggressive and fearless, too.

As he backed warily around the room, Ray's mind worked busily. How was he to get out of this worse-than-silly, this dangerous, situation?

"I can't keep on backing around the room the rest of the night," Ray told himself impatiently. He wasn't exactly frightened, but this certainly was not a situation he would have chosen.

Just then his eye fell on the broom standing, conveniently, within reach of his staff. He gave it a hard jerk, kicked it behind him, farther from the advancing bushmaster, and picked it up. The snake just then was surging, loops reared, between the rungs of a chair. Ray thrust the broom straight in its face.

Surprised by the attack, the serpent paused and pulled in its head. Coiling, it rattled its tail against the floor. Ray followed up his advantage with several more quick pokes. The snake decided, suddenly, that it had had enough. It turned and made for the tier of cages. Guiding it with the pole, Ray directed it into its own cage and slid shut the panel.

Ray was not surprised to find that his knees were trembling. Then he grinned: he was remembering that his thrilling encounter, some five years before, with Mr. Eggling's bad-tempered water snake had made him feel much the same way.

There still remained the boas. Ray pushed back the bathrobe and lifted the smaller snake out on the crook of a staff. It was a beautiful light tan, with chocolate-colored saddles. Moreover, it was perfectly gentle. Moving its head back and forth with what Ray took to be interest in its new surroundings, it allowed itself to be placed in the big cage next to the now tightly coiled bushmaster.

The larger boa, too, appeared good-humored, in spite of its formidable size. Ray felt a legitimate collector's pride as he looked at it. He could hardly wait to get Hugh Downey up to see it; it was larger than any in the menagerie's collection.

Slipping the crook under it, Ray pulled hard but gently. The big serpent's head and the first yard of its thick body were hoisted up. It looked around with an air of mild inquiry. Resting on the edge of the crate, it started to ooze down the side. Ray hauled out another three feet of it, and, clasping it in his arms, heaved the big fellow out of the crate. It weighed so much he staggered as he started to half carry, half drag it down the hall.

Suddenly he was halted by a sharp jerk. Looking around, he saw that the boa had caught the rail of the banisters with its tail, and was twisted firmly around it. He yanked. The snake held tighter. A tug-of-war was on the point of developing when footsteps sounded on the stairs. Ray's parents came into view. Too curious to wait longer, they had violated his explicit orders.

"Ray!" both shouted. It was a disquieting sight. A flashy-looking snake, eleven feet long and thick as a fire hose, was stretched taut in the hall. Their only son, clasping it by its middle, was pulling on it for all he was worth. The reptile, in a protest that was actually mild but looked hideous to them, was waving its head back and forth and flicking its long, blackish, forked tongue.

It was at that point that John Ditmars took his first, and last, flier in serpent management. Snatching Ray's staff from the floor, he gave the tightly twisted tail a sharp jab. Astounded by an attack from the rear, the serpent let go with a flourish. Caught off balance, Ray crashed heavily into the door and lurched through it into the snake room as the serpent, well startled, looped itself anxiously around him.

Uttering cries of consternation, Ray's parents rushed after him. They found their son, still enfolded in the big boa and sagging under its weight, quietly laughing as he stroked and soothed it. A few moments more, and he had induced it to cast off and crawl peaceably into its cage.

"Oh, Ray, what a frightful sight!" his mother exclaimed weakly, as she sank into a chair.

Ray grinned. "That's a very gentle, good-tempered snake, Mama," he explained. "If ever a snake had an excuse to lose its temper and strike, that one did, the way Pop was punishing its tail."

"I never did care for snakes," John Ditmars growled, wiping beads of perspiration off his pale forehead.

Ray had acquired, along with his new snakes, new problems. He had to figure out what kind of food the new members of his collection would eat, and how to induce unwilling snakes to feed.

Snakes are exacting about their food. Some will eat only cold-blooded prey like fish and frogs; others, warm-blooded victims like rodents and birds. Some will eat cold- or warm-

82

blooded quarry indiscriminately, so long as it is just the right size. Some are cannibals, but are fussy about the kind of snakes they will take. Some like lizards, some insects, some snails. Some, in captivity, steadfastly refuse food and starve. All decline to eat when nervous or startled.

In caring for his collection, Ray was guided principally by sympathy and interest in his charges. There was, he later explained, something about the appearance of a reptile that suggested to him the food it would accept; or its relationship to another species might give him a clue. Sometimes his hunch would be worthless, and the snake would be half-starved before he had figured out the right diet.

Mouse- and rattraps, even roach traps, which accommodating proprietors let him keep in neighborhood groceries, supplied some of his snakes; frogs and fish, which he first purchased, then bred himself, took care of others. For some of the larger specimens he had to buy rabbits. Sometimes he had to coax a nervous reptile to eat. It was a triumph of reassurance and patience when he finally induced Doctor Allen's cranky rattler to eat. He placed a skinned rabbit in its cage, and stooped before it a full half-hour, motionless and with aching knees, while the creature turned its head to glare first at him, then at its food—and finally swallowed it.

Hugh Downey, now his firm friend, sometimes came to visit him and inspect his collection. Often the advice of the veteran snake handler was invaluable.

"That fellow?" Downey would say. "Try him on snails—that's all that kind will touch." Or, "Watch for sores in the big fellows' mouths. Snakes are apt to get them after long shipment without water." And Ray would go down to First Avenue, to a place he knew where he could get live snails, and come home with a sackful of them; and he would purchase a bottle of the commonly advertised mouthwash that Downey had recommended for the boas' mouths.

Another occasional visitor of Ray's was Jack Sonwell, member of a "snake charming" troupe. On Fourteenth Street, near Third Avenue, was Huber's Museum, one of those minor showplaces where, for a dime admission, an unexacting and usually credulous public could witness the performances of itinerant showmen. When snake charmers were featured, Ray would sometimes drop in and watch with mild interest while alleged Indian princesses manipulated their tame boas and pythons. One day, seeing "The Sonwells and Their Rattlesnakes" billed, he went in.

The Sonwells had a dozen big Florida diamond-back rattlers, among the most deadly of North American serpents. They walked among them and as the snakes struck at them Ray saw, with an uneasy thrill, that the reptiles' poison fangs had not been drawn. A bite, which the performers were risking with apparent nonchalance, would almost certainly be fatal. At the close of the performance, he introduced himself to Jack, a man a little older than he, and invited him to visit his collection.

From that time on Ray and the Sonwells, especially Jack, were friends. They came to see him now and then, and on one occasion he traded one of his flourishing young diamondbacks for a large one of theirs that was refusing to eat.

"Jack," Ray warned one day, "I wish you'd be more careful with those deadly brutes of yours. You think you're keeping out of range, but the wood of that platform's so smooth that they're likely to slide as they strike, and get you."

Jack laughed easily. "Don't worry, Ray. We pretend to be a little careless, just to give the audience a thrill, but as a matter of fact we're mighty cautious."

"I hope you really are," Ray observed seriously.

The Sonwells left New York and Ray didn't see them for several months. Then, a few days after their return to Huber's, he got word late one afternoon that Jack had been bitten during the performance.

Sick with apprehension, Ray got on the elevated and hurried to the hospital. Waiting in the faintly antiseptic-smelling corridor for Jack's nurse to see him, he felt desperate at the realization of his helplessness. The diamond-back's bite was almost certain death. Some venoms, Ray knew, had an antidote, but the work was still in the early experimental stages. The antidote was not obtainable in this country, and it took months to prepare. Barring a miracle, Jack Sonwell would be dead in a matter of hours. Nobody, not even his doctors, could do a thing on earth about it.

The nurse, when she appeared, had no encouragement to offer. "I'm sorry, you can't see him. His condition is desperate," she said.

Ray went home, quiet and very pale. The next morning, when he inquired after Jack, he learned that he was dead.

THIRTEEN

HIS FRIEND'S DEATH was an ugly shock to Ray, and it made him wonder if he could contribute anything to the work that had already been done towards finding a remedy for snake bite. This was a problem that had been agitating people, in a not very urgent way, for centuries. Deaths from it were numerically few, and unimportant compared to those from more ordinary causes, so the problem at no time seemed a very pressing one; on the other hand, they were often strikingly horrible. The effects, always violent, varied widely, depending on the kind of snake and where its fangs entered; it might take a victim minutes, or days, to die. Some people recovered, but they were the lucky ones.

The ancients, even the most enlightened of them, had naïve ideas on the treatment of snake bite. The remedies offered by Pliny are a sample.

"For poisonous bites," the learned Roman wrote, "it is customary to employ a liniment made of fresh sheep droppings, cooked in wine. Rats cut in two are also applied. These animals possess important properties, especially at the epoch of the ascension of the stars, seeing that the number of a rat's fibers wax and wane with the moon.

"Of all birds, those that afford most assistance against snakes are vultures. The black ones are the weaker. The odor of their feathers when burnt puts snakes to flight. Provided with a vulture's heart, one need not fear encounters with snakes, and can also defy the wrath of wild beasts, robbers and princes.

"Cock's flesh, applied while still warm, neutralizes the venom of snakes. The brains of the bird, swallowed in wine, produce the same effect. The Parthians for this purpose make use of chickens' brains. The fresh flesh of the pigeon and the swallow, and owl's feet burned are good against snake bites.

"If one has been bitten by a snake or any venomous animal, another method of cure is to take salt fish and wine from time to time, so as to vomit in the evening."

In those days, if the snake bite failed to kill, there was a good chance that the remedy might do it.

Unfortunately, up to the last decade of the nineteenth century, nothing much more effective was developed. Chromic acid, chloride of gold, the alkaline hypochlorites, and, particularly, potassium permanganate, came into use. These chemicals, however, had to come in actual contact with the venom to destroy or modify it. Since venom is assimilated by the bloodstream from the very instant of its injection, the efficacy of these remedies was, necessarily, greatly restricted.

Not much scientific work was done on snake venoms, and their chemical and physical properties were little understood. It was not until 1882 that the discovery was made that supplied the vital clue to their nature, and provided the starting point for further work. It was made by Doctor S. Weir Mitchell, of Philadelphia, widely celebrated both as doctor and writer, who came upon it quite by accident.

Doctor Mitchell was making a call, one afternoon late that year, on a patient who was also a tenant of his. Absent-mindedly, he reached in his pocket, pulled out the key and started to insert it in the lock. Suddenly he recollected himself, dropped it back in his pocket and rang the bell. Waiting for the door to be opened, he glanced down at the rope door mat, an old one that was beginning to ravel. A loose coil from it lay like a snake across the top step and his idle eye fell on it. Although it had been twenty years since he had done any work on snake venoms, the thought flashed into his mind:

"Snake venom is a *double* poison, not a single, simple one!"

Mitchell went to work on his hunch that same afternoon. Five months later, he and his colleague, Doctor Edward

Reichert, published a preliminary paper announcing that the venoms of the several different species they had tested contained at least two toxic elements, in proportions that varied according to the species of reptile. Their definitive paper on the subject appeared in 1886 and is a landmark in the advance of knowledge about venoms.

In it they pointed out that the most important effects of venom are on the circulatory and respiratory machinery of the body. The two poisonous elements they identified they called venom-globulin and venom-peptone. The globulins, they stated, have, among other effects, the following: they destroy the coagulability of the blood; alter its red cells so that they can no longer perform their physiological job; produce changes in the capillary walls so that the modified blood seeps through them, thus creating the hideously bruised effect characteristic of certain kinds of snake bite; and paralyze the nervous center that regulates breathing. Some of the effects of the peptones, the doctors said, were the breaking down of tissue; the speeding up of putrefaction; the increase of blood pressure through irritation of the capillaries; and the increase in the rate of breathing by exciting the nerves that control it.

Some of their conclusions, of course, have been superseded by later work, but it gave the medical profession a more accurate idea of the chemical composition and pathological effect of venom, and laid the foundation for later studies.

One of the conclusions reached by Mitchell and Reichert was melancholy, and deserves quoting:

"The activities of venoms are manifested in such diverse ways and so profoundly and rapidly that it does not seem probable that we shall ever discover an agent which will be capable at the same time of acting efficiently in counteracting all the terrible energies of these poisons."

In plain English, the two best-informed men in the country thought that the chances of ever doing a great deal for the victims of snake bite were extremely slight.

Within ten years they had been proved wrong.

The year after the publication of their paper an investigator at the University of Michigan medical school showed that pigeons could be immunized against venom by inoculating them with minute amounts of it. His was the first step in the successful line of experimentation that led, at last, to the development of antivenin. At the end of another half-dozen years, Doctor Albert Calmette, of the Pasteur Institute in France, and his co-workers had demonstrated that, by vaccinating guinea pigs and rabbits with cobra venom, a strong immunity could be conferred on them. They found, too, that the blood serum of vaccinated animals contained antitoxic substances capable of transmitting the immunity to other animals.

Calmette then decided to vaccinate horses to obtain the serum in large quantities. Vaccinating horses with repeated shots of venom, he found that after sixteen months' treatment they could withstand eighty times the lethal dose. Blood was then drawn from them and the serum, after separation from this blood, tried out on rabbits. It worked. The rabbits were immune to many times the lethal amount of venom. The Pasteur Institute at Lille began to produce the serum to ship to regions, particularly India, where snake bite was relatively common. As early as 1896 it was claimed the new antidote had saved the life of a man so far gone from a cobra's bite that artificial respiration had to be used to keep him alive while the serum began to take effect. Slowly, over a period of years, the serum was improved and widely distributed; but that all happened too late to do poor Jack Sonwell any good.

Familiar with this story, Ray reflected that if he did some experimenting with venom, he too might learn something interesting. That he had neither a chemical laboratory nor chemical training did not discourage him. What did give him pause momentarily was the idea of grasping a rattler or a moccasin just back of the head and extracting its poison.

89

Weir Mitchell had described nis method of venom extraction in one of his papers, and Ray decided to follow it. It was simple, demanding only quickness and sureness of hand, but it allowed of no fumbling. He planned to make the experiment one night after dinner, and wisely refrained from mentioning it to his parents.

The necessary equipment was simple, consisting only of a glass tumbler covered with a tightly stretched piece of chamois, and the usual handling staff. Selecting one of his smaller and more amiable rattlers, he reached into its cage with the staff and conveyed it to the table top. It coiled and buzzed, and Ray, with swift precision, swung it half out of its coil with the staff, pressed its head down firmly, and with a dart of his hand, seized it by the neck so close behind the head that it could not turn. While the serpent thrashed resentfully, he took the glass in his other hand, raised it to the snake's gaping mouth and pressed the chamois against the fangs. As they penetrated, a few drops of amber poison spurted into the glass. Breathing hard, Ray released the snake and restored it to its cage.

That was the beginning of his venom collecting. He used a different glass for each species, and poured the venom into test tubes. He quickly learned, however, that poison kept for a short time in a fluid state spoiled, giving off a strong, disagreeable smell. That situation was easily remedied by drying the stuff in glass containers and cautiously, to avoid inhaling any, scraping off the crystalline flakes and dust of dry venom.

To insure himself against unexpected interruption, he worked with the door of the snake room locked. A bite was a possibility he didn't even contemplate. Only through his own carelessness could he be hurt, and he had recently had a lasting lesson on the penalty of carelessness. So, carefully and curiously, he "milked" his rattlers, his moccasins, his copperheads, even his sinister fer-de-lance, and soon had a lengthening rack of test tubes hanging in the snake room, containing venoms ranging in color from amber to greenish yellow. Only the diabolical bushmaster was not called on for contributions; after the almost invariable custom of its kind in captivity, it was stubbornly starving itself to death. Ray feared that handling or otherwise disturbing it would only hasten its end.

As his collection of venoms expanded, an idea began to take shape in his head. Judging from the color of the poison, its toxic power varied from snake to snake of the same species, depending on the relative conditions of the reptiles; and it varied, too, he suspected, in the same snake at different times, depending, for one thing, on how recently the creature had been milked. He decided to keep careful track of the venom of his dozen moccasins, and maybe he would have an opportunity to experiment with its strength and check his theory.

Kate Swan was a vivacious, energetic little lady, always, as befitted one of the star feature writers of *The New York World,* on the lookout for a good story. The first time Ray saw her she was going down the throat of a whale.

The whale—or its skeleton, to be accurate—was suspended from the ceiling of the main hall of the museum, and Miss Swan had gained access to it by means of a ladder, courteously provided by the superintendent, Mr. Wallace. She was planning a feature story about whales, and wished to determine whether the creatures really afforded adequate accommodations for a human being. There was that story about Jonah, but she wanted to see for herself.

Ray and a small group of the museum staff gazed upward as she picked her way over the iron braces that gave a precarious foothold through the throat and into the rib cavity. Miss Swan stood erect, stretched out her arms as far as she could reach them, and pronounced the whale a truly capacious animal.

When she had come down to earth again, Mr. Wallace introduced Ray.

"Raymond would make a good story for you, Miss Swan.

He's a snake fancier, and keeps a big batch of poisonous ones in his room."

"Really, Mr. Ditmars? I'd love to see them. Perhaps there would be a story in it."

"I'd like very much to have you come. I have some rather unusual specimens. When would you like to see them?"

A few nights later Mary Ditmars escorted to her son's room the woman who was to present him, for the first time, to the newspaper-reading public. Kate Swan was startled and thrilled as she entered the snake room to see the blond young man holding a great boa, swabbing out its gaping mouth with some cotton, dipped in mouthwash, twisted around the end of a penholder. The reptile was submitting to the operation with perfect gentleness. Ray finished the treatment and shook hands with his caller.

"He's had a sore mouth," he explained, "but it's almost well now. I'm keeping up the treatment until the inflammation's entirely gone." He held the big, gentle snake toward her, and hesitantly she touched its beautiful head.

Ray showed her everything. He pointed out his rack of dried poisons, took down from the wall the skull of one of his deceased rattlers and explained its venom apparatus, told her about Calmette's promising work, even demonstrated how he extracted venom. He gave her a small, harmless green snake to hold, and observed with approval that she did not quail, but, like a sensible woman, stroked and petted the little creature. He told her of some of the queer characteristics of snakes. When she admired his display of snake skins, he explained why the big boa skin, the one from the menagerie, held a place of honor; and, with melancholy, pointed out to her all that remained of the suicidal bushmaster. Finally, he let her help him skin an eleven-foot boa that had recently arrived in such bad shape in a second shipment from Trinidad that it had died the day before. Altogether, it was a most successful interview.

A day or so later, he received a letter from her.

"My dear Mr. Ditmars," she wrote. "To my amazement, Mr. Brisbane, the managing editor, was struck with your affairs. I wrote an exceedingly commonplace yarn but two expressions caught B's attention and he has personally ordered a peculiar illustration . . .

"It is not supposed to represent what you actually do—but I warn you now so you won't be scared when you see it. I can tell you, you are an object of immense interest in this office this week."

The following Sunday—the historic date was February 11, 1897—Ray got up early and, filled with anticipation, hurried out into the cold, dark street to get the paper carrying his name in print for the very first time. When he saw the "peculiar illustration" concocted by the heated imagination of a staff artist under the influence of Mr. Arthur Brisbane, he was glad that Kate Swan had warned him.

Never in a lifetime full of snakes had he seen so many in one picture. By actual count there were twenty-three. A figure which Ray recognized as a fanciful representation of Raymond L. Ditmars occupied the center of the picture. From the floor around, cobras, hoods spread, reared. Two large pythons closely girdled the central figure, while copperheads and moccasins in startling profusion emerged from his pockets, and a couple of things Ray thought were anacondas ascended his legs. On one outstretched hand there rested the head of an immense boa constrictor. The other hand was recklessly engaged in brandishing a diamond-back rattler. The caption at the top read VENOMOUS SNAKES ARE HIS PETS, and the one at the bottom made Ray blush. It was, PROFESSOR R. L. DITMARS, CURATOR OF THE AMERICAN MUSEUM OF NATURAL HISTORY, AND HIS CRAWLY PLAYTHINGS. Professor! Curator! He was not yet twenty-one.

The text, happily, was not lurid like the drawing. Kate Swan had done a good job. Her story was interesting, full of detail, and accurate, although it did make Ray feel foolish when it referred to him as "Master of the Snakes" and "Prince of Serpents."

When he showed the page spread to his parents, John Ditmars, for the first time in his life, got a hearty laugh out of Ray and his snakes.

" 'Peculiar illustration'! Oh my word!" he exclaimed. "What a masterpiece of understatement! But it's a nice story, son. It will help build you up as an authority in your field."

" 'Professor,' " Mary Ditmars said with a thoughtful smile. " 'Curator.' Maybe you really will be sometime soon, dear."

FOURTEEN

THE FIRST RESULT of Kate Swan's article left Ray breathless. Weir Mitchell, the great Weir Mitchell, came to call on him! As he showed the handsome, elderly doctor around his snake room, Ray could hardly believe it was true. He had many times thought of writing him to ask about some of the problems of snake venom that bothered him, but he was too modest to do it. Mitchell was famous, he was wise, he was busy; it would be an imposition, Ray feared, to intrude on his time even by letter.

And now Doctor Mitchell had sought him out on his own initiative. He was sitting at the Chinese table, admiring the snake cages, examining the array of venoms, listening with encouraging interest as Ray diffidently mentioned his notions about the variable toxicity of venoms.

"It's a good point, Mr. Ditmars," Mitchell said, studying the special set of moccasin poison. "It's one that ought to be cleared up, particularly if the antivenin—you know about Calmette's work, of course?—is to be successfully standardized."

"These test tubes are all labeled, you see, doctor, with the full circumstances under which the venom was extracted. If the color means anything, there are varying degrees of difference in the strength of the venoms."

They talked for a long time and when he left, Mitchell carried away with him, as a gift, all the tubes of venom that had most interested him. Ray felt very proud to be able to make even such a small contribution to venom research. Also, his parents were impressed. Ray's latest and most dangerous activity evidently wasn't just a useless playing with fire, if the famous Doctor Mitchell saw some good in it.

The limitations placed by his small salary on his career as a snake collector were growing increasingly irksome to Ray. And soon a way to relieve the financial crisis occurred to him. He had several times taken snakes, usually large, harmless kings, to initiations of his school fraternity, Chi Sigma Chi, at which they had created much interest and excitement. Everyone wanted to handle them, and Ray found that he always had to give a short talk about them. Why shouldn't he try to become a paid lecturer? Maybe Dr. Henry Leipziger, director of evening lectures for the New York City public schools, would let him give a few.

No record remains of the launching of this enterprise, except the herpetologist's own brief remark that the first lecture, illustrated with live specimens, was a success. A more fully documented account, however, covers another lecture which he delivered about this time.

Three New York doctors called on him one Sunday and asked him to speak before a medical society. Ray was excited, and flattered that medical men should seek him out and offer him a fee for a lecture. With the idea of giving them their money's worth, he packed two satchels of snakes to take to the lecture. In one were his harmless reptiles. In the other he bundled Doctor Allen's big diamond-back, now the lustiest, most lethal rattler in his collection.

It was Ray's first appearance before a strange professional group, and he was nervous. To the audience, the fair young man on the stage looked even slighter and younger than he actually was. He handled his harmless reptiles, however, with reassuring skill, and, they thought, was putting on a good show. When he recounted his brush with the bushmaster, they shuddered appreciatively.

At Ray's announcement that he would now demonstrate how venom was extracted, everyone stiffened with an interest well mixed with apprehension, particularly when the thin, youthful lecturer went on to explain that the diamond-back was the most deadly of all North American serpents, and that he was fortunate in having an unusually large and handsome specimen.

In complete silence Ray loosened the strings of the rattler's bag and, by upending it with his pole, dumped the creature out on his table. As it coiled and quivered its warning, he went through his adroit routine of pinioning its head, grasping it by the neck and pressing the chamois-covered glass against the huge, wicked-looking fangs. When they pierced through the chamois, half a dozen drops of amber poison squirted into the glass.

Murmurs of awed interest, a loud gasp, even a brusquely muffled cry reached the busy lecturer, now engaged in stuffing his wrathful stooge, tail foremost, into the bag. Letting go the big head and snatching away his hand, Ray jerked the neck of the bag upward and gave it a twirl to close it. Only then was he able to look out, anxiously, at his audience. Had he *really* held their interest? Had they *really* been impressed? Had he, in his first paid, professional lecture, "put it over"?

His question was answered by the tableau at the back of the room. A little group of doctors was gathered in an agitated knot around a gentleman in their midst. Pale and limply lolling, he was being supported in his seat on both sides, while a glass of water was being held to his blanched lips.

The poor man had fainted.

Ray's social life, up to the time of Kate Swan's article, had been conventional. Its formal phase had opened two or three years before when, appearing for the first time in a dress suit, he had taken his sister Ella to a museum-sponsored lecture given at the elegant Waldorf-Astoria Hotel.

For some reason which nobody remembers now, although he had his first tails, Ray didn't have a silk hat; therefore he borrowed his brother-in-law's. Jim Mathews was a big man and his topper rested well down over Ray's brow, so Ray wadded the hatband with a long twist of paper. Feeling very adult, very well dressed, and not a little self-conscious, he escorted Ella the length of the famous Peacock Alley, in whose brilliant mirrors so much of the wealth and fashion of New York was nightly reflected. It was not until he reached his seat and took off his borrowed hat that he realized, with a pang of chagrin that turned him scarlet, that a length of stuffing had emerged from the hatband and was trailing down his neck.

Having survived this embarrassing beginning, Ray took readily to social pleasures. He was gay and good-natured, and interested in so many things that he could talk to even the shyest person. Although he had never taken lessons, he enjoyed the piano, playing it with energy and sentiment and composing with considerable talent. He knew plenty of girls and had fun with them; he even fell in love, slightly, now and then, but never took it seriously.

Thanks to Kate Swan, his highly normal social life began to expand in an unconventional direction. He made friends with circus people. The article had appeared in February, when many traveling circuses were holed up for the winter and the performers, weary snake charmers and tired reptiles among them, were thriftily living in small apartments and boardinghouses. From snake charmers Ray received a flurry of letters asking advice about indisposed serpents.

Making the rounds to inspect the patients and offer advice, Ray found out a lot about circus snake charmers. Most of them, he learned, were hard-working—it is hard work, and monotonous, heaving a seventy-five-pound snake around night after night—middle-aged women who earned a modest living by traveling with a circus and handling their big tame snakes. There was no "charming" involved in their performances. The reptiles, far from being under any occult influence, were simply gentle creatures well accustomed to handling. It was really the customers who were charmed, and that, after all, was just what they came for.

On his sick-calls Ray found, in almost every case, a boa or python with a sore mouth. He prescribed the treatment he had learned from Hugh Downey, politely declined payment, and often, over a cup of tea, listened to accounts of circus life.

It was the letter from "Mademoiselle Olga," asking if he knew where she could get a good boa, which led to his most interesting visits. When he presented himself at the door of her neat apartment he was invited in by a pleasant woman with gray hair, who introduced herself as Olga. Ray, who had supposed the glamorous young blonde decked in snakes, whose picture he had spotted on the wall as he entered, was Olga, looked confused. Olga laughed.

"It's the blond wig," she explained. "It takes twenty years off my age. I have two daughters as old as you."

Her pythons were beautiful creatures, in excellent condition. Inspecting the reptiles critically, Ray thought that he and Olga could do a piece of mutually satisfactory snake-trading.

Olga wanted a big boa for her act. His larger boa, which was eating him into the poorhouse, had entirely recovered from its sore mouth and would probably suit her very well. On the other hand, he needed a python to fill a gap in his collection, and one of her smaller ones would fill the bill and at the same time have a thriftier appetite than the snake it was replacing.

"I think we can arrange a swap," Ray told Olga. "That big boa of mine should be just the snake for you." He enlarged on its merits.

Olga was interested, but wouldn't commit herself.

"I'll tell you what I'll do," Ray suggested. "I'll bring him down to you tomorrow night after dinner, and, if you decide he's what you want, it's a deal."

All the way home in the elevated Ray wondered how he was going to convey a snake weighing more than half as much as he did from the Bronx to Greenwich Village. To send it by the express company was out of the question: the weather was cold and the snake might be fatally chilled. To try to carry it in a wooden box on the elevated would probably involve him in a battle with the conductor; besides, between the weight of a substantial box and the reptile's own, he would be crushed to the ground.

The train rattled to a stop, then jerked off again. Down the aisle, proceeding with the precarious, lurching gait peculiar to patrons of the elevated railway, came a large woman, red-faced and red-handed, clasping in her arms a big wicker basket filled with laundry. Settling into a seat, she disposed the basket on her knees, and wondered why the young gentleman opposite gave her such a nice smile.

Carrying a laundry basket in the "el" might not give him the perfect air of scientific dignity, Ray reflected the next evening, but he didn't care. It was a fine way to get a big boa constrictor around. The conductor passed staggeringly down the aisle, and Ray gave him the innocent look of a young man bound on a household errand for his mother.

When Olga saw the boa she was in an ecstasy.

"What a beauty! And so gentle, so handsome! He's exactly what I've been looking for for several years." She laid the big snake over her shoulders, and it turned its head back and forth with its usual bland and friendly interest. Disengaging herself, Olga draped it over a chair back.

"Have you time to meet some of my friends, some circus people who live in this building?" she inquired.

"I'd be delighted to meet them," Ray assured her.

"I'll call them in," she said, and hurried out of the apartment.

When the guests arrived, Ray found some of them at first sight startling, particularly the fat lady, the giant, and a tall man, dignified as a church warden, whose skin was bright blue. The occasion developed into a party. Olga produced sandwiches and cakes and coffee, and everyone talked and laughed and treated Ray in the friendliest manner, not at all like an outsider. He had a grand time.

After the guests had helped Olga wash up, the business of selecting Ray's python began. Olga took her snakes out one by one and, draped in reptilian neckpieces, demonstrated their gentleness. Ray finally decided on a handsome eight-footer.

"That's my Teddy. He's kind as a dove," Olga told him.

Ray's new friends helped him pack the dovelike Teddy into the wash basket, making quite a farewell ceremony of it, and he shook hands all around and invited everybody to come visit his collection and keep in touch with Teddy.

At the museum, Ray was still confined to the insects. Aside from that, his life was getting more and more interesting. He corresponded with Mitchell. He continued to collect venoms. His new circus friends, admitting him to their circle on terms of equality, paid him visits and produced a sensation among the neighborhood children. He exchanged more shipments with Mr. Mole, bought an occasional snake, and supported his collection, if not in luxury, with scrupulous care. He was developing a small photographic studio, too, with a sanded stage, and finding the enterprise an expensive one. About the only thing, in fact, that didn't cost him money was playing the piano.

There was no escaping the fact that his salary was not adequate to sustain his manner of life. He would have to give up the more costly of his interests, or get a better job. Between the alternatives the choice, of course, was clear.

Mr. Jesup and Doctor Beutenmüller protested vehemently over the latter idea. He was too precipitate. He didn't realize how impractical it was for an embryo scientist to abandon his connection with a functioning scientific institution like the museum. He had warm friends there, he was accumulating valuable experience, he was establishing the foundations of a promising career. Ray knew their arguments were sound, but the fact remained that his wages couldn't support his work, and his studies had come to a standstill.

Finally, they let him go, with good wishes and regretful head-shaking. So, on January 1, 1898, Ray went to work for the Kny-Scheerer Company, an optical instrument company, for the fine salary of fifty dollars a month, and the tempting lure of a raise to sixty at the end of six months.

FIFTEEN

THE GREAT ADVANTAGE of the Kny-Scheerer job was that it was at 17 Park Row, in the section of downtown New York where most of the newspapers were clustered in that day. Ray had always written well and easily, and what he was able to see of a newspaperman's life appealed to him. It was, he thought, the kind of independent life he would like himself. By the time his six months were up, he had obtained a job with *The New York Times.*

Henry Lowenthal, the managing editor, had looked him over, and liked what he saw.

"I'll give you two weeks' trial, young man," he said.

"Thank you, sir!" Ray said. Then he asked, "Does it have to be just trial, Mr. Lowenthal? The idea of being out of a permanent job makes me very uneasy."

The editor smothered a smile. "My dear boy," he inquired dryly, "then what in the world are you doing in the newspaper business?"

In spite of his fears, Ray did well in his probationary period. Combined with the ability of expressing himself, he had natural news sense. Lowenthal recognized in him the makings of a good reporter. When the two weeks were up, Ray was told he had a permanent job.

He did the usual work of a green young reporter, covering the police courts and minor fires, accidents and brawls; but in the eyes of his new associates he had a special distinction— not every cub had a collection of twenty-six snakes, many of them venomous.

Sometimes, when he had a lecture to deliver, he would bring a satchelful of snakes to the office and leave it beside his desk in the editorial room, where the reporters, in a sort of orderly madhouse, worked. If anyone was interested, he would take out his specimens and show them around the office, arousing a certain amount of carefully camouflaged consternation among the antisnake element. There were murmurs of protest, but they did not reach the force of organized revolt without some cause.

One day Bacon, a reporter whom snakes rendered very apprehensive, saw a satchel on the floor and thought he heard it squeak as though on the point of bursting open. Feeling courageous, like a man dealing promptly with a dangerous emergency, he snatched it up and locked it in the steel cabinet where biographical records were kept. An hour later there was an angry commotion. Another reporter, one with an out-of-town engagement, couldn't find his bag and had missed his train. At the height of the disturbance Ray entered, and was immediately taken to task by Bacon for leaving his snakes in an about-to-burst satchel.

"But I didn't bring any snakes in today," Ray protested.

"Oh yes you did!" Bacon insisted. "I've got them right here in the cabinet."

He produced the suitcase. Taken aback—it looked just like his own—Ray opened it. Its contents were a shaving kit, a change of underwear and two clean shirts.

"NO MORE SNAKES!" was the unanimous demand.

"All right, then! If you're all so scared of a few little snakes that you get stampeded into locking up an inoffensive suitcase full of clean clothes, I'll find somebody less timid to leave them with." Ray felt rather huffy for a few minutes.

Several days later he came into the editorial room and announced cheerfully:

"You boys won't have to worry about my snakes any more. I've got a new place to leave them now."

"Where?"

"The County Recorder's office. Mr. Goff said I could leave them with him."

At the roar of laughter that met this innocent declaration, even the city editor came running out of his cubbyhole to see what was funny.

Ray might scare his colleagues with his unwelcome reptiles, and he might amuse them by the unheard-of procedure of getting a prominent city official to mind them for him, but he was popular among them. He was a good worker, and a good companion, and during his year on *The Times* he made a number of friendships with newspapermen that were pleasant then and valuable later.

His hours, noon to midnight, left him little free time, and he had to plan it with care. He began his day by getting up about ten. After breakfast, he had time to pull out and turn the glass cage panels that needed polishing, before taking the trip downtown to work. Having finished his long shift, he would arrive home about one-thirty in the morning, and there would be the cages to inspect and clean. At the end of an hour of this work, he would tumble into bed for a short, sound night's rest.

His day off was usually devoted to field trips to catch frogs for some of his snakes, or occasionally to a lecture before a high school science class. When the day off and the lecture did not coincide, he would swap shifts with another reporter, or Mr. Lowenthal would give him extra time. The managing editor, always sympathetic and encouraging to young men in his office, liked his work and respected the reputation he was beginning to acquire.

A couple of times a week Ray took up a collection in Chinatown and Bowery eating places for his mouse-eaters. That part of New York swarmed with rats and mice, and by placing circular traps, capable of ensnaring several victims at a time, in restaurants selected for their high rodent-production records, Ray was able to supply a number of his reptiles with all they could eat, free.

Between the inexhaustible supply of free mice and his larger income, Ray found with satisfaction that he was solvent again. His schedule was hard, but he didn't care. He liked newspaper work and felt that he was good at it; and it meant everything to him to continue to augment and improve his collection.

The city editor had a job for Ray.

"Ditmars, I've got something in your line. Go up to the Bronx and talk to Doctor Hornaday and write me a story on the new zoo's progress."

Ray realized later that the city editor, with those few words, had that day projected him into his future.

In 1894, when Theodore Roosevelt was president of the Boone and Crockett Club, one of its members had remarked:

"New York City ought to have a *real* zoological park."

Most of the men present that fall afternoon, relaxing in their comfortable chairs or warming their backs at the fireplace, were sportsmen and big-game hunters. The idea, so casually advanced, took hold of their imaginations at once. The little menagerie in Central Park had only a tiny collection of animals, not too well displayed and of limited educational value. Surely New York, the nation's greatest city, ought to be able to show something better than that.

The idea grew. By April 26, 1895, a charter had been obtained for the projected scheme. The New York Zoological Society, as the new organization was called, was to open a zoological garden, free to the public, which would provide a scientific approach to the study of living creatures. It was to stimulate public interest in the knowledge of animal life, and it was to co-operate with other organizations in preserving wildlife and encouraging sentiment against its wanton de-

106

struction. Two hundred and sixty-one acres of wilderness at the southern end of Bronx Park, land easily adaptable to the Society's use, were selected for it. In June, 1898, ground was broken. By the time the city editor of *The Times* sent Ray Ditmars up to interview his old acquaintance, Doctor Hornaday, the park's progress was visible.

Doctor Hornaday, receiving the reporter on that late December day in his temporary office in the Elk House, was enthusiastic and communicative, and in a peppery frame of mind over delays, most of them occasioned by the severe winter weather. Where the aquatic mammals' pond should be, there was an expanse of black muck, frozen rock-hard. Contracts for walks, roads, sewers had been approved so late in the season that no work would be possible on them before spring. The actual collecting of animals had made little progress—the exhibits at that point consisted of a bear cub, a wolf pup and a snapping turtle in a tin bathtub—because few of the houses for their accommodation had progressed sufficiently. But the ground was cleared, buildings were under construction and hopes were justifiably high. In spite of having fallen behind schedule, the promise of the zoological park was exhilarating.

Ray had a long talk with Doctor Hornaday, and reflected on the way home, with embarrassment, that he had done a good deal of talking himself, about R. L. Ditmars and snakes. Back at the office, he wrote a news story filled with facts, figures, and enthusiasm.

Ray's account of the zoo's progress appeared on Monday morning, January 2, 1899. Five days later Doctor Hornaday wrote to him:

"Dear Mr. Ditmars:
"I am delighted to find you on *The Times* which has always been one of our staunchest and most helpful friends. . . .

"Your 'story' is very good and helpful, and very correctly written. . . .

"I have been thinking about you in connection with our Reptile House. Would you like to be Keeper of Reptiles? If so, we had best meet soon, at our Wall Street office, some day when I go down town, to talk over the matter.

"Very truly yours,
"W. T. Hornaday."

Would he like to be Keeper of Reptiles! Keeper of Reptiles in the zoological garden that on its opening would be—his own story promised it—"the finest in the world!" It was a prospect beyond his wildest dreams.

Hesitantly he invaded Mr. Lowenthal's office to ask his advice.

"It's an unusual opportunity, Ditmars. The job will be big or little, whatever you make of it."

"Do you think I should take it, Mr. Lowenthal?"

The managing editor looked at his cub thoughtfully. It would be too bad to lose him.

"By all means," he advised.

SIXTEEN

On July 17, 1899, Ray Ditmars was hired as assistant curator of reptiles at the New York Zoological Park.

Will Beebe, whose poise he had envied at that Linnaean Society meeting several years earlier, was assistant curator of birds. Doctor Hornaday, who as director held the title of curator of snakes, mammals and birds, was an acquaintance of six or eight years' standing. With Henry Fairfield Osborn, chairman of the park's executive committee, Ray had had long and kindly association at the museum. Had he selected them himself, he could hardly have hoped for more friendly colleagues with whom to start his new job, and his life's work.

To the young man who found himself suddenly in charge of it, the Reptile House seemed too good to be true. It was the intention of the Zoological Park's founders that this zoo, unlike many others at that time, should place the same emphasis on reptiles as on birds and mammals and exhibit a representative series of them from all parts of the world. Funds for their purchase were adequate, and the building to accommodate them was to be in keeping with the importance of the exhibit. The house had been begun the previous August, and on the raw December day when young Ditmars interviewed Doctor Hornaday its foundation walls were finished and its steel floor beams in place. Ray spent every spare moment watching the progress of the building over which he was to preside. Its buff brick walls steadily rose to enclose the central hall with the alligator pond and the huge snake room separated from it by three big arches.

His delighted parents could hardly believe it: their son was getting the one, the perfect, job in the world for him—and he was being paid a hundred dollars a month! Only twenty-three, he was an acknowledged expert in his field. And he was giving his collection to the zoo. Henceforth the top floor of the Ditmars' house would be like the top floor of any other well-regulated house. It was a very restful prospect.

Although the Reptile House was not completed yet, Ray, as soon as he joined the staff of the zoo, set to work to form a collection with his own forty-five snakes, representing fifteen species, as a nucleus. Now there was no more need for laborious thrift—nor was there much time. The opening of the zoo, twice postponed, was scheduled for November 8, 1899. He could buy anything he wanted that would enhance the interest and value of the collection, but he had to do it fast. He plunged into a welter of correspondence and cables.

While the reptiles were being gathered together and the Reptile House was being made ready for them, they were temporarily housed in a shelter in the animal yard, a large fenced-in space at the north end of the storehouse building, divided into wire enclosures and equipped with temporary sheds. Pelicans, a caribou, alligators, elk, snakes, lived there in elbow-rubbing proximity until their proper quarters were ready. While the arrangement was satisfactory to Ray as long as the warm weather held, he became uneasy about it with the advance of fall. Constantly hovering over his charges, however, he steered them all through the difficult preopening period, with the exception of one, a python that succumbed to a cold snap in October.

In those last several months before the opening, everyone was desperately busy. Forty teams and their drivers and dozens of workmen labored on roads, sewers, clearings, buildings. Curators and keepers coddled their charges unremittingly. The officers in charge of construction toiled from early morning to sunset. Doctor Hornaday hovered over all, directing, urging, and in one way or another getting things done. When the big day came, the roads were passable, the grounds were presentable, twenty-two permanent installations for the animals were ready, and eight hundred and forty-three creatures, from the safety of pen and cage, calmly inspected the excited crowds that flowed through the park to goggle at them.

Doctor Hornaday himself admitted that "no event in connection with the opening of the Zoological Park was watched by the public with keener interest than the completion and opening of the Reptile House." After the short ceremony during which Professor Osborn, speaking from a bunting-draped temporary platform, proudly assured his listeners that New York City now had the largest zoological park in the world, the crowd broke up, and many of its members trooped to the Reptile House. Ladies in long full skirts and jackets with leg-of-mutton sleeves, accompanied by gentlemen in derby hats, poured through the doors into the hall where the alligators dozed in the pool with the wide sanded banks, and through the arches into the jungly fern-hung interior of the huge snake room.

Ray, dressed in his best and with his new blond mustache groomed to perfection, circulated in the crowd. At last, he reflected, he was in a position to do some missionary work on behalf of snakes—to explain their peculiar beauty, their utility, their place in the natural scheme. Watching the fascinated crowd as they studiously read the labels, gazed through the plate-glass fronts of the cages, and shuddered and stared at the unaccustomed creatures within, Ditmars was sure that he had before him the prospect of a constructive and happy life.

Young Ditmars' primary concern for the first few months in his new job was to expand the collection. He succeeded in this so well that by the first of the year he had acquired more than four hundred reptiles. After closing hour, when the visitors left the Reptile House, he and Charles Snyder, his head keeper, would lock the doors and make the rounds to inspect and feed their temperamental specimens.

An idea of the curator's catering problem can be gained from the menu for 1900. That year he had to provide three hundred and eighty-nine mice, one thousand four hundred and ten rats, one thousand two hundred and seventy-three English sparrows, three hundred and sixty-six rabbits, five hundred and thirty-one pigeons, two hundred and thirty-two chickens, eight hundred and twelve toads, four hundred and eight frogs, twenty-six thousand nine hundred live fish, fifty-five pounds of earthworms, one hundred and twenty-two large pumpkins, eighteen thousand mealworms, and more than a ton of green vegetables.

There were plenty of problems besides catering. Some of the reptiles ate readily, some were fussy or frightened, some refused food altogether. Some developed sore mouths. Some serpents had to be kept dry, some needed bathing tanks. Some liked to drape their gaudy lengths over high branches, some preferred to lie in the sand, others were at home only in beds of dead leaves that blended with their own colors. The requirements and whims of each reptile had to be fathomed and taken into account.

Sympathy, observation, common sense, intuition guided Ditmars and his helper in caring for their varied and sensitive charges. There was still no book that described their habits and requirements.

"I'll write one myself," the young herpetologist decided, and began collecting notes on his observations.

In August, 1900, Ray had his first vacation from the Zoo. With Charles Snyder, he went to the South Carolina swamps to collect specimens.

Ray had counted his money and found that he had enough to finance himself frugally, since, at the invitation of one of its members, he would be able to stay at the Pinelands Club near Robertsville, South Carolina. Always independent about money, he intended that this expedition, and all his subsequent ones, should be paid for out of his own pocket. If he could not regard a collecting trip as a success, he preferred to have wasted his own funds, and to be answerable only to himself.

Driving in a light, tough buckboard loaded with their collecting apparatus, and accompanied by Negro guides on horseback, Ditmars and Snyder went on daily expeditions into the countryside surrounding the club. The ditches on either side of the causeway through the swamps were particularly productive of snakes and both young men returned night after night to the clean civilization of the club muddy to the waist from jumping into the swamp to grab some harmless water snake.

A reptile that the young curator wanted for the Zoological Park was a harmless water snake whose long head, swollen at the temples and set with small pop eyes near the snout, made it look more horribly threatening than even the venomous water moccasin. These snakes lay, entwined in friendly clusters, on fallen logs, or floated perpendicularly in the water, anchoring themselves by the tail to some submerged aquatic plant. Agile and apprehensive, they could be approached only with the utmost caution. Stalking them, the young naturalists found, was not only a delicate but a painful operation due to the swarms of bloodthirsty mosquitoes that settled on neck and face and hands and tormented them almost past endurance.

Ray, angling patiently with his noose attached to a bamboo pole for an especially fine specimen, bit his lip grimly as a big hungry mosquito bit his nose. Stung almost to desperation, he refrained from giving it the smack that would exterminate it—and scare the shy snake out of reach. Gently, almost imperceptibly, he lowered the noose over the reptile's head, while Snyder, holding his breath, watched the operation. Then, somehow, the loop touched against a bramble, trembled, and communicated the alarm to the alert snake. With a lightning-like motion it snapped back its head and dove into the water.

"Great Scot!" Ditmars shouted—it was the strongest exclamation he ever allowed himself—and squashed the mosquito against his nose with a vicious swat. Snyder, doubled up with laughter, missed his footing on the crumbling bank, and rolled, with flailing arms, into the water. Ray lent him a hand as he rose, sputtering, and hauled him out. Gasping with mirth, the two young men sat down to recover themselves.

"This is really the life!" Ditmars said, delicately removing the remains of the deceased mosquito from the end of his nose.

"I'm certainly sorry for all those poor city-bound wretches who don't know *Agkistrodon* from *Natrix*," Snyder said happily. "Just look what they're missing."

"Just look!" Ray agreed, eying his sticky companion.

Not all of their mishaps on this first expedition were as carefree as this one. One day Ray, leaving Charlie behind to build some crates, set out with four Negroes for a sand island, a curious spot like a desert in the midst of the swamp, scattered with low brush and patches of cacti. His guides advised him to start at dawn so as to be back by nightfall, since the river was rising and would flood the swamp. The four-hour journey across the lowgrounds to the sandhill was uneventful.

While the Negroes speared carp in the near-by lagoons, Ray spent several hours driving his rig about the sandhill, collecting plants for a botanical friend and chasing lizards.

Toward the middle of the afternoon his guides suggested that Ditmars start back, since the rising water would soon flood the causeway. Spot-Nose, the pinto horse he was driving, knew the way out as well as they did, they said, and would get him safely home. They, being on horseback, would fish a little longer and go out by another trail impassable to the buckboard.

With scarcely a misgiving, Ray mounted the wagon, loosened the reins, and clucked to Spot-Nose. The horse trudged off, and Ray settled himself for the long drive. Spot-Nose meandered steadily along the trail which Ray could recognize by the blazes on the tree trunks. After a while, however, he noted uneasily that the blazes had disappeared. Was the water rising faster than the Negroes had thought? He decided that it was, alarmingly, when the trail led into an expanse of water. His unpracticed eye could no longer follow the course of the submerged causeway. The scrawny horse, however, waded in and unhesitatingly began to thread his way among the cypress knees. Ray sat tight, waiting for the jolt that would indicate that they were off the track. Finally, feeling the responsibility laid on him by the superiority of the human over the equine intelligence, he tightened the reins and tried to guide Spot-Nose, who rewarded him for his presumption by laying back his ears with an angry squeal and kicking.

The water was coming up fast. For a moment the wagon floated and Ray considered unhitching the horse and riding him out, leaving the buckboard and his specimens to whatever watery fate might overtake them. The horse, however, had a different idea; he laid his ears flat and pressed steadily forward. It dawned on Ray, then, that the animal knew what he was doing.

"All right, old man," he said. "From now on it's all your show." He slacked the reins, lighted his pipe, and began to smoke furiously to discourage the mosquitoes that were gathering around him in the twilight.

Hours—two long, unbelievably deliberate ones—passed creepingly. Darkness came down. Ray smoked steadily, and steadily Spot-Nose sloshed through water that sometimes covered his hoofs, sometimes reached his chest. Finally, the splashes of the horse's hoofs ceased, and Ditmars heard the gritty sound of the wheels revolving on dry, sandy ground. He pulled on the reins, and the horse obediently stopped. With stiff legs that felt strangely weak, Ray descended and went to the horse's head.

"Good old boy! Fine old fellow!" he said feelingly, and rubbed the animal's nose.

Spot-Nose tolerated the caress, then averted his face and stamped. Taking the hint, Ray climbed into the wagon again.

"You have no sentiment, Spot-Nose," he said reproachfully.

Ray lay on his back in his familiar room and contemplated the ceiling out of vague, blue eyes. His recollection struggled with the details of his recent trip. It had been most successful. There was the 'gator's nest, the first he had ever seen, a mound of dead twigs and moss five feet across and a yard high, with thirty-seven spotless white eggs buried a couple of feet deep in the close-packed, disintegrating mass. He had carried twelve of the eggs back with him, to hatch them at the zoo. He had brought back, too, ninety-two snakes of fourteen different species, nine of them new to the park's collection.

His teeth chattered as a chill shook him, and he reached for another blanket. Huddled and shivering, he grinned weakly. A dozen 'gator eggs, ninety-two snakes—and one very superior case of malaria. Oh, yes, a most successful trip!

SEVENTEEN

THE LITTLE GIRL was slight and pretty, and had dark hair and big brown eyes. Her name was Clara Hurd. When she was about a dozen years old, she used to hang around the tall brownstone house at 1666 Bathgate Avenue for a glimpse of Raymond Ditmars. He was blond, slender, handsome, with light blue eyes that never rested on her. He was a reporter on *The Times* then, and her hero. He never noticed her—she always scooted out of sight when he appeared.

When Mary Ditmars came to call on Clara's mother, Clara usually managed to stay in the room. She heard a great deal about the good-looking young reporter, and eagerly absorbed each scrap of information. She often wondered if she would ever get to know him. When he was appointed to take care of all the snakes at the splendid new Zoological Park, she thought she probably never would—he was too exalted now.

She could, however, admire him from a distance. On hot summer nights, when windows were wide to catch any weak, wandering breeze, and the hesitant dusk was filtering through the street, she would cling to the iron fence that surrounded the Ditmars' house and peer through the lighted parlor window. When she saw Ray at the piano and heard his pleasant music, she felt unreasonably happy; when she saw his mother pass across the window, she darted away in a panic.

After Mrs. Hurd died, Mary Ditmars still came to call on Clara and her older sister, Laura, and still, with maternal fondness, told them stories about her handsome son. It became increasingly clear to Clara that there had never in the world been anyone quite as wonderful as Ray Ditmars.

When he had the accident she was frightened. It happened

about a year after he joined the staff of the Zoological Park. He was pickling the head of a venomous snake in preserving fluid and dropped the jar. Somehow, in clutching for it, he had run a piece of glass deep into his arm. The wound had become infected and he was dangerously ill. He might lose his arm, he might even die. Her hero with an empty sleeve—or dead! Clara could hardly bear to think about it.

Ray knew very little about the anxiety he was causing. Most of the time he was irrational. Among the phantoms that filled his feverish mind there would sometimes intrude disconnected reflections of his surroundings, but none of them made sense to him. There were his mother's face, strange and pale and frightened; Ella, with her sleeves rolled up and her hair disarranged, offering him something on a spoon; strange men with little satchels who hurt him; simple street noises—the shouting of children and the clop of horses' hoofs, strangely inappropriate to the dim, vast swamp in which he was struggling. He was carrying something that he couldn't identify and couldn't lay down. The weight was excruciating; it was crushing his arm, and he couldn't shift it.

Ella took charge of the sick-room. It was she who had driven to the park to bring Ray home after the accident. It was she who sat beside him, coaxing him to take champagne in a tablespoon when that was all he could swallow, and spent her nights on a cot in his room, alert to every breath he drew. Finally, it was she who saved his arm.

"You *can't* amputate it!" she declared passionately. "He'd rather die! I *know* he would!"

The doctor shrugged helplessly. "Then it's your responsibility. Anyway, we'll do what we can. He may squeak through."

He did squeak through. But it was more than three months before he was up again. When he was well enough to go out, he invited his mother to go driving with him behind his trotter, Victor, that he had bought shortly before the accident.

Mary Ditmars clapped her hands. "What fun, Ray! And let's take Laura Hurd. She's such a pretty girl, and I know you'll enjoy her company."

So they stopped and picked up Laura, and the three of them rolled through the fall sunshine along the Pelham Parkway. Ray reflected, with earnestness if not originality, that it was certainly grand to be alive—and whole. He slapped the reins against Victor's glossy flank and smiled at Laura.

"I hope you'll come driving with me often, Miss Laura," he said.

When they got back to the Hurds' house, Clara was home from school. Seeing her idol at close range, she was almost tongue-tied.

"I'm glad you're well again," she managed to murmur. Then she sat and looked at him in transparent admiration. Close inspection revealed no flaw. Everything about him was attractive—his slim, well-groomed hands, his smooth blond hair, his blue eyes, his clear complexion, his well-cut clothes, and, best of all, the gentle, charming smile he gave her.

"Oh, I do hope he'll come soon again!" she thought.

And Ray was saying to his mother as they drove away, "She's a darling, Mama, the little one. Like a soft baby chick."

"She's a sweet little thing," Mary Ditmars agreed absently. Then she added, "I'm taking Laura to hear your lecture at the high school next week."

"Fine!" Ray agreed. But he was still thinking of Clara.

What Ray enjoyed most about his work at the zoo was the fact that something was always happening. The alligator eggs hatched and the babies were in the pool. He went home one night, leaving behind him one fer-de-lance, and the next morning found two dozen more, the size of angle worms, wriggling around their mother. A ship's captain might telephone from the pier that he had a shipment that would interest the zoo, or there might be—a melancholy occasion but interesting—a post-mortem to attend.

One day a python died, and Ditmars attended the autopsy performed by Doctor Harlow Brooks, the park's pathologist. The doctor observed that from the appearance of its lungs the reptile seemed to have had tuberculosis. He removed some lung tissue to examine microscopically in his laboratory, and remarked to Ditmars that he would also try to propagate the germs, whatever they were, in a culture medium.

"Probably several different kinds of bacteria have invaded the lesions, and we'll have a hard time identifying the one that caused the trouble," he said.

Ray had been looking on sadly. His fine python, bent like a hairpin on the autopsy table, was neatly laid open from chin to tail. Maybe, if he'd known more, he could have saved it.

"What's a good book on bacteriology, Doctor?" he inquired.

"Delafield and Prudden is the classic. It's stiff going for a layman, though."

So Ditmars bought the bacteriology textbook of Delafield and Prudden, and burned much midnight oil over it. The references led him to other books, the cost of which shocked him, but he persisted. There was a certain fascination about the subject. It was hard to believe that living organisms, visible through the microscope only as a tiny rod, a comma, or a little wiggle, could incapacitate or kill a man or an animal.

Sometimes a problem that cropped up in the day's work would assume the proportions of a crisis. On arriving at the Reptile House one morning he found that Mose, the big alligator he had had in his own collection for six or seven years before presenting it to the zoo, had been attacked and badly slashed by another of the 'gators in the pool. From a long gash in its abdomen, its intestines trailed on the ground, and the shocked curator could see its lung through a tear in its side.

An alligator is not a creature to inspire affection, but Ditmars was fond of his old friend. He thought it unlikely that an animal so badly mangled could live, but he decided to do all he could to save it. With the help of Charlie Snyder and chloroform, he held it down and prepared to stitch the wounds. Knowing very little about the interior of 'gators, he wasn't quite sure that he was replacing everything where it belonged, but he tucked the entrails neatly inside, drew together the edges of the wounds and sewed them shut. When the operation was over, he had the creature placed in a shallow tank of tepid water. Within ten days Mose was feeding again, and thirty years later he was still hearty.

Ditmars' interest in venoms and antivenin remained keen and was, indeed, stimulated by the news that his early observation on variability in toxicity had been confirmed. With an understanding increased by his bacteriological reading, he followed the investigations being done at the University of Pennsylvania by Doctor Simon Flexner and Doctor Hideyo Noguchi. Working on venoms obtained from the Philadelphia zoo and local sources and from Doctor Calmette, and with Calmette's cobra antivenin, they were learning more and more about the actions of the poisons and of the antidote.

There was never a dull moment at the Bronx Zoo, and the newspapers knew it. The reporters soon learned that, when they asked the assistant curator of reptiles for news, he would give them something with legitimate news value, and give it with unassailable accuracy. The sympathetic and accurate treatment that the press gave the Zoological Park in its early days was especially important in emphasizing its character as a huge museum of live exhibits, each of which had its own interesting scientific background. There were, naturally, comic accounts of animals and tall stories that amused the public and endeared the creatures and the zoo to them; but also there were many interesting and informative stories that contributed to public knowledge.

It was, incidentally, during these early days that the expression "Bronx Zoo" came into popular use to replace the more ponderous title, "New York Zoological Park." Manfully, even testily, dignified elderly gentlemen associated with the great scientific enterprise struggled against the colloquialism, but it was too useful to be abandoned. It is a title now far more commonly used than the original.

Snow was thick on the ground the afternoon of Victor's memorable escapade. Ray was driving with Laura along the Pelham Parkway in the light sleigh that supplanted the carriage in such weather. Victor's swift hoofs seemed rather to repudiate the earth than to touch it.

Around the bend, unexpectedly, came an apparition. It looked like a carriage, but it chugged and clanked, and proceeded, shockingly, without a horse. Automobiles were still rarities after the turn of the century, rarities guaranteed to give even the most phlegmatic horse a thorough fright. Victor was not a phlegmatic horse. As the noisy monster approached he uttered an explosive snort and stood erect on his hind legs. Laura gave a small shriek.

"Steady, boy!" Ray commanded, and gripped the reins firmly.

But Victor had had too nasty a jolt to be calmed by mere words. He took the bit in his teeth, with a few well-placed kicks severed connections between himself and the sleigh, and bolted. Ray hung on, soared over the dashboard, and landed at full length on the ground.

It was not until he felt that he had given adequate expression to his fright and disapproval that Victor stopped. Ray staggered to his feet, and Victor gave him a friendly little poke with his nose in his bruised ribs.

When Ray, with his unrepentant horse, limped back to the sleigh, Laura was alarmed.

"Oh, Ray! Are you hurt? Are you sure? Look at your coat —not a button left! And your knees! You're sure nothing's broken?"

Ray smiled reassuringly. "No damage. Except to the sleigh," he added ruefully.

"Those horrible things!" Laura exclaimed, reverting to the source of all their woe. "They oughtn't to be allowed on the highways!"

Ray gazed pensively into the distance into which the horse-less carriage had disappeared.

"Oh, I shouldn't be too hard on them, Laura," he said. "I've been thinking of getting one myself."

EIGHTEEN

IT WAS, FINALLY, a Stanley Steamer that Ditmars bought. The machine was the wonder of the neighborhood, and gave its owner immense satisfaction—for a while.

The occasions were rare, of course, when an excursion in it went according to schedule. It was not unduly pessimistic to look forward with confidence to a flat tire or two, but Ray insisted that it was simply morbid to expect the thing to blow up. He had great faith in its ability to get him there and back —eventually. This faith was somewhat disturbed by his experience when he took Clara to see *East Lynn*. It was the first time she had ever been to the theater, and Ray had promised Mr. Hurd to bring her home early. Hoping now to marry her, he didn't want to do anything to irritate her stern father.

To Clara it was a marvelous adventure. She was enchanted by the lights, the well-dressed people, her escort, and the play. She enjoyed every minute of it, and wept heartily.

"I wish we could stop somewhere for a bit of supper," Ray said as they got into the Steamer to go home, "but I told your father I'd bring you straight back."

"Never mind, Ray. It's been a wonderful evening," Clara assured him, with a final sniffle. Ray drove into the street. The automobile gave a gurgling cough and died.

The fun was over then. It took them until two o'clock to cover the twenty-odd blocks from the Metropolis Theater to the Hurds' house. Eventually, a milk truck came along and towed them part of the way. When it turned off, they were left sitting beside a beer garden, whose patrons and management had long since departed for the night. With the aid of a sympathetic pedestrian Ray pushed his dead Steamer through a gap in the hedge, into the garden. There, with never a backward glance, he deserted it among the empty tables and the stacked chairs. They walked the rest of the way home.

The light in the parlor was still on as they mounted the steps. At their approach the door burst open, to reveal Mr. Hurd looking, to their startled eyes, twice life-size in his majestic wrath.

Clara darted up the stairs without a single word. The instinct of self-preservation was uppermost, and it was a situation that Ray could handle better alone, anyway. Shrewdly taking advantage of the fact that indignation had rendered Mr. Hurd temporarily speechless, Ray did some plausible talking. Even so, the interview was painful. Finally, he became indignant.

"I see no reason for you to doubt my word that we had a breakdown, sir! I shall call for you in the morning and take you to see for yourself!"

By morning both men had cooled off. Agreeably enough, they went to the beer garden, where a bewildered proprietor, looking rather like a bird that has found its nest full of cuckoo's eggs, was staring at the Steamer.

Mr. Hurd eyed it gloomily. "I don't like the looks of this thing. I'm not at all sure it isn't dangerous. When you get it going, I shall insist upon having a ride in it before I trust my daughters to it again."

"Yes, sir," Ray agreed.

A few days later he took Mr. Hurd for his test run. They were bowling swiftly along the street at perhaps fifteen miles an hour, and Ray was just beginning to feel relaxed and pleased, when Mr. Hurd uttered a loud exclamation.

"Look at the steam-gauge," he yelled. "The thing's about to explode!"

"Nonsense!" Ray said nervously. "It's always like that!"

"Great guns! Let me *out!*"

Ray pulled over and his passenger hastily debarked. He stood on the curb, breathing heavily, and glared at Ray.

"To think," he exclaimed, "that my girls have ridden in that . . . that . . ." words failed him, and he concluded weakly ". . . that *vehicle!* Young man, I forbid you ever, under any circumstances, to get either of my daughters into that death-trap again. Is that quite clear?"

"Quite clear, sir," Ray sighed.

"Get a horse!" commanded Mr. Hurd, and stalked down the street.

So Ray got another horse.

Harry D. was a pacer, and he neither ran away nor threatened to blow up. He had a white harness and drew a smart sulky, and Ray raced him on the speedway. That he was able to afford the luxury of a race horse was due to increased prosperity.

His management of the reptile collection had been so satisfactory that Doctor Hornaday had appointed him assistant curator of mammals at the beginning of 1902. Accompanying this increase in responsibility were kind words from the director and a substantial raise in salary.

Ditmars up to that time had had relatively little experience with mammals, and he found himself with a whole new set of problems. So he had spent a month with Olga's circus, mostly in the company of the animal men, picking up lore, information and pointers. Mostly, however, he learned as he always had, by doing. He had plenty to do.

There was an immense amount of routine in supervising the feeding and care of the ever-growing collections. In the beginning, he had regarded crises as extraordinary events; but after a while, when he realized how frequent they were, he came to look on them, too, as part of the routine.

Alice, the Indian elephant, provided one of the most diverting crises that distinguished the early days. To keep the big pachyderm healthy and happy before the completion of her roomy permanent quarters her keeper took her for daily walks. The two of them were strolling amicably together, one day, past the puma's enclosure. The puma was a kindly beast and it was, moreover, asleep. Alice's consternation was complete, therefore, when it suddenly, perhaps under the influence of a nightmare, gave a horrifying screech. With her little ropy tail standing out straight behind her, Alice bolted for cover. The handiest cover was the Reptile House.

Alice headed for it with her excited keeper puffing in her wake. She lumbered swiftly up the wide granite steps and plunged into the doorway. The doorway, naturally, was too narrow for her. There she stuck. A few scared people admiring the snakes poured quickly out the opposite door.

First, she had been frightened out of her wits by the puma's demoniac yowl. Now she was forcibly restrained against her will. Alice's alarm gave place to wrath. With a heave of her mighty bulk, she burst into the building, carrying the entire door frame, set with swinging doors, on her back. Inside, she slammed herself against walls and pillars until the door frame, demolished, dropped off. By now she was in a mood for destruction. She began on a lizard cage, three feet long and all glass, one of two dozen standing on a big table. Then she pushed the whole table over. The cages burst, and lizards, followed by assorted harmless snakes, exploded in every direction.

Alice's next project was to tear up the visitors' guard rail anchored in the floor. She was applying herself earnestly to that when she slipped on the smooth concrete floor and fell. Keeper Richards quickly sat on her head. Her tantrum spent, Alice quietly subsided. Once again she was her usual gentle, manageable self.

It took Ditmars days to repair the ruin and restore order among his lizards.

A less spectacular and far more serious problem was caused by the outbreak of dysentery among the anthropoid apes.

The bacteria causing the disease were readily identified in the park's laboratory, but it took several days of laboratory tests to discover that the germ was an intestinal parasite of the Galapagos tortoises, whose pen drained into the apes' temporary enclosure. By then all but one of the apes was dead, although the tortoises did not seem to suffer at all from the parasite.

Catering to reptilian appetites was, of course, an endless problem, one aggravated by the fact that snakes often have large litters of young. By 1903 the collection, due to births, purchases and donations, had increased to almost eight hundred specimens, and the curator's procurement problem proportionately. It took constant ingenuity to meet it.

He did meet it, however, one way or another. One solution, the last resort, was to kill some of the specimens; on one occasion he had no choice but to kill the baby rattlers because of a mouse shortage. Sometimes, on the other hand, it was possible to outwit a snake with an exacting appetite. The king cobra, for instance, was the victim of a benevolent deception. Strictly cannibalistic, he was also so greedy that it was impossible to keep him supplied with enough snakes to maintain his finest condition. The curator solved that problem by killing a black snake, stuffing it full of frogs and feeding that to the unwary cannibal.

Czarina, the big reticulated python, was in her own person a chronic crisis. She couldn't shed, she had a sore mouth, she wouldn't eat, and she was strong and hostile. Her shedding problem was met by turning steam into her cage, which softened her old cuticle and made it possible for her to move out of it. By having keepers hold her firmly at two-foot intervals, Ditmars was able to get at her mouth to treat and eventually cure it. Getting her to take a little nourishment was a harder problem: you can force-feed a snake, but you can't make it retain its food. Czarina regularly disgorged. Ditmars out-

128

witted her, too. Instantly after the force-feeding, he turned the hose on her, a device that so surprised and angered her that she forgot to regurgitate. As for the problem of her disposition, that was insoluble.

Treating the sore mouth of a nonpoisonous snake, even when large and mean, was easy compared to treating that of a venomous one. One of the hooded cobras had engaged in a brawl with the other two over their food, and was bitten through the lower jaw. Although certain snakes are more or less immune to their own venom, the wound was serious because it became infected. Taking his life in his hands, Ditmars treated the injury and eventually removed a section of diseased bone. Until it recovered sufficiently to eat normally, the reptile was kept alive with beaten eggs squirted down its throat by a syringe. It would, of course, have been easier to kill the snake than doctor it, and the risk involved in handling a big cobra would easily have justified such a course. There were only three hooded cobras in the country at that time, however, and the serpent was valuable. Anyway, Ditmars sympathized with it. It was typical of him that he should have preferred to restore it to health and to whatever happiness a reptile knows.

Driving down Broadway behind Harry, on the way to the Sportsmen's Show at Madison Square Garden, Ray gave Clara the engagement ring. She used her ungloved left hand to gesticulate freely the rest of the afternoon—until they got near home. Then she drew on her glove and slipped her hand in her muff and became noticeably silent.

"What's the matter, Chicky?" her fiancé asked.

"It's papa. I'm afraid he'll say I'm too young."

"Just leave him to me," Ray advised. "I'll talk to him."

The next morning Ray, ready for the sober business of breaking the news to Clara's father, rang the Hurds' bell. Clara let him in.

"Have you told him?" Ray inquired.

"No. Oh, dear. Oh, no." Her left hand was a fist, concealing the ring.

"Now be calm, Clara," he said kindly. "It's nothing to be nervous about. Where is he?"

"In the dining room. He hasn't finished breakfast yet." She ran ahead into the parlor and, jerking the ring off her finger, threw it under the piano.

Ray groaned and followed her into the dining room. Mr. Hurd, filled with the satisfaction that follows a good meal, surveyed him benignly.

"Good morning, my boy," he said genially. "What brings you here so early?"

"Some news, sir, good news, I hope you'll think. Clara and I want to get married, and we both hope you will make us happy with your consent."

Mr. Hurd gaped with astonishment. "Certainly not!" he exclaimed forcefully. "At least not for two years. You're much too young," he said accusingly to Clara.

"But, Papa, I . . ."

"No! But in two years it may not be a bad idea," he added grudgingly.

"Thank you, sir," Ray said. His gravity was threatening to crack into a wide smile. "I'm certainly glad the match meets with your approval."

Mr. Hurd gave him a sharp look, and began to laugh. "No, really, Raymond. Not a bad idea a bit! I'll be all for it. I think a great deal of your parents," he added awkwardly, and patted his mouth with his napkin to cover his perilous lapse toward sentimentality.

"Didn't your beau give you a ring?" he turned to Clara.

"Yes, Papa. It's under the piano."

It was Mr. Hurd's turn to groan.

Not daring to move the piano for fear of crushing the stone, the two men got down on their knees and poked for the ring with Mr. Hurd's cane. Eventually, they recovered it.

Mr. Hurd, with middle-aged stiffness, rose to his feet and flicked the dust from his knees.

"What a morning!" he sighed.

Ray sighed too. "Yes, wasn't it!" he agreed feelingly.

Ray and Clara thought two years was too long a time to wait. So did Mary Ditmars. Fatally ill, she was in a hurry to see her son married. The three of them converted Mr. Hurd to their point of view, and the wedding date was set for February 4, 1903.

It was to be a very quiet wedding. Because of Mrs. Ditmars' long sickness no one felt festive, Ray least of all. The time that he could spare from his work he divided between her and Clara. In the early evening he would go to the nursing home where his mother was staying, and read to her or, leaving her door wide, would play her favorite tunes on the piano downstairs until her bedtime. Then he would stop on his way home to see Clara, and hear about her shopping expeditions, her trousseau, the wedding plans.

When the day came, there was only a handful of family and close friends in the Hurds' parlor to see Clara Hurd and Ray Ditmars married. The affair was so quiet, in fact, that some of the newspapers felt it necessary to enliven their non-eye-witness accounts of the wedding of the young curator with details of a rattlesnake skin-draped altar, snake-skin decorations and other fantasies. They made for interesting reading, and bothered the principals not at all. They were too interested in each other to think of looking at the papers.

NINETEEN

IT WAS 1904. Raymond Ditmars was a family man now, with a wife, a new baby, Gladyce, and a minute apartment to support. In addition, he had a reputation to build. It was all very well to be known as a man who knew how to take care of snakes, but he wanted to be known as a scientist, too.

He wrote articles for the Zoological Society's publications, and an occasional popular one for a magazine. He gave lectures on snakes to high school classes and to clubs. He supervised the care of some eight hundred reptiles—he had been promoted to curator in 1903—and more than six hundred mammals. The big thing scientifically, however, that he had on his schedule was the book about North American reptiles for which he had been collecting material for the past three or four years.

In handling the work he had a particular idea: it was to present his information in such a manner that the book would be interesting and comprehensible to laymen and, at the same time, so complete and accurate as to be valuable to technical workers. Impatient with the use of scientific language obscure in meaning to all but specialists, he wanted to tell about snakes in an understandable style that would awake the sympathy of the general public. It was part of his lifelong campaign to break down the widespread prejudice against reptiles.

Another man might have thought the conditions trying under which he produced this work that was immediately to become a standard. Not above domestic chores, every evening Ditmars cleared the table and helped his wife with the dishes. Then he collected books, photographs, notes, jars of pickled snakes, from the buffet and chairs where, for lack of other space, they were stacked during the day, and spread them on the dining-room table under the gaslight.

Sometimes he would write until his hand ached and midnight had passed; sometimes he would open his preserved specimens and, in an atmosphere reeking of alcohol, count rows of scales or take measurements. Clara always kept him company. Sitting in a big rocker on the other side of the table, she would read until her eyes got heavy, and then drop off to sleep. She woke only when she heard the baby's squall from the bedroom, or the shuffle of papers and the scrape of her husband's chair as he prepared, at last, to put his work away.

"I wish I were better company for you, Ray," she would say regretfully.

"That's all right, Chicky. I like to be able to look up once in awhile and see you there."

He took the pictures for the book himself, mostly at the zoo, and developed them in the bathroom at home, in the thick of kerosene fumes emanating from the red developing light. The text, he thought, would come to a quarter of a million words; and he estimated that, since he could devote only his spare time to the book, it would take him about two years to complete it.

Naturally, he could not leave a young wife, however devoted and patient, dozing in the rocker every night for two years. They both needed diversions. They went to parties; friends visited the crowded little apartment; finally, one day in 1906, another baby, Beatrice, arrived, too, and they had to move to larger quarters. They found an apartment on Union Avenue in the Bronx.

The principal diversion, however, was an automobile. It was a secondhand Rambler, bought from a man who said, vaguely, that it had gone "quite a few" miles. Its paint was shiny, its brass gleaming, its engine noisy and irregular. The young couple were very proud of their purchase, though a little distrustful. They remembered the kind of trouble you could get into with a balky automobile.

Ditmars decided that to be able to deal with possible emergencies, he should know how the thing worked internally. Squeezing two nights a week out of his crowded schedule, he took a course in the combustion engine at a near-by night school. A can of gritty soap took its place beside the developing fluid in the bathroom, and a large chart of the working parts of an engine displaced the pictures from one wall of the dining room. It was not until he received his diploma that the Rambler was allowed to go more than half a dozen blocks from the garage.

Its use thereafter was frequent. Ditmars put on his duster and gauntlets, trappings required of every well-dressed motorist, loaded his wife and babies into the car and set out for a drive. As he developed confidence in his ability to deal with any ailments the car might develop, the family excursions lengthened into snake-hunting expeditions in the country. A thoroughly domestic man, Ditmars was happiest when his family was with him; so he was fortunate in having a wife who hunted rattlers with as much *sang-froid* as another woman would have gone picnicking, and children who associated with snakes as willingly as with any other pets.

The Rambler brought him into contact, for the second time in his life, with the law: he was arrested for driving seventeen miles an hour. In those days, that was speeding. A cold rain had begun to fall as the family was returning from a jaunt in the country, and the children, in the open back seat, were tucked under a tarpaulin. The arresting officer rejected the anxious father's plea that he was in a hurry to get them home, but the judge took a more humane view.

"An adequate excuse," he decided. "Case dismissed."

Ditmars, before whose apprehensive mind the prospect of a large fine had been dangling, went home with a kindlier feeling toward the law than he had had in some years—in fact, ever since it had deprived him of his first water snake.

Work on the book proceeded steadily, subject to those interruptions to which a family man is always exposed. The most alarming one was Gladyce's illness. When she was three years old, she had infantile paralysis. For hours every day her mother leaned over the child, massaging her until aching back and stiffening fingers compelled her to stop. Then she would call the zoo.

"Ray, I can't go on any longer."

"All right, Clara, I'll be right home."

"You're not too busy?"

"I'm busy, but it will have to wait."

And Ditmars would hurry home, toss his coat on a chair, and take up the treatment where his wife had left off. They were harrowing days, the worst he had gone through since his mother's death a few months after his marriage. When his little girl was up again, showing none of the dreaded after-effects of the disease, the relieved father could hardly bear to be separated from her.

He developed the habit of taking her to work with him. She would sit in his office by the hour, playing with a harmless snake, a baby 'gator, a turtle or some small mammal which he was keeping there for special treatment, while he attended to his work. When he left the office to inspect his creatures or visit the zoo's hospital, she trotted at his side. The yellow-haired little girl with the blue eyes and the big smile became almost as familiar a figure around the park as the herpetologist.

Being a sensible child, when she got tired she didn't fuss, but lay down on the couch in the curator's office and went to sleep. On one occasion, after she had been coming to the zoo regularly for a year or more, her father started home one evening, bothered by the obscure feeling that he had forgotten something. He had a lot on his mind: the book was almost done and there were a couple of questions about the index; he was working on an article about the rate of growth of alligators that was going to upset some established conceptions; the precious bushmaster was about to consummate its suicide by slow starvation, and he was desperately anxious to save it. In the press of problems Ditmars couldn't quite put his finger on the cause of his uneasiness. It accompanied him throughout the drive home, and crystallized only when his wife met him at the door and asked accusingly:

"Where's Gladyce?"

He snapped his fingers. "*That's* what I forgot! She's asleep in my office." He turned and ran to the car, pursued by his wife's indignant exclamations.

All the way back to the park he reproached himself bitterly. How could he have been so careless with his dear little girl? Poor little thing, she must be frightened to death, in the dark and surrounded by wild animals. She was perfectly safe, of course, but children had such vivid imaginations. She was probably screaming herself into hysterics right that minute, calling his name in the dark, and getting no answer. He opened the throttle wide and clenched the wheel.

He drew up in front of the Reptile House in a spray of gravel and raced up the steps. Poor baby! How could he ever make it up to her? His heart was thumping painfully as he threw open his office door and snapped on the light.

On the couch, just where he had left her, lay Gladyce, her yellow curls spreading over the pillow and her lashes, in the strong light, throwing shadows on her round cheeks. She opened her eyes and smiled.

"Hello, Pop," she said sleepily.

With a mixture of pride and incredulity he flipped over the leaves of the big book. It was almost five hundred pages long. It had eight color plates and more than four hundred photographic illustrations. It was *The Reptile Book*, by Raymond Lee Ditmars.

Admiringly his wife hung over his shoulder.

"Oh, Ray, isn't it beautiful! Aren't you proud?"

He smiled. "Lots of people write books, you know, Chicky, I'm not the first one."

"You're the first one to write this kind of book."

"That's right." His eyes took on a reminiscent look. "I'd have given anything for this sort of a book when I was first fooling around with snakes. I hope it's going to fill a need."

This modest wish was fulfilled beyond his expectation. The book, which appeared in 1907, was favorably reviewed everywhere, and at once and generally acclaimed as outstanding. From the White House came a letter from Theodore Roosevelt.

"In these days of nature fakers it is genuinely refreshing to come upon a book like yours," the President wrote. "I have a very strong belief in having books which shall be understood by the multitude, and which yet shall be true—in other words, scientific books written for laymen who have some appreciation of science . . . It seems to me that your volume exactly fulfills these requirements."

The Reptile Book quickly became a standard work. With its publication Ray Ditmars was established.

TWENTY

DURING THE TIME that he was working on *The Reptile Book*
Ditmars became acquainted with Noguchi. This brilliant
young Japanese, at the conclusion of his work with Flexner
at the University of Pennsylvania, had gone to Copenhagen.
There, in 1904, he and Doctor Thorwald Madsen, working
with rattlesnake venom Noguchi had brought with him from
the United States, produced a serum that was specific for rattlesnake bites. (Calmette's antivenin, based on cobra poison,
was of only limited effect in the treatment of snake poisons
which acted against the blood rather than the nerves.) Word
of this work had been received with interest in United States
medical circles. Even Elihu Root, in the midst of a busy
political career, took notice of it. "It occurs to me," he wrote
to his friend Weir Mitchell, "that a supply [of the new serum]
might be useful in American politics." Ditmars, of course,
was intensely interested.

When Noguchi returned to the United States, he continued
his venom research in New York, under the auspices of the
Rockefeller Institute for Medical Research. It was natural
that he should apply to the curator of reptiles at the New York
Zoological Park.

In the building on Lexington Avenue and Fiftieth Street
that temporarily housed the Institute's laboratories, Ditmars
and Noguchi milked rattlers. The Japanese doctor, despite
the disadvantage of a hand crippled in infancy, manipulated
the strong, struggling reptiles expertly. The two men took
turns extracting venom, sometimes handling as many as a
hundred snakes a day. Ditmars later recalled that Noguchi
was always cheerful and that, when he had finished with his

snake and dropped it into the barrel, he would point to the next one with a smile and a little bow and say:

"Your snake, sir."

One of the world's leading experts on venoms, Noguchi was enthusiastic about the possibilities of antivenin. "The use of antivenin in human cases has a most encouraging prospect," he wrote. Views had changed in the thirty years since Mitchell and Reichert had stated that little, probably, could ever be done for the victims of snake bite. As Calmette remarked in 1907 in the book on venoms and antivenin that recapitulated his work, antivenomous therapy was already established in current medical practice. In each country where snake bite was an important cause of mortality, laboratories for the preparation of the serums were functioning.

The United States was not one of those countries. There were no accurate statistics on the incidence of snake bite in this country, but it was estimated that fewer than five hundred people, of whom between fifteen and thirty-five per cent might die, were bitten yearly. Accidents, however, were increasing, because, with the rising popularity of automobiling, hiking and camping, more people were getting into rural areas where they encountered venomous reptiles. Ditmars felt, reasonably enough, that preventable deaths ought to be prevented, whether they were few or many, and that serum should be provided against the bites of the three venomous snakes of North America accountable for the vast majority of deaths— the rattler, the copperhead and the water moccasin.

It was twenty years before he saw the establishment of a laboratory for the manufacture of antivenins in this country. He could congratulate himself, then, that his activity in drawing the attention of herpetologists, doctors and the public to the need for it had been instrumental in bringing it about.

By 1907, the year *The Reptile Book* appeared, the New York Zoological Society's zoo was one of the finest in the world. Ditmars was proud that he had brought the reptile collection into second place, with eight hundred and ninety-seven reptiles and one hundred and thirty-four species.

Maps prepared by the curator, showing the world distribution of various snakes, hung on the walls of the Reptile House. Directions were posted telling what to do in case of snake bite. Snake skulls and fangs were on display, as well as tubes of antivenin and the apparatus necessary to treat snake bite. School children, with their teachers, made scheduled trips to the zoo for illustrated lectures on birds, mammals and reptiles, which were followed by tours of inspection of the cages. The institution, exhibiting some of the rarest of the earth's creatures, was playing an increasing role in popular education.

New York's millions loved the zoo and visited it in droves. There were always crowds hanging around Billy, the Alaskan brown bear; Gunda, the Indian elephant with the big tusks and the bad reputation; little Congo, the pygmy elephant whom big Alice babied and bossed; the pair of African rhinoceroses which had cost the zoo five thousand dollars apiece; the comic and cumbersome Galapagos tortoises; and the antic apes.

Purchases and births replenished the collection; deaths depleted it. The mortality rate, however, was satisfactorily low. Animals were segregated as soon as they seemed sick and epidemics were usually arrested before they got started; and Ditmars' sympathetic and skillful supervision helped to keep the creatures in top condition. The animals were, indeed, usually in such good health and spirits that, as Doctor Hornaday plaintively said, their natural pugnacity was increased, and there were occasional fights with fatal outcomes. When a specimen with a fine pelt died, one or the other of the little Ditmars girls was likely to blossom out in a new fur coat.

It was 1909. Doctor Ditmars—people were beginning to

call him "Doctor" now—was off to Europe on a purchasing mission. For company he had, not his family, but the mammals and reptiles he was taking for exchange.

He leaned on the rail, straining his eyes across the widening stretch of oily water that separated the ship from the pier, and waved as long as he could distinguish the fluttering handkerchiefs of his wife and little girls. As they blended into anonymity among the crowd, he felt suddenly lonely, and he wished he were on his way back.

Arriving in London on May 17, he took a room at the Midland Grand Hotel. Then he had dinner in its dining room and went to the theater to see *An Englishman's Home*. When he returned to his room, he cast a hostile eye over its Gothic *décor*, and wrote his wife a long letter. Characteristically, he filled it with remarks about locomotives and fire engines.

"The cars [in England] look exactly like modified children's toys," he reported. "Our train was painted yellow and had a red engine. The engines have no cowcatchers and most of them have the cylinders inside and out of sight under the boiler. They are painted all kinds of screaming colors. The engines have no bells, as it is against the law to walk on the R. R. tracks. The engineers seem to be stuck on the whistles and the air along a railroad line is filled with ungodly shrieks."

And as for the fire department! "The firemen look like Roman gladiators dressed for a gorgeous parade. *They wear great helmets of polished brass,* and you can see them coming a mile away. The engines look like playthings—and the top of the chimney is not much higher than your head. However, they are very strong pumpers and easy to draw. Only two horses are used. Each engine carries its own line of hose in a big box in front of the baby boiler—which is not bigger than a dish pan."

He confessed that he was appalled by London's traffic, impressed by the skill with which the "bobbies" handled it. He found English money simple and could even pronounce it correctly ("ha-penny" and "tuppence"). He imparted his thoughts on London theatrical audiences ("remarkable polite"), and on his hotel ("too blooming swell for me"). The last half page of his letter was covered with x's, representing hugs and kisses.

Visiting the London zoo, calling on animal dealers, making a hurried dash to Liverpool, and establishing headquarters where he could assemble his purchases for shipment kept Ditmars busy, but he worked a little sightseeing into his schedule and frequent letters home. He longed for the children—"if only I had them with me I'd hold them on my best trousers and not think of the creases"—and already was instructing his wife to hire a car and bring them to meet him at the pier on his return.

With a ticket a yard long, he set out for a hurried visit to continental zoos. Crossing the Channel to Holland, he was delighted by the spotless Dutch towns through which the train carried him, and by the cheerful peasant girls with their blue dresses, braids of fair hair, and rosy complexions who waved from the fields. "I'm in love with Holland," he wrote of his ancestral land.

After stopping briefly at the Amsterdam and Brussels zoos, he hastened to Paris, which he described as "a real live town." In four hectic days and nights he attended to his business and succeeded in covering many of the sights. He had to omit his visit to Doctor Calmette and the Pasteur Institute at Lille because of lack of time, so the dried rattlesnake venom he had brought for the French doctor was dispatched to him instead of personally presented.

Cologne, Frankfort, Dresden, zoos, scenery, castles sped past. Then Berlin for two days, where he saw some of the ladies of the royal family driving through the streets in a big auto which "was going like a fire chief's machine—with the muffler wide open." He was impressed by the German capital's festive air and cleanliness, the beautiful avenues, the soldiers in brilliant uniforms, and especially by the zoo. But home, even in the midst of new sights, was uppermost in his mind. "Go to Hanover tomorrow, which takes me 300 miles *nearer home*. . . . Don't forget, when you get my wireless from the incoming ship you are to go to Seadale's garage and he is to bring you and the children down to the pier."

Then Hanover, where it rained hard enough to depress him and keep him indoors; Alfeld, where he bought a rare South African zebra and a magnificent kudu, and was touched and charmed by the friendly hospitality of the pretty little inn at which he lunched; and Hamburg, where he was entertained by Carl Hagenbeck, the great animal dealer, who took him over the Tierpark with the splendid collection of beasts, and the military band that played for the orderly throngs.

And finally London again, the last lap of the long trip. He rushed to the zoological garden to pick up the mail that had been accumulating for him, and read his wife's letters over and over. She and the children were well; everybody was eager to have him home. Only two weeks more, and he would board the *Minnehaha* and start back to them.

In that time, he had crates made for his purchases; celebrated his thirty-third birthday by dining at the Hotel Cecil "which makes the Waldorf-Astoria look like two cents"; visited the Duke of Bedford's estate, Woburn, where the deer herds were exhibited wandering over an extensive range; and made a special tour of the Tower of London under the guidance of a learned young Oxford student. It was interesting, but he was glad when it was over: he missed his family almost unbearably. With forty-eight cases of mammals, birds and reptiles, he boarded the *Minnehaha* for home on July 3.

He observed, on the way back, that no matter how adversely the motion of the vessel might affect him, none of his charges showed any signs of uneasiness. The principal event of the voyage was the escape of a pair of mangabey monkeys.

The frantic chase led all over the ship, put grease on Ditmars' cherished and only custom-made pair of English trousers, disturbed and amused the passengers and exasperated the captain. Finally the refugees ascended a mast, and were coaxed down, when thoroughly hungry, with a large bunch of bananas. The spectacle of their capture was so ludicrous that the captain, who witnessed it, was restored to good humor, but by that time the unhappy curator was too seasick to care.

Cleaning the cages, feeding the animals and making himself presentable again after this menial toil consumed most of Ditmars' time on the way home. South American skunks, Tasmanian devil, Tibetan red fox, bleeding heart pigeons, bower birds, Patagonian burrowing owls, hangul deer, giant salamander, monitor, kudu, zebra, lemur, tortoises, crocodiles, serpents—all the creatures got as much care and attention as though they were first-class passengers, instead of freight in the hold.

As the ship drew near Ambrose Light, their exhausted chaperon received a wireless. "Are you bringing many animals?" the Associated Press wanted to know.

"Fine series of rare mammals, birds, reptiles," Ditmars wirelessed back. It sounded tame, so he added, with the trained instinct of a good reporter, "and a Tasmanian devil." That ought to make a snappy lead, he thought. Later, news stories all over the country justified his hunch.

Liberty and the towers of Manhattan rolled slowly over the horizon. Quarantine was passed. Hanging over the rail and staring across the narrowing strip of water, he could distinguish his wife and little girls on the pier, frenziedly waving their handkerchiefs. He snatched out his own, and waved it wildly. He was home again, at last.

TWENTY-ONE

MOST OF Raymond Ditmars' collecting trips took him no more than a couple of hundred miles from New York City. Work and play were, literally, the same to a man who loved his job as he did. His idea of a good holiday was to hunt snakes and insects.

During these years he usually spent his two weeks' vacation with his family in Sullivan County, New York. Every season they selected a boardinghouse in a different part of the county, and with that as their base of operations scoured the country in the car. The little girls, who could tell a rattler or a copperhead from a nonvenomous snake as well as their father, sometimes went along, sometimes were left behind to amuse themselves catching bugs and garter snakes while their parents explored the rocky south ledges of promising-looking hillsides for rattlers, or the banks of likely-looking streams for water snakes.

The doctor and his wife looked on snake hunting as a sport on a par with angling, indeed superior to it, for the trophies remained alive and could be exhibited and studied after the fun of the capture. Catching rattlers took skill and care, and was dangerous even though the hunters carried antivenin kits. There was no particular art, however, in capturing the harmless species of snakes. All that was needed was quickness in seizing them, and the stoicism to ignore their bites. When, on overturning a stone, they would find several specimens together, the best thing to do was to snatch at them with both hands, grabbing as many as possible. The snakes, held by the tail or well back from the lead, often had room to turn and bite, but the wounds were superficial and healed quickly.

On one occasion, however, Ditmars developed a painful infection on his finger from the bite of a snake which, presumably, had some septic remnant of its prey adhering to its teeth.

Mrs. Ditmars and the children took care of the captives, and had all they could do to handle the two weeks' catch, which often amounted to three hundred snakes and a thousand or more insects. At the end of the vacation, they would travel back to the city in a car stacked with luggage, snake cages and insect boxes, and perhaps adorned by a young maple in full leaf, nourishment for the bugs.

"What would happen if we had an accident, Pop?" Beatrice piped, as they entered the familiar Bronx after one trip.

Ditmars shuddered. "Don't ask Pop such awful questions. I can't bear to think what would happen."

Beatrice subsided, smiling agreeably. She could bear to think of it. It would be fun. There would be snakes all over the street—rattlers and green snakes and black snakes and water snakes—and katydids and spiders hopping all around, and everyone would run back and forth and yell and be terribly excited. Everybody except Pop, who would be calm, and capture them, and make everything all right. There would be nothing to it.

"Almost home," Mrs. Ditmars sighed. It had been a long trip, with punctures, clutch trouble, and an argument with the guard at the Nyack ferry, who hadn't wanted to let snakes aboard.

"Just a few more minutes," the doctor answered, turning from Tremont into Webster Avenue. City streets were not very smooth in that day and he hit a bump—hard. There was a crash behind as a cage of harmless snakes, strapped on the back, slipped its moorings and dropped to the street.

"Ohhhhhh!" groaned the doctor.

"Wheeee!" shouted the children.

The car stopped. Passers-by took one look and fled. The

patrons of a corner saloon swarmed into the street to see what the commotion was, and immediately swarmed in again, demanding that the doors be locked. Two policemen, calling on St. Patrick, ran to assist the curator, scooping up the reptiles which were proceeding full speed ahead in as many directions as there were snakes. The combined efforts of the four Ditmars and the two policemen were needed to recapture the fugitives. When snakes and passengers were once again stowed in the car, Ditmars turned to his younger daughter.

"Does that answer your question, dear?" he inquired mildly.

Sometimes Doctor Ditmars felt like a juggler, he had so many things going at once. He was preparing a new book, *Reptiles of the World*. He lectured constantly and had to think up new subjects for his talks. Impressed by the insect exhibits he had seen in several European zoos, he arranged some of his own. He displayed some disease-bearing insects of this country, such "musicians" as katydids and crickets; venomous things like tarantulas, spiders and centipedes. He coddled frail animals, made performers of intelligent ones, answered questions on the telephone, extracted venom, gave stories to the reporters, went on hunting trips.

His salary was not then, and never became, large. Ten years before, he had begun lecturing to provide more comforts for his reptiles; now he continued it to provide them for his family. Accustomed to platform appearances, he no longer had stage fright or worried about "putting it over." His lectures were in demand and enthusiastically received, and as his reputation spread, he made increasingly distant trips to deliver them.

Nineteen-twelve was the year Teddy Roosevelt, forsaking the Republican Party, ran on the Bull Moose ticket, and the Zoological Society, perhaps inspired by some outraged Republican in its fold, spurned the offer of a bull moose for the zoo. It was the year, also, of the fiftieth anniversary of the Confederate victory at the Second Battle of Bull Run, in which John Ditmars had fought.

Now, as in his youth, the naturalist's enthusiasm embraced a number of unrelated topics. The year before, fearing—quite without justification—that audiences would get saturated with snakes and animals and not want to hear any more about them, he decided to equip himself to lecture on another subject, the Civil War. Learning of a fine collection of negatives of Civil War pictures in the custody of the War Department, Ditmars, with the assistance of ex-President Roosevelt, his friend since the appearance of *The Reptile Book*, obtained permission to make lantern slides from them to illustrate his talks. His first Civil War lecture was in July, 1911, on the fiftieth anniversary of the First Battle of Bull Run, at the armory of the Sixty-ninth Regiment. The audience was so large and the armory so enormous that he was hoarse for a week afterward. The anniversary of the second battle turned out to be considerably more strenuous. As a treat for his father, Raymond took him to Virginia to go over the battlefield.

In his seventies, John Ditmars was a hardy old man, and the recollection of Stonewall Jackson's flanking operation, the bewildered Pope's confusion, and the Confederate victory all lent him new energy. With his son panting behind him, he strode over the old battleground.

"The first time, in '61, we scared them off with Quaker guns," the old rebel recalled with a dry laugh. "Poor McClellan, his name was mud after that. But in '62 we didn't fool them, we just whipped them. It took us days to make an inventory of the stuff we captured. We formed in those meadows," he waved his hand, "and they were coming over the knolls yonder. We could hear their drums—that was one of John Pope's notions, music up to the moment of action." His recollections were minute, his energy inexhaustible.

In the little inn at Manassas Junction where they put up for the night, the younger man, tired in every joint, crawled into bed and looked at his elderly father with fresh respect.

"Aren't you tired, Pop?"

"Tired? No. Tomorrow, Ray, we'll go along this way," his bony forefinger picked out the road on his map, "and I'll show you how the action went along the Warrenton Pike."

The old gentleman turned out the light, and the springs creaked as he got into bed. He lay silent a while, remembering.

"Ah, Lee," he sighed finally, "there was a *man!*"

From that time on, covering old battlefields and reconstructing the action was another of the herpetologist's hobbies.

One of Ditmars' most popular lectures about this time was an instructive miniature vaudeville act he had worked out to demonstrate the agility and skill of certain little creatures. Head Keeper Charles Snyder and he built a small red stage and apparatus for the performers, with the necessary electrical appliances, and a Chinese friend of Ditmars' painted a gorgeous twelve-foot drop curtain. A motion picture projector and colored spotlights supplied background effects, so that each actor seemed to be performing against the background of its native habitat. Cookie, the lemur, a relative of the monkeys, traveled along a slack rope and "skinned the cat" on it as he might have done in his native forest; the jerboa, a small desert rodent whose method of locomotion is much like a kangaroo's, sprang over the hurdle to an amazing height, against a desert picture thrown on the backdrop. Snakes, waltzing mice, and other small creatures showed off natural abilities surprising to the average audience. Ditmars often closed the show by noosing a "prowling" rattler and extracting its venom. All the paraphernalia of the act, including the performers, could be compactly packed in cases to fit into the lecturer's car.

Carrying snakes around to lectures is no occupation for a

man who objects to good-natured banter in the press. Ditmars didn't mind it. One St. Patrick's Day episode gave the reporters a fine opportunity for fun. According to the widely published account, Doctor Ditmars and Mr. Snyder, on their way to speak at a school in New Jersey, were walking across town on Twenty-third Street to reach the ferry, when they were blocked by the parade in honor of the saint who drove the snakes from Ireland. As they tried to dodge through it, they were halted by a policeman, who demanded:

"Where do ye think ye're goin', buddy?"

"I'm Raymond Ditmars of the Zoological Park, and I have an appointment to lecture in Elizabeth."

"What have ye got in that bag?" inquired the policeman suspiciously.

"Snakes. Want to see?"

"No! It's a sacrilege that ye're carryin' such things this day! Get across with ye. Get them out of the state!"

Accordingly, Ditmars and Snyder dashed across the street in front of the advancing ranks of a band, which was loudly tooting *The Wearing of the Green.* Later, when he opened his suitcase preparatory to giving his lecture, Ditmars found "three of his snakes dead, and several others in a state bordering on hysteria"—casualties, so the papers said, due to exposure to the strains of the Irish band.

Reptiles of the World, published early in 1910, met with excellent critical response. Through his books, his lectures, and his work at the zoo, Ditmars was pressing his campaign to create popular sympathy and understanding for wild creatures. But it was when he got the idea of presenting animals to the public by means of motion pictures that he made his greatest contribution.

The idea developed naturally. His vaudeville act could present only creatures small enough to be portable, and large enough to be seen clearly by audiences from a little distance.

Gunda, the savage elephant; Silver King, the magnificent polar bear; the rare musk oxen; insects with interesting ways; life processes like the hatching of snake and spider eggs and the development of tadpoles into frogs—all these could be presented to lecture audiences only by motion pictures. No one had ever made a systematic, educational series of zoological films showing members of the main branches of the animal kingdom going about their daily lives. This was what Ditmars had in mind.

"Won't it be a huge job, Ray, and terribly expensive?" his wife asked.

"Yes, but think what wonderful educational pictures they will be. And if the idea is commercially successful, we can begin to build, too." For several years they had been wanting to build a house in Scarsdale, outside New York City.

The winter's lecture receipts were capital for the new enterprise. Ditmars bought a motion picture camera and some film, and hired an assistant named Andy, who was something of an electrical wizard. Then they set to work.

On a tiny improvised stage in the Reptile House, the curator and his assistant took close-ups showing the life histories of local spiders. When they had a series of those, they did a reel showing the different means of locomotion among such creatures as chameleons, tree toads and swifts. Then frogs' eggs developed to tadpoles, tadpoles to frogs, before the patient recording eye of the camera. By that time Ditmars began to run out of money.

"I'm going to try to sell the several thousand feet that we've already taken to one of the motion picture companies," he told Andy. "They're excellent pictures, and there's certainly never been anything like them before."

"Good luck, Doctor," Andy said absently. He had taken the camera to pieces to see what made static marks on the film, and was preoccupied with his own problem. Some hours later he was contentedly smoking a cigarette and contemplating his successful operation, when the doctor returned, looking dejected.

"No sale," he reported, laying his cans of film on the little stage. "They all said they were remarkable pictures and very interesting, but every one of them wanted to make undignified changes, like introducing comedy and adding funny titles."

"What's undignified about comedy? It was good enough for Shakespeare."

"I'm making scientific films, not slapstick," Ditmars told him austerely.

"You're making them, but you're not selling them," Andy pointed out. "The trouble is, you haven't the commercial slant. Those fellows in the movie business know that laughs sell better than education, so they want laughs. Why don't you take their advice? You have wonderful stuff in those cans, and with a little rearranging you could sell it easily."

"For instance?"

"For instance, those frogs with suckers on their feet—give them a horizontal bar to walk on; and those aquatic frogs that swim on their backs, they're natural acrobats; and the cock-eyed chameleon that can roll each eye in a different direction; and the kangaroo rats you used in your vaudeville act, and a dozen others. You have enough stuff for a whole jungle circus —and there's your title, *The Jungle Circus!*"

"And my scientific reputation?" the startled curator asked.

"Oh, *that*." Andy grinned. "If any highbrow criticizes you, you're doing films like this to interest children in zoology."

So *The Jungle Circus* went into production. Jerboas took professional-looking hurdles before the grinding camera; acrobatic tree toads swarmed up ropes like gymnasts; a bluebottle fly, stuck by the wings to a chair fastened on a beetle's back, clutched and rolled with his feet a dumbbell made of cork and straw, giving the effect of juggling. The audience, small toads chilled to passivity by fifteen minutes in the refrigerator, watched the performance from plaster models of toadstools, and at the end dispersed in alarm when a skunk came shuffling onto the stage. Patience, ingenuity, and minute care, as well as skill, went into the making of *The Jungle Circus*. It was a smash hit. Ditmars used it as the finale to a few reels he billed as *The Book of Nature*, which presented studies of animals, reptiles and insects hunting, eating, attending to the affairs of their daily lives. He used the pictures in his own lectures, and distributed them commercially through the motion picture companies which were now enthusiastic.

The films were so successful that, by 1913, the house in Scarsdale became a reality; moreover, it was equipped with a movie studio for the continuation of the work.

The motion picture records of living animals, which Ditmars spent years in taking, became his main piece of work outside of his duties as curator. By arrangement with the Zoological Society, he made pictures of most of its animals, the large ones right in the zoo, the smaller ones in his studio at Scarsdale. He often sought insects at night, and photographed them in the open, by the glare of a powerful spotlight attached to his car. The entire family participated in one capacity or another in the film production. Gladyce and Beatrice experimented with singing insects, sorting out those bold enough to perform under lights, and assuming the care of delicate ones, and they became expert in the handling and training of small mammals. Mrs. Ditmars no longer dozed in a rocker while her husband worked. She spent her evenings in the studio, making ingenious suggestions and sometimes intervening perilously.

One evening the doctor and Andy were filming a Ringhals cobra, a deadly reptile that spits its venom toward the eyes of an enemy. The serpent was on the stage in front of the camera. Mrs. Ditmars, out of harm's way, was at the back of the studio.

"It's uncanny, the glassy glare of that snake's eyes," she

remarked. "It would be wonderful if the camera could look him straight in the eye and catch it."

"We can try. We'll put on driving goggles and move the camera closer," Ditmars agreed.

"Look!" Andy said vehemently. "I'm as close as I intend to get to that brute."

"Here, let me crank it," Mrs. Ditmars offered.

Ditmars held the snake off, while she moved the camera to within four feet of the stage. The snake was released, and Mrs. Ditmars began to crank the camera. She was not satisfied with the reptile's performance.

"More action!" she decided. She flicked her handkerchief at the cobra. Instantly it reared and struck with such force that it slid and fell off the stage almost at her feet. She jumped to a bench, and the snake glided under it.

"Good!" she said, quite unmoved. "That must have made a beautiful picture."

"Clara!" Ditmars exclaimed, aghast. He captured the snake with a pole and returned it to its cage. Only then did Andy, looking pale, come down from the filing cabinet on which he had taken refuge.

The picture, when it was developed, was extraordinary. The cobra darkened the entire screen with the spread of its hood, and the glassy eyes glittered malignantly. Then, savagely, it struck, seemingly in the spectators' faces. It was a scene that always wrung a gasp from audiences, a gasp that would have been even more frightened had they realized the peril involved in shooting it.

The studio fixtures became increasingly elaborate as Ditmars expanded his motion picture enterprise. The studio was equipped with mercury and arc lighting, motor-driven projectors for editing film, vaults for storing it, complicated lighting arrangements, various types of cameras and specially designed apparatus for recording the life histories of the smaller forms. Since the films attempted as much as possible to show animals in their natural surroundings, Ditmars built appropriate stage sets which could be taken down and stowed away until they were needed again. To picture a prairie rattler in the proper setting, for instance, he constructed a set representing prairie dog burrows by molding several mounds of cement over mesh forms. One of these "burrows" connected with a runway opening into the reptile's box beneath the stage. When he was ready to shoot, the rattler was released into the runway and crawled slowly into the camera's view out of what appeared to be a deserted burrow.

Sometimes long negotiations were necessary before Ditmars could obtain an animal, not in the zoo's collection, to film. It required permission from the government to import a mongoose, the ferret-like little mammal of India which fearlessly attacks venomous snakes. Their importation is banned by law for fear they may multiply and become a menace to poultry and birds as they have in certain West Indian islands where they were introduced to combat the fer-de-lance. When the mongoose was finally received, the doctor staged a fight between it and a cobra in a set of his own construction representing an opening in the jungle. Unfortunately for the element of suspense, the mongoose killed the cobra almost instantly. Ditmars, feeling like a prizefight fan when the championship bout ends in a knockout in the first round, had to go to the trouble of buying a new cobra. The second engagement was suitably prolonged and dramatic, the mongoose emerged the winner, and a fine film was added to the series on the natural enemies of reptiles.

But even long negotiations could not produce a bushmaster. The last one the zoo had been able to get had died of starvation, as usual, in 1911. Eager to film this handsome viper, the curator made repeated attempts to obtain a specimen—without success. It was an effort to which he returned persistently in the following years.

Some of the pictures involved real danger for the man

behind the camera. Gunda, who had tried to kill his keeper and very nearly succeeded, had to be caught in a good humor and filmed with speed and caution because Ditmars, sympathetic even to the most violent of his charges, didn't want the big elephant recorded, in disgrace, wearing leg chains.

The curator's worst moment, probably, was shooting a large chimpanzee the zoo had just acquired. She weighed more than a hundred pounds and could outfight a strong man; and, like most chimps approaching full growth, she was becoming savage and unmanageable. Since her former owner, a skillful animal trainer, was present, Ditmars felt safe in entering her cage to photograph her tricks at close range. She had done a number of difficult acrobatics, had been induced to sew, and was marking on a slate when she became restless. At a sharp command from the trainer, her temper flared. With a yowl, she hurled the slate across the cage. The stiff hair on her back stood up and her yellow eyes, lighting on the startled curator, seemed to blaze. Ditmars was further alarmed to see the trainer, tiptoeing cautiously behind the beast, slip out of the cage.

He was alone with the enraged ape. As the brute, making savage sweeps with her powerful arms, began to tramp slowly around him and the camera, he had time to remember that big chimps had mangled and killed larger men than he. The circles were getting smaller and the ape seemed to expand under his eyes. A motion on his part would have precipitated the assault. Tensely, he stood ready to throw the heavy camera in her face should she attack, when the door rattled and the trainer's voice cracked:

"Look out!"

Astonishingly, the chimp collapsed with a whimper on the floor. Ditmars dared to look around and saw the man, as badly frightened as he, pointing a gun at her—a toy gun with a red stock and a shiny tin barrel.

"She's afraid of firearms," he gasped, "and this thing has her bluffed. Let's get out of here!"

A few such scares notwithstanding, Doctor Ditmars filmed wild creatures for thirty years without an accident, producing an unparalleled series of zoological pictures systematically illustrating animal life in its various phases.

Most of the movies he made on his own time, often working until eleven or twelve at night, and always appearing at his office promptly the next morning. Occasionally, he had to take some shots at the park during the day, but it was an expenditure of its time that the Zoological Society did not begrudge. The pictures, which Ditmars alone financed, were his personal property, and all the income from them, which eventually became considerable, his too; but the society benefited from them. Although the use of his films brought good fees, he always showed them free at all Zoological Society functions. Commercially distributed, they brought the name and the work of the society before hundreds of thousands all over the country; they forwarded its aim in instructing the public in zoological knowledge; and, at least once, they were largely responsible for obtaining a large sum of money for the society.

Doctor Hornaday attributed it to the Ditmars films that Andrew Carnegie contributed lavishly to the pension fund. The elderly steelman, who was applying a vast fortune to philanthropic and educational purposes, had long been interested in the zoo. When he asked Ditmars to show his pictures at his house, one April day in 1914, Ditmars ran off the reels that were completed. Carnegie was fascinated; he asserted that it was the most interesting exhibition of the sort he had ever seen. A few days later, when one of the Zoological Society's officers called on him to ask for a contribution to the pension fund, Carnegie gave him a hundred thousand dollars.

TWENTY-TWO

THE BRONX ZOO, even as early as 1914, began to feel the effects of the First World War: the European animal markets were closed to it. At the same time, its immense popularity—two million people visited it that year—was an incentive to the director and the curators to maintain the high standard of their collections. With some of the most important sources of replacement eliminated, it was uphill work. Ditmars' collecting trips became even more important than they had been.

To the curators of the zoo, this trying period brought special problems in addition to the usual ones. No European, Asiatic, Malayan, African or Australian reptiles could be bought to replace those that died. A virulent kind of tuberculosis killed every orang-utan and chimpanzee in the collection. Gunda, bloodthirsty beyond control, had to be shot. Comic, endearing Congo, in constant pain with neuritis, was put out of his misery. The disabilities of his advanced years were making the old age of Sultan, the magnificent lion, a burden to him, so he was mercifully chloroformed. Billy, the Alaskan brown bear, one of the zoo's oldest and most popular residents, fell and broke his hip. It failed to heal and humanity required that he, too, be shot. And Dinah, homesick and depressed, starved herself to death. She was not the first gorilla in the zoo, but she was the most popular. Brought back from Africa just after the outbreak of the war by Richard Garner, the man who advanced the theory, to which little credence is now given, that the sounds monkeys utter can be classified as language, she had been on exhibit for eleven months. It was an unusual length of time, in those days, for a gorilla to survive captivity. A baby herself, she had a puppy for a companion and pet, and her keeper, feeling foolish, took her for airings in a baby carriage when she was ailing. Her public mourned her deeply; no one more than Ditmars.

To climax the bad luck, Ditmars sustained a disappointment that always rankled. From boyhood he had been interested in volcanoes. In 1914 and 1915 Mount Lassen, in the Cascades, erupted. Eager to see a volcano in action, Ditmars hurried to California, weighted down with movie equipment. By the time he arrived all volcanic activity had passed. Not even a streamer of smoke issued from the mountain. He consoled himself with a snake hunt in the desert.

The next year, 1916, was somewhat brighter. The Bronx Zoo, co-operating with the Zoological Society of Philadelphia and the National Zoological Park of Washington, sent an agent to Africa, who was able to restore the depleted collections with the purchase of some fine animals. Ditmars himself got an exceptionally good catch of reptiles on his vacation at the Pinelands Club in South Carolina.

This was the first long trip on which he took his little girls. Now about twelve and ten, they were thrilled at the prospect of the boat journey to Savannah. By the time Ditmars had herded his family onto the boat at New York and seen that all his equipment was properly stowed, he felt that he had done a hard day's work. Beatrice, he noticed uneasily, what with excitement and too much candy, had contracted hiccups.

"No more candy for you, Beatrice," he told her.

"Yes, Pop," she said obediently.

Later when the ship was moving through the lower bay, he found his younger daughter on deck, radiant with excitement and plastered down the front of her dress with a sticky mess. She had secreted a handful of chocolates in her pocket, where they had melted. Ditmars took her to her mother, for cleaning and retribution.

"That was *very* naughty of you, Beatrice, to hide the candy in your pocket," he rebuked her. The child's mother looked at him with an expression that abruptly reduced him to sheepish silence. He knew just what she was thinking: she was remembering the night not long before when she had discovered a gooey slice of apple pie in his pocket. Disliking it, and unwilling to hurt the cook's feelings, he had slipped it off his plate and into his pocket, intending to dispose of it after dinner. There, two days later, his wife had found it.

The Pinelands Club was much as it had been on his last visit to it some fourteen years before. There was the same hospitable atmosphere; and the Negro guides, stiffer and more grizzled now, were the same. The canny pinto, Spot-Nose, whom Ditmars still remembered with warmth, had gone wherever good horses go, but there were sturdy, scrawny animals like him to take the party into the lowgrounds.

For two weeks the doctor and his wife and George Palmer, one of the Reptile House keepers who accompanied them, worked through the lowgrounds for 'gators, rattlers, cottonmouths and harmless snakes. At first, for safety's sake, the little girls were left behind at the club where, immediately, Gladyce captured a huge diamond-back rattlesnake.

She did it quite without fanfare. Walking in the grounds near the clubhouse one afternoon, she saw the reptile coiled under a tree, bulging and sluggish from a recent meal. Knowing her father would want it, she went in, asked for a large box, and cautiously placed it over the snake, weighting it with a stone. When her parents drove in later, after a disappointing day's hunt devoid of rattlers, she announced, conservatively:

"I've got a snake for you, Pop. I think it's a diamond-back."

Ditmars was startled and a little skeptical. He raised the box with due precautions, however, and revealed the largest diamond-back he had seen in years. For the only time in Gladyce's recollection, he almost lost his head. He trembled, laughed, scolded and congratulated her all in one breath.

"But there was nothing to it, Pop. All I did was put a box over him."

"Great Scot! He might have killed you!" Pale and agitated, he wiped his brow. "If you children can turn up diamond-backs in innocent front yards, front yards are no place for you. We need you on our trips. From now on, you'll go into the lowgrounds with your mother and George and me, where we can supervise your exploits."

Ditmars, as always, donated his catch to the zoo. The collection was further strengthened by a series of Trinidad reptiles sent by R. R. Mole, the West Indian editor and herpetologist who, almost twenty years before, had sent young Ditmars his first tropical snakes; and by a fine collection of South American snakes from Doctor Vital Brazil, director of the Institute of Serum Therapy at São Paulo, Brazil, where the antivenins for South American snake poisons were prepared.

The organization that would make antivenins specifically for North American snakes still had not come into existence. Whenever a case of snake bite occurred within reach of his help, Ditmars donated a tube of Doctor Calmette's polyvalent antivenin which, it is to be remembered, was produced from a mixture of venoms in which the neurotoxic cobra venom predominated. Not as effective for rattler and other hemorrhagic venoms as for neurotoxic ones, still it worked partially. In 1909, to the wonderment of the doctors treating the case and of the New York newspapers, it had saved the life of a snake charmer who had been bitten by a rattler during a performance at one of the dime museums on Fourteenth Street. In 1916 the accident was closer to home: John Toomey, an experienced keeper of mammals and reptiles, was struck by a large rattler while he was cleaning a cage full of newly arrived Texas diamond-backs. It was the first accident of its kind to occur at the zoo.

It was the morning of January 27. Ditmars was in his office

looking over his mail. About nine-thirty he heard a yell and the scuffle of hurrying feet, and went out to investigate.

In front of the diamond-backs' cage he found Toomey and Charles Snyder. Toomey's hand was bleeding and Snyder had twisted his tie around his wrist and was holding it tightly.

"One of the diamond-backs got him," Snyder said shortly. "Better call Doctor Blair and Doctor Van der Smisson quick." Doctor Blair was the Zoo's veterinarian, Doctor Van der Smisson its official physician.

Toomey was led into the curator's office and made to lie down. Another ligature was twisted about the injured arm above the elbow.

"Take it easy, John. This will be all right," Ditmars reassured him. He looked at the injury. The snake had torn Toomey's hand so badly, both with its long fangs and its incurved, nonvenomous lower teeth, that it was impossible to tell into which of the ragged wounds the venom had been injected. All were bleeding freely, and Snyder was already drawing off what poison he could by sucking.

Doctor Blair came on the run. After a quick examination he decided, "We won't open those wounds any further. It would involve a lot of tissue destruction and they're bleeding well anyway. We'll bathe them with a solution of potassium permanganate."

Twenty minutes after the accident, when Doctor Van der Smisson arrived, Toomey felt no discomfort beyond the pain caused by the tight ligatures and a burning in his hand. The symptoms of snake bite had not yet set in. The physician ordered a tube of Calmette's antivenin to be liquefied.

Forty-five precious minutes crawled past while the dry yellow crystals deliberately dissolved in distilled water. In a little more than an hour from the time he was struck, Toomey received the first injection of Calmette's antivenin, and the painful ligatures were removed. In another half-hour the usual symptoms set in. He sweated, shivered, vomited and became deadly weak. His hand and arm swelled badly. At one o'clock Doctor Van der Smisson gave him another injection of the antivenin. He was extremely weak, but still conscious, when the ambulance arrived to take him to the hospital.

"Don't worry, John," Ditmars encouraged him. "You'll be back shortly, perfectly well."

For a while it looked as though the curator was a bad prophet. At the hospital Toomey sank into a coma and had to have injections of strychnine. The swelling in his arm extended over his chest to his abdomen and discolored fright-fully. The rattler venom was having its characteristic hemor-rhagic effect; its less severe action against the nervous centers, however, was counteracted by the Calmette antivenin. Still, Toomey was a dangerously sick man. Van der Smisson wanted a specialist's opinion.

"I'm calling Langmann," he told Ditmars.

"Good," Ditmars agreed. He had known Doctor Gustav Langmann, an authority on venoms, for almost twenty years, and had on many occasions supplied him with venom.

Doctor Langmann had good news: Doctor Brazil himself was in town, attending the Pan-American Congress, and prob-ably had some specific antirattler serum with him. Doctor Brazil, run to earth the next morning, did have the specific serum, hastened to the hospital and immediately injected it— it was in fluid, not crystal, form—in the sick man. Toomey's improvement was spectacular. In a few hours his chills and nausea ceased; in a dozen more the swelling was reduced by a third and the lurid discoloration began to fade to a dull brown. From then on his condition improved steadily. In three weeks he was discharged from the hospital, suffering no ill effects beyond some stiffness in his hand. He had had a horribly close call, and had provided the opportunity for some interesting observations.

The first was that the rattler's bite responded far better to specific rattler antivenin than to the polyvalent type. The second was that serum in liquid form, although it had to be replaced more often, was preferable to the crystalline because no precious time had to be spent in dissolving it. The third was that Ditmars' often-repeated instructions on what to do in case of snake bite had been well learned. Everybody did just the right thing, and did it quickly. Prompt first aid had definitely contributed to saving Toomey's life.

Shortly after the accident, Ditmars received from Doctor Brazil two hundred and fifty tubes of antirattler serum. Fifty tubes of it he gave to the Army; the rest he kept in refrigerators at the zoo and at his home, for distribution as it was required. That summer, two cases of snake bite in New York were successfully treated with antivenin from that stock, and two people with a very good chance of dying were quickly restored to health.

Reciprocally helpful, Ditmars sent Doctor Brazil some Texas rattlers and a quart of dried venom. Because of legal bars, the antivenin manufactured in Brazil could not be sold in the United States. There was nothing, however, to prevent its being given away. The idea of the hundred or so yearly fatalities from snake bite in the United States troubled Ditmars. These painful deaths were unnecessary when current scientific knowledge could so easily avert them; yet they were not being averted. The curator decided that, until such a time as an antivenin laboratory was organized in this country, he would distribute antivenin produced at Doctor Brazil's laboratory on his own initiative. In return, he would ask the beneficiary for two and a half dollars, considerably less than the antivenin's cost, to be used to purchase a rattler for Doctor Brazil. The expense to Ditmars was not great; even had it been much higher he would have felt it a privilege, in fact a duty, to assume it. At the same time, he repeated his warnings in papers and magazines: if you are bitten by a venomous snake, twist a tourniquet above the wound, between it and the heart; incise the punctures so that they bleed freely; apply suction, mechanical if possible, otherwise by mouth—if you have no abrasions on lip or mouth through which the venom might enter; then, as soon as possible, inject antivenin.

The entrance of the United States into the war made life at the zoo more complicated than ever. Ditmars found himself in charge not only of reptiles, mammals and insects, but also of Company A, Zoological Park Guards. Devised as a contribution to the protection of New York City, and uniformed and armed with Springfield rifles at the expense of the Zoological Society, the company, with a certain amount of expectancy, drilled smartly under the Barnard-conditioned eye of Captain Ditmars, and held target practice two days a week at the Yonkers rifle range. Never called on for martial action, the overworked curators and keepers of the Guards had their exercise for their pains, and the not negligible satisfaction of knowing that, had need arisen, they would have been prepared to meet it.

At the same time Ditmars, whose proficiency in still and motion photography was highly professional, was doing confidential work involving the analysis and interpretation of photographs with the Army Signal Corps. He stayed later than ever in his studio, and took frequent trips to Washington. His family hardly saw him any more.

Wartime problems multiplied at the Zoological Park. There was a shortage of coal, a serious thing for the tropical members of the collections whose quarters had to be kept hot. Doctor Blair, the invaluable veterinarian, left the zoo to become an Army officer, and many experienced employees joined the service. There was an embargo on imports, including zoological specimens, which made the replacement problem more acute than ever; and there was a cut in the zoo's maintenance appropriation. By the time the Armistice was signed director, curators and keepers were at their wits' end, but Doctor Hornaday was still able to assert stoutly that, in spite of losses, the general excellence of the collections had been maintained and that there were even creatures to spare among many of the species. Illustrating his point, the Zoological Society sent a generous shipment of mammals, birds and reptiles to the war-depleted collection of the Royal Zoological Society at Antwerp.

A period in history was past. To Ditmars, it was punctuated not only by the ending of the war, but by the deaths of Andrew Carnegie and Theodore Roosevelt. The one had been a stanch patron of the Zoological Society; the other, his cordial friend. The old men were dying, the young moving into middle age. He was well into his forties himself. His little girls were growing up. Now they went to the movies with boys, instead of with their grandfather who, still an unreconstructed rebel, had recently amused and embarrassed them at *The Birth of a Nation* by standing stiffly at attention during the playing of *Dixie*, stalking indignantly out of the theater at the first strains of *Marching Through Georgia*.

Ditmars' life moved comfortably back into its prewar channel. He lectured to YMCA boys, church members, Sing Sing convicts, school children, college students, teachers' groups, scientific societies, men's smokers, women's clubs. He added more reels to his *Book of Nature*. He worked on a new motion picture, *The Four Seasons*, four reels showing the effects of the turning of the seasons on mammals, birds, reptiles and insects. He made profitable arrangements for the release and distribution of his films. He visited snake dens in New York and Pennsylvania and, in regions where venomous reptiles were common, distributed tubes of Doctor Brazil's antivenin among the local doctors and gave them instructions in its use. He coped expeditiously with the crises that for twenty years had been everyday occurrences in his life, and looked on them, after his wartime preoccupations, almost as relaxations.

Usually the comic element was uppermost in them. There was that affair of the skunk and Washington Irving High School, for instance. Every fall for several years, the zoo had supplied a number of reptiles, birds and small mammals for the vivarium the school maintained for its zoology classes, and received them back at the end of the school year. This postwar fall a skunk was requested. These amiable little animals, their offensive power removed by a simple operation, make agreeable pets. Ditmars selected one, presumed harmless, which had been presented to the zoo several years before, and sent it to the school along with the other creatures, in charge of a keeper. As the unsuspecting man transferred it from its traveling box to its new cage, before an eager audience of children and teachers, the little beast took offense. It expressed resentment by the only means at its disposal. As if by magic, the spectators dispersed, leaving the confounded, incredulous keeper alone with his skunk and one teacher who, holding her nose, told him to get out, fast. Disgraced, keeper and skunk were conveyed back to the park by a compassionate taxi driver, where the one underwent an extensive deodorization treatment, the other some simple surgery. Ditmars' apologies to the school were graciously accepted, his offer of an absolutely guaranteed skunk firmly declined.

An element of danger, sometimes entering into the emergencies, lent zest to the accustomed routine. Answering the telephone one morning, the curator was told by the panic-stricken animal dealer on the other end that two king cobras were loose in his unloading room.

It was a serious emergency. The king cobra is the largest and most poisonous of all venomous snakes, and is alert and aggressive as well as deadly. The idea of two such monsters wandering free in downtown New York didn't bear contemplating. Without delay Ditmars and Snyder hurried downtown equipped with a couple of staffs with nooses on the ends and a strong suitcase containing two burlap bags. They found the dealer stuttering with alarm.

"A shipment's just arrived from India, and I took the crates upstairs to the unloading room. This big teak box was heavy, as though it had a python in it, so I knocked the lid off without thinking much about it. I tell you, it gave me the turn of my life to see that thin olive body in it, instead of a thick, sluggish python! I jumped for the door, and the cobra reared up, fighting mad, and I just caught a glimpse of another one looking out as I slammed the door. I called you right away," he added trustfully.

"How about the room? Where can they get out?"

"The windows are covered with fine, heavy mesh, but I don't know about the floor. It may have rat holes, and the place is stacked full of broken crates and stuff where they can hide."

"An appetizing prospect," Ditmars remarked to Snyder as they climbed the dingy stairs, "trying to find a couple of deadly snakes in a jumble of old lumber."

The animal dealer pointed out the door of the unloading room and stood well back as they swung it open and entered gingerly. There was nothing in sight, and the two men closed the door before beginning their search. Peering around, they saw almost at once a fold of dull green protruding from beneath a broken box. The only way to get at the snake was to poke it, and bring it out with a rush.

"Better open the door, Charlie," Ditmars advised. "We may want to get out of here in a hurry."

Snyder softly moved to the door and, taking the handle, pulled. The door did not open. The dealer had locked them in!

Ditmars was furious. Controlling himself, he rapped gently on the door, not daring to make any vibrations by vigorous pounding. There was no answer.

"Very well," he said in a hard voice. "There's nothing to

do but catch these things. If this one rushes us, swing to disable it. I'd hate to hurt it, but we can't take a chance." Already he was turning over in his mind a few of the scarifying remarks he intended to address to the dealer. He prodded the coil.

The cobra hissed explosively, and started to pour from beneath the box, dilating its hood slowly and hesitating between anger and surprise. Before it could make up its mind, the noose was over its head and tightened. Furiously the reptile surged forward. Seizing the stick, it bit it savagely, not once, but with the repeated chewing motion of its kind, spilling its deadly venom freely. Snyder swung his stick and pinioned the big reptile's head, and Ditmars grabbed it by the neck. The fifteen-foot body lashed and tossed frantically until Snyder got hold of the tail and began stuffing it into one of the bags. At that moment the other cobra, unnoticed until then on a high stack of boxes, reared up and took a good look at them.

"Swing for it!" Ditmars yelled, thrusting the first cobra farther into the bag. With a motion quick as sleight of hand, he withdrew his hand from the straining neck and twirled the bag, closing it over the snake's head. In the same moment Snyder precariously pinioned the neck of the second snake. Full of fight, it jerked free, and made a savage, sweeping strike that sent both men scrambling back for safety.

"Phew!" Snyder whistled.

"Once more, now!" They advanced on the snake again. Snyder for a second time succeeded in pinning the creature down. As it thrashed violently about, Ditmars got his pole against its neck just behind the head.

"Grab it, Charlie," he panted.

Snyder grabbed. The snake was captured. Without further trouble they backed it into the second bag. Breathing hard, both men looked at each other. The keeper shook his head.

"I'm sure glad we don't do this every day," he said.

Ditmars was smiling grimly. "And now," he said, "I shall take great pleasure in smashing that blasted door to kindling!"

Using the heaviest piece of wood they could find as a battering ram, they went to work on the heavy door. A panel was split and their feelings were already greatly relieved, when it opened suddenly. The dealer peeked in.

One glance at him was enough to still the scathing words on Ditmars' tongue. He was an elderly man, and he was trembling visibly. His putty-colored face was beaded with sweat. It was obvious that he was scared to death.

"The snakes?" he quavered.

"It's all right," Ditmars informed him gruffly. "We've got them."

Color came back into the man's face, poise to his bearing. He actually smiled.

"Those are very fine specimens, Doctor Ditmars, and cheap at a hundred dollars apiece. It'll be a long time before you find a bargain like that again."

Ditmars caught Snyder's eye. The head keeper gave him a slow wink. There was still that little matter of the locked door to be adjusted.

"A hundred for the pair of them," Ditmars offered.

"But they cost *me* that much. I have to make something on them. Eighty-five apiece."

Ditmars turned to his assistant. "It seems we can't do business here today, Mr. Snyder," he remarked pleasantly. "Take the snakes back in there and liberate them."

That closed the deal. The locked door was avenged.

The herpetologist and his helper, carrying the cobras in the suitcase, went back to the Bronx on the subway. In spite of a few bad moments, they were not inclined to make much of their adventure.

"After all," Ditmars summed it up, "it's all in the day's work."

TWENTY-THREE

THE LIFE of a chaperon is always arduous, and that of a chaperon of wild animals is harder than most. He has to cope with their considerable capacity for mischief, and he cannot reach them by appealing to their reason. He has to be calm, patient and resourceful, and it helps if his wife is, too. In June, 1921, the curator, with Mrs. Ditmars, went to San Francisco to purchase some animals and escort them back to the zoo. The experience was an exercise in ingenuity and patience.

The S.S. *Granite State,* arriving from Singapore and other Oriental ports, had a large collection of beasts aboard. A pair of orang-utans, a couple of twenty-foot pythons and some anoas, pygmy water buffalo of the Philippines, were the specimens that Ditmars particularly wanted. Competing with the representatives of other zoos, he purchased them. There then arose the necessity of dealing with the quarantine regulations applying to the anoas. Formalities occupied several days.

June temperatures on the coast were variable, the orangs sensitive to change. They had to be kept in a place where they would not be exposed to the nightly drop. Ditmars found space in a theatrical warehouse for the larger one, an adult male weighing about a hundred and fifty pounds. The cage, placed in front of a sunny window, was anchored to the floor with stout pieces of lumber to keep its occupant from moving it by shaking the bars that closed its front. The orang was given an Army blanket in which to enshroud himself when it became chilly. One of the warehousemen agreed to keep an eye on the big beast, and Ditmars was to drop in three times daily to feed and water him and oversee his welfare.

The other orang, a baby, had a snuffly cold. Plainly he had to have special attention. Ditmars took him to the hotel and, over the heartfelt protests of the manager, started to his room with him.

"Pets are not allowed!" the hotel man declared with the strongest emphasis.

"But, my dear sir," Ditmars insisted politely, "it isn't a pet. It is a specimen for exhibit in a zoological garden."

"Our regulations do not permit . . ."

"A regulation covering orang-utans? If you can show me a rule that bars orangs from this hotel . . ."

"Of course I can't! It never occurred to the management that anybody would *want* to keep an ape in his room!"

"Look," Mrs. Ditmars intervened coaxingly, "he's just a poor sick baby." The little ape turned watery eyes to her and sneezed pathetically. "He won't be any trouble, and he will probably die if he doesn't get the right care. You wouldn't want the poor little thing to die, would you?" She smiled charmingly at the harried manager.

"Oh, all right," he said wearily. "But please take your pet —your zoological specimen, or whatever it is—up and down in the freight elevator."

The sick baby enlivened their stay at the hotel by yanking the telephone out by the roots, but the manager was too beaten to protest further. He merely put the damage on the bill, without comment.

Ditmars solved his catering problem by arranging with a Chinese restaurant to dry loaves of Graham bread and cook rice for his apes. When he went to call for the food, one of the Chinese offered to carry it to the warehouse for him.

"It's for an orang-utan, you understand," Ditmars explained, slowly and clearly. The Chinese smiled and nodded without surprise. "A big ape," Ditmars added, more loudly

172

and with gestures. He had the feeling that he wasn't getting his point across.

A watchman let them into the ghostly interior of the warehouse. They made their way to the big south room where a single electric bulb shed a dim, dingy light over struck scenery and shrouded pianos. The interior of the cage was in shadow, the orang invisible within it. The Chinese, curious, stepped up to the bars to peer through, and the appetizing smells of freshly boiled rice and dry bread rose temptingly from the kettle he was carrying. Immediately, a putty-colored face fringed with ragged red hair and circled in a loosely draped Army blanket materialized inches from his nose. A hairy arm, inordinately long, plunged through the bars and an inhuman hand sank to the wrist into the rice. At the unnerving specter, the Chinese uttered a single little sound, like the peep of a scared bird, and fled. The ape, casting aside its blanket, went to work on the kettle of food. From then until his departure, the curator served his orang's dinner single-handed.

Negotiations with the Southern Pacific Railroad secured Ditmars accommodations to Chicago on a crack train, with permission for his apes, snakes and other animals to travel as excess baggage on the same train. (The anoas, at the expiration of the quarantine period, were to travel in care of the express company's employees.) The passenger traffic manager of the railroad wrote a letter asking all employees to extend any courtesy, however unusual, that Doctor Ditmars requested.

The big ape in his strong teakwood cage, the indisposed baby in a little traveling house that Ditmars had had built in San Francisco, the snakes and the squirrels and the rest of the company were loaded into the baggage car, and the curator and his wife went to their stateroom several cars back. The train pulled out.

"Well, I guess our troubles are over," Ditmars said contentedly.

"We're not home yet," Mrs. Ditmars said with foreboding.

A rap at the door brought them both to their feet. It was the conductor and the brakeman. Both looked eager and a little self-conscious.

"We wonder if you'd show us your snakes?" they asked.

"Gladly," Ditmars answered with a heartiness that sprang largely from relief. He had been afraid that something untoward had happened, already.

The three men went to the baggage car, where the rattling and swaying of the train was much more perceptible than in the Pullmans. Opening the box in which the two pythons were traveling, and raising his voice above the noise of the speeding train, Ditmars said:

"You've no doubt seen snakes like this a dozen times at circuses, only probably not so large. Pythons are often used by the snake charmers. This fellow, rearing up and wagging his tongue at us, is a black-tailed python. The other is a regal python."

Sensing a curious lack of response on the part of his audience, he turned around. He was just in time to see the conductor and the brakeman crowding each other in frantic competition to get through the door.

About midnight the first night out, there was another knock on the stateroom door, this one with an unmistakable note of urgency in it.

"Told you not home yet," Mrs. Ditmars mumbled sleepily in the dark.

Ditmars stumbled out of bed and opened the door to a porter, who apologetically informed him that he was needed up front. He reeled through the swaying, green-hung aisles to the baggage car where he was confronted by the conductor, no longer eager or self-conscious, but irate. He was nursing one knee. His story, stripped of the reproaches with which he told it, was this. He had been passing through the baggage car, minding his own business. The orang, curled up on the floor of his cage with only his frowsy head sticking out of the blanket, looked like a disreputable and sleepy old bum. The conductor, never thinking to give the cage a wide berth, was striding past it when the beast, suddenly aroused, darted out one long arm, grabbed him by the ankle and jerked him to the floor with a crash that, but for the intervention of Provi-dence, would have cracked his kneecap.

Ditmars apologized for his ape's bad behavior. The con-ductor told him severely that he would accept the apology only on condition that the solid front that fitted over the bars of the cage be put on. The holes bored in it would, Ditmars knew, give the orang barely enough air, but the night was chilly, so, sighing, he complied and went back to bed.

In the morning, when he arrived in the baggage car to give the ape his breakfast of bananas, apples and cooked oat-meal, the cage was surrounded by wreckage.

"The big fellow did it when he woke up," the baggageman said, grinning. "He sat up and wanted to look out, so he smashed his shutter. Then he patted his blanket into a cushion and sat down on it, just as patient as you please, to wait for his breakfast."

Untroubled in conscience by his accumulation of misdeeds, the orang ate a hearty breakfast with visible relish. His keeper wondered what he would do next. It was not long before he found out.

When the train stopped at Ogden, Utah, the incorrigible ape grabbed a bundle of newspapers from an unwary boy passing through the baggage car and entertained himself, and a large crowd of excited spectators, by tearing them sheet from sheet and tossing them around in billows. Ditmars appeased the newsboy with liberal payment. The incident, recounted in the local papers and wired to Chicago, assured the orang of the best attentions of the press for the rest of his journey.

His best prank he saved for another midnight. The curator and his patient wife, when the knock came, were ministering to the baby ape, now ill with pneumonia, which they had taken into their stateroom for closer attention.

"What is it this time?" Ditmars inquired resignedly of the porter.

"Your big monkey, he's got a knife!"

Ditmars ran through the train to the baggage car without waiting for further explanation. The heavy bread knife with which he cut the stale loaves for the apes had been slipped behind a slat in the car. A thoughtful baggageman at a recent stop, fearing that a trunk he was loading would hide it, had laid it on the orang's cage. The beast, inquisitive, had reached through his bars to get hold of it and had begun to experiment with his interesting toy. As Ditmars appeared he was flourishing it with terrifying energy, jabbing it deep into the floor of his cage and making passes at the luggage just out of his reach. No one wanted to go near him, so long as he was waving the heavy steel blade. It was his chaperon's problem to wheedle him into giving it up.

A shiny brass oil can with a long spout sufficed to distract the simian attention. Clutching his new toy with passionate interest, the orang relinquished the knife which Ditmars quickly removed from his reach. Knowing that the worst thing his obstreperous charge could do with the oil can was to get a mouthful of unappetizing lubricant, Ditmars went back through the swaying cars to his stateroom, his wife and his sick baby ape.

The journey came to an end after four feverish days, with the baby on the way to recovery and the rest of his charges in good health. Both Ditmars and his wife were a little sorry when it was over.

Ditmars didn't have to go to California or even as far as the zoo to have monkey troubles. There were usually some right around home. Ever since the children had been small, the house had been full of pets. Besides the cat and the dog rou-

176

tine in most suburban families, there were such things as harmless snakes, insects like crickets or katydids, and delicate specimens from the zoo, usually monkeys.

Most monkeys are mischievous in youth, uncertain of temper as they grow older. The conditions of their captivity have to be exactly right or they become ill. Ditmars never recommended them as pets: the monkey, treated with ignorant kindness, usually had a wretched life, and the owner, sooner or later, was likely to be attacked with temperamental savagery. Still, he frequently kept monkeys at home himself, to give them the individual care impossible at the zoo, owing to the jealousy of cage mates.

There was little he did not know about their propensity for wanton destruction. He had seen an orang wrench loose the crossbar of its trapeze and, using it as a lever, wreck the cage; a baboon snatch hat, umbrella or purse from an incautious onlooker and rend it, with pointless fury, into shreds; and the lemur, his office pet, pour ink and glue together, swig off all it could swallow, and daub the rest over desk and walls. Whenever he left the house he made it a point to see that the monkeys currently in residence were locked into their cage.

His single oversight was followed with dire results. As the family came in late one evening, after an absence of several hours, they heard a scurrying sound. At the spectacle revealed, when the light was switched on, there arose a chorus of dismayed cries. The house looked as though a tempest had swept through it. Huddled together on the back of an overturned chair, in the midst of the wreckage, sat the pair of guilty-looking monkeys.

The curtains were down, and in ribbons. Books had been yanked from the shelves and their pages snatched out. Flowers were madly strewn over the entire downstairs and the vases, full of water, smashed on the floor. Plants had been stripped of leaves, overstuffed furniture disemboweled, lamps knocked over. The worst shambles was the dining room; scarcely a whole piece of glass or china remained. With truly inspired devilishness, the monkeys had even scattered the ashes from the fireplace over the rugs.

The horrified family gazed speechless on the ruin, and the monkeys, subdued and scared now, peered at them apprehensively. Mrs. Ditmars spoke first.

"Ray, I don't know whether to laugh or cry."

"When in doubt, Chicky, always laugh," he advised.

She tried an uncertain smile, and he grinned at her. At that she really broke into a laugh.

"See how absurd they look, just like naughty children!"

The monkeys, realizing that the crisis was past, raced to Ditmars and, with gibbering little noises, sprang into his arms.

It took the best part of a week, and no trivial expense, to restore the house.

Red, the baby South American howling monkey, was a creature of a very different character and one that gave the whole family amusement and satisfaction. He had been brought from British Guiana to New York by a returning explorer when he was about three months old. He was a sorry sight, emaciated, depressed and decrepit.

Inspecting him in her father's office, Gladyce observed, "He won't live if he stays here. He needs special care. I'm going to ask Doctor Hornaday to let me take him home."

Doctor Hornaday had no objection and Gladyce, buttoning the forlorn little beast into her coat, drove home with him. Too dispirited even to bite, he submitted cheerlessly to a bath. Then he let himself be persuaded to try a mixture of cod-liver oil, water and condensed milk. After the first taste, he wanted more.

"He's going to be all right," Gladyce told her father. She was right.

She undertook his entire care and education, and they became inseparable. She taught him clean habits, supervised his diet and bathed him regularly. He was like a grateful and affectionate child. He had the run of the house, was never kept in a cage, and, being careful and neat, did no damage.

The records of the London zoo indicated that the average life of a captive of this species was between three and four months. Their reputation for delicacy was well documented. Their digestions were precarious, and a lack of vivacity and resilience of spirit prevented them from adjusting to cage life. Red, however, upset all precedents. He could eat and digest anything, including frankfurters, mustard, sauerkraut and sarsaparilla which some well-meaning children fed him at the beach one afternoon, and most of a lemon pie, which he reprehensibly stole from the pantry later the same day. He was a hardy traveler, accompanying the family wherever they went, and he was always happy and friendly. When he died in an influenza epidemic, after two years in captivity, he left an unparalleled record for longevity and a family mourning one of the most cherished pets they had ever had.

Receiving celebrities at the zoo, both human and animal, making films and delivering lectures filled up all the chinks in the herpetologist's busy schedule. Marshal Foch visited the zoo, accompanied by a nervous wildcat, the gift of admirers in the West, whose disposition and digestion were being ruined by the excitement attendant on the French hero's triumphal tour. Irene Castle, the dancer, paid it a call, and "adopted" a Galapagos tortoise, wisely refraining, however, from taking her unwieldy pet away with her. A duck-billed platypus, a rare Australian egg-laying mammal, was acquired, along with its conveyance, a box complicated beyond belief, which simulated the platypus' natural home. It was the first time this unusual creature had been exhibited alive outside Australia, and for the seven weeks of its survival the zoo seethed with visitors.

In his studio Ditmars was working on a new five-reel picture called *Evolution,* showing the development of life from single-celled forms to man. His films were widely popular—*The Four Seasons,* presented at the Rialto in New York, had to be held over several weeks—and, using them to illustrate his lectures, he was addressing a total of some fifty thousand auditors a year by 1923. When he returned from his lecture tours, he was sometimes so hoarse that he could hardly speak.

The reptile collection, too, received constant attention. Although reduced in numbers from its prewar high, it was more representative than before. A trip to the Mohave Desert in the summer of 1922 produced a fine series of desert reptiles, including rattlesnakes, Gila monsters and nonvenomous serpents. Ellis Joseph, the animal dealer who had scored the *coup* of delivering the platypus, sent an extraordinary group of true sea snakes from Australian waters, rarely displayed venomous reptiles related to the cobras, with compressed, paddle-like tails and brilliantly banded bodies. There were many other rarities in the reptile collection, as well as excellent series of cobras and constrictors.

Ditmars was crowding more and more activities into his time. His only relaxation was journeys to New York State and California on collecting trips—a sort of busman's holiday. That, however, was the way he liked it. His fun and his work were the same.

TWENTY-FOUR

THE FILE on Ditmars' desk in the Reptile House became more and more bulging with newspaper clippings and with the correspondence relating to each story. The herpetologist was collecting and authenticating death-by-snake-bite stories in an effort to learn how many occurred yearly in this country. There were still no accurate statistics, and guesses ranged anywhere from twenty to a hundred. His own figures, totaled at the end of the year, indicated that a hundred and fifty was a likelier number. And that did not take into account the people permanently injured by what Weir Mitchell had called "the terrible energies" of venoms.

Ditmars was trying, unsuccessfully, to induce laboratories to make antivenins. The demand for them was so small, those approached argued, that they could not be produced on a satisfactory commercial basis. Several scientific foundations, too, had declined to make them, on the grounds that their scientists would benefit humanity more by working on some of the dozens of diseases that caused more deaths than snake bites.

Ditmars offered to furnish all the snake venoms it could use to any organization in the United States that would assume the production of antivenins specific for North American reptiles. Still there were no takers. The United States remained dependent on the Brazilian Institute of Serum Therapy for its antivenins.

Dr. Afranio do Amaral, of the Institute, was interested in the United States' problem. On his visit to New York in 1922, Ditmars had discussed it with him, and showed him his file of figures and clippings illustrating this country's need for antidotes. Amaral had promised that the Institute would produce antivenins not only for rattlesnake bite, but for that of the copperhead and the cottonmouth as well. It was a generous offer, considering the amount of research and manufacturing the Institute was already doing to provide Brazil with antivenins, and it was one that Ditmars gratefully accepted. His share was to provide venoms, so for a starter he extracted the venom of two hundred copperheads and one hundred water moccasins and shipped the dried stuff to Brazil.

The Reptile House at the New York Zoological Park was widely known by now as the distribution center of the country's antivenin supply, and its director as the man to apply to for information about snake bites. He broadcast his warning in articles for popular magazines. If you are going into a region where venomous snakes are to be found, wear high boots and, in climbing, be careful where you place your hands. In case of bite, go through the routine: tourniquet, incision of the punctures, suction, then antivenin.

Not infrequently the telephone at Ditmars' house in Scarsdale would ring in the night, and a frantic appeal for antivenin would come over the long-distance wire. The herpetologist would rouse one of his daughters, give her a tube of the proper antivenin, and start her on the long drive to the station in New York. While she was on her way, he would get the station on the telephone, find out the fastest train between New York and the place where the victim was, and arrange for its conductor to get the antivenin from his daughter and take it in charge. In a matter of hours, the fluid, handed off the train at its destination, would be exerting its powerful antidotal effect in the veins of the victim.

The arrangement—having the antivenins produced in Brazil and distributing them personally—was not ideal, but it worked. It was successful in saving lives, and that was the important thing.

Ditmars went to California in the summer of 1923 with his wife and daughters. As usual, he collected interesting reptiles in the desert, but the highlights of the trip were not zoological.

One of them was a handsome old Indian in Glacier National Park who took Mrs. Ditmars' eye. He was, a guide explained, Chief Two-Gun White Calf, whose profile appeared on nickels. One of the most picturesque pieces of scenery in the park, he was known to dislike being photographed. Mrs. Ditmars, hopefully, made friends with him and soon, to the astonishment of her husband and the guides, the old chief was offering to pose for her, with her daughters on either side of him. It was a great diplomatic triumph, suitably recorded by the camera.

It was on the way to Ensenada, Mexico, with other friends, over a primitive road that made their heavy car strain and shudder, that the Ditmars began to feel that the West was still wild. At a bare little canteen in the desert, where they stopped for lunch, the cook took their order—there was nothing available but chile con carne and tamales, so it was quickly given—and placed it in front of them. Suddenly there was an uproar at the door. The peaceable tourists were astounded to behold a Mexican, clad in the most colorful western tradition, riding his horse through the door. Yelling something in Spanish, he flourished a big pistol with flamboyant recklessness. The cook shouted, "Under the table!" and, collaring Gladyce and Beatrice, hauled them into the kitchen. Through the door they could still see the Mexican, executing noisy maneuvers on his horse, and their father, grinning, photographing him. Waving his pistol, the rider shouted in Spanish, "Thanks! Send me the papers when my picture appears." He spurred his excited horse through the door and galloped away, leaving an unnerved audience and a couple of overturned chairs behind him.

The girls and the cook emerged from the kitchen, the rest of the party—except Ditmars, who was calmly putting away his camera—from beneath the table. The cook sighed deeply.

"He is not a bad man, just a bandit. He means no harm. But when he becomes excited or drunk he sometimes shoots. It is better to take no chances."

"What did he want here? Was he going to rob us?"

"No, no. He owed me money, so he came to bring me two steers. He left them in the yard. He is really an honest fellow."

In Ensenada there had been, three days before Ditmars' arrival, one of those local political upheavals sometimes called revolutions. Disappointed at missing the excitement, the travelers looked hopefully around for signs of revolutionary action, but saw none in the primitive little place. They were even more disappointed to learn later that, on the very afternoon of their departure, another revolution had occurred, and a rebel gunboat had dropped a couple of shells among the adobe. houses of the village. Ditmars was beginning to think that he positively repelled excitement: Mount Lassen had stopped erupting when he tried to see it; a genuine Mexican revolution had gone into abeyance in his presence; and it had been thirty years since his only hurricane. He never thought of his zoological adventures as particularly thrilling; they were a regular part of his life.

Among Ditmars' luggage was a suitcase containing snakes, each individual in its own bag. He had caught them on his trip in the desert, and was particularly pleased with a rare king snake of a kind he had never exhibited. Because it was hot crossing the desert, Ditmars left the suitcase open one night. He and his wife were dismayed, on returning from breakfast the next morning, to find the woman in the section next to theirs in an almost hysterical state. A snake had somehow got between the panes of the double window of her section and was flaunting itself, in a quiet, spiteful sort of way, before her terrified gaze. Ditmars, with a sinking heart, recognized his prized king snake. Hasty and surreptitious examination showed that the reptile had escaped through a burst seam in its bag. Assuming the guileless, sympathetic air of an innocent fellow-traveler, the curator tried to get at the snake by raising the window. It was stuck fast. The porter was summoned, and the conductor. Their combined efforts were unavailing.

"But where could it have come from?" the distressed lady wailed.

"I really couldn't say," Ditmars answered, with rare equivocation. His wife and daughters, he was glad to note, were simulating just the air of shocked surprise appropriate to finding a snake loose—more or less—in a Pullman car.

"No such thing ever happened before, madam," the conductor panted, still straining at the window. "Well!" he puffed, giving up, "we'll stop the train and get at it from the outside."

So the train was stopped and the interested passengers debarked to watch while the outer window was forced up. The rare, harmless king snake, exposed on the sill, dropped to the roadbed.

"Kill it! Kill it, quick!" somebody cried.

Ditmars preferred losing his prized rarity to admitting that he was at the bottom of all the disturbance, but it was too much to stand by and see it killed.

"No!" he said sharply. "It's a harmless thing. Let it go."

As the snake glided quickly from the right of way he looked dolefully after it, and Beatrice heard him mutter:

"There goes my little snake, and I can't do a single confounded thing about it!"

How it had crawled between the double windows no one was ever able to figure out.

By 1924 Ditmars had been associated with the Zoological

Park for twenty-five years. Writing books and pamphlets and popular articles, lecturing to adult audiences, holding conferences with teachers, addressing classes in the city schools, making zoological motion pictures—in all these ways he was constantly contributing to the spread of popular knowledge of the animal world. It was about this time, too, that he added broadcasting to his activities. Judging from his mail that many people were curious to know what a rattlesnake sounded like, he took one to a broadcast and induced it to sound its warning before the microphone. The radio station was astonished when this novelty drew four hundred fan letters in a week.

While he was used to appreciation, Ditmars nevertheless felt a little thrill of encouragement whenever he received it. On the completion of the forty-two reels of his *Living Book of Nature,* after a dozen years of work, his old friend Doctor Osborn wrote him about "these wonderful films," and Doctor Hornaday sent him a letter glowing with admiration of his achievement. Praise from such critical sources was something to be highly valued. Ditmars was happy to know that his work in popular education was so warmly appreciated. He wished, ruefully, that his attempts to get antivenins manufactured in this country would proceed as successfully.

TWENTY-FIVE

THE AMOUNT of dried rattlesnake venom in the jar was the equivalent of a fluid gallon of the deadly stuff. Ditmars had milked several thousand resentful rattlers to obtain it, and there was enough to produce a thirty-year supply of antivenin. As far as he knew, it was the largest amount that had ever been collected in one receptacle, and he was quite impressed with it. In the summer of 1925, he delivered it himself to Dr. Vital Brazil at the Institute of Serum Therapy near São Paulo, and discussed with the South American doctor various problems involved in maintaining a steady supply of antivenins to the United States. His whole family went along. The twelve-day voyage on the Munson Line's *Southern Cross* was uneventful, the July weather pleasant. It was exciting to enter the Rio de Janeiro harbor and see the beautiful city framed against jungle-covered hills; and exhausting to go through customs in an unfamiliar tongue.

The Rio zoo, outside the city at the foot of the hills, was an outdoor collection, with many interesting and unusual specimens. The Ditmars, and a couple of shipboard friends, were making a tour of it on foot under the guidance of its courteous director. A sudden wind arose, heavy clouds blew up and the sky darkened ominously.

"Run!" commanded the director, after a quick glance overhead. He led the way at a brisk trot down a winding path bordered by tree ferns. His visitors pelted after him, spurred by the flash of lightning and the threatening explosion of tropical thunder. Ahead loomed a thatched building. The director opened the narrow door and bundled his guests through it just as the rain crashed noisily down.

"Safe," he exclaimed with satisfaction, "in the anacondas' den!"

A silence, open to several interpretations, greeted this intelligence. To the Ditmars family, association with large reptiles was too much of a commonplace to deserve comment. The other lady and gentleman, however, would rather have taken their chances with a hundred cloudbursts. In the dim light, Ditmars could see yards of reptiles, some as big around as his thigh, others as slender as his wrist. Interested, he inquired:

"How many serpents are there in this enclosure, Señor Director?"

"Twenty," the director answered proudly. "Just wait till the light returns and you shall see how large they are."

A convulsive twitch at his coattails disclosed to Ditmars that someone was clinging to them, someone not at all happy in the situation. Soothingly, he remarked:

"All harmless, of course. Tell me, Señor Director, your opinion of the maximum length to which South American snakes may grow."

"It is often much exaggerated. Our largest here is an anaconda about twenty-two feet long. In my experience they do not grow much longer than that." Shop talk followed, absorbing to the specialists, diverting to the rest of the party. By the time the rain stopped and they could leave the anacondas' retreat, the scared members, boldly eying the surrounding reptiles, were hazarding guesses as to their weights.

The Serum Institute's serpentarium at Butanan, near São Paulo, which Ditmars and his party reached after an overnight train ride, was an interesting place. Low walls and moats enclosed grass plots dotted with little round huts where the snakes lived. Notices admonished the spectators, of whom there were always a number hanging over the walls, not to throw stones at the reptiles. They deserved respectful treatment. Thanks to the serum made from the venom rendered by these serpents, it has been roughly estimated that deaths from snake bite in Brazil have dropped from nearly five thousand a year to one hundred.

Doctor Brazil, director of the Institute of Serum Therapy, was greatly pleased to receive such a large supply of snake venom from his North American colleague. He had a present for Ditmars, too: a collection of South American venomous serpents. Before their inspection of the snake farm, Doctor Brazil showed his visitor some rare snakes that he kept in his office. One in particular, crimson with yellow bands, took Ditmars' eye.

"What a beautiful creature! I've never seen anything of the sort before."

"It is a rare and harmless species of *Liophis*," explained Doctor Brazil. "I will be honored if you will accept it for your collection."

Ditmars was delighted with the gift. Doctor Brazil put it in a linen bag and gave it to him at once, warning him that the snake, a fish-eater, should be fed as soon as possible since he had not been able to obtain any fish for some time. For the next few days it lived in Ditmars' suitcase, while he attended to his business and pleasure.

The business, naturally, related to snakes and antivenins. The pleasure consisted principally in meeting and being entertained by people connected with the Institute, and in making short trips into the near-by country to capture snakes and study local insects. Secretly, Ditmars hoped that he might even stumble on a bushmaster. It had been a dozen years or more since he had exhibited one. The big, showy vipers, implacable in their hatred of captivity, fascinated him, and he knew he would never be satisfied until he had reconciled one to cage life. He particularly wanted to capture a specimen himself, sure that, using a pole with a hook on the end rather than a noose, he could avoid shock to the sensitive reptile. So he kept a hooked pole at hand on his short trips into the Brazilian jungle—and saw no sign of a bushmaster.

When his business was finished and his snakes were boxed for traveling, Ditmars and his family returned to Rio. The curator was still carrying his crimson-and-gold serpent in his suitcase. Releasing it on his bed at the hotel, he observed with anxiety that it was much too thin for its own good. It needed a meal at once.

With Gladyce he undertook a quest for aquarium stores. They plodded doggedly around the city, and couldn't find any.

"Maybe the markets will have fish," Gladyce suggested.

So they went to the market district. At booths where pets were on sale, Ditmars explained that he wanted some small, fresh-water fish. He searched diligently, but obtained no fish. At lunchtime he and Gladyce, weary and empty-handed, limped back to the hotel.

"Not a single fish!" he reported to his wife. "We've combed the city. When I've rested a little I'm going to take a streetcar to the end of the line and try to find a pond in the country where I can seine some."

Mrs. Ditmars had spent a restful morning sleeping late and doing a little idle shopping in the Rio stores with Beatrice. She looked at her husband sympathetically.

"Poor dear, you do look worn out. Did you happen to see that fountain not far from the hotel? I saw some nice little fish in that."

"Clara! I couldn't do that!"

"No? Not even after dark?"

He smiled at her thoughtfully. "Well, when you put it that way . . ."

That afternoon Raymond Ditmars, naturalist, author and lecturer, shopped for a seine with which to sneak fish out of a public fountain in Rio by night. Stopping in the shelter of a hat store doorway to light a cigarette, he saw just what he wanted—a sailor straw of open weave. What more unsuspicious-looking net could a loiterer near a public fountain carry than the hat on his head?

The night was dark when, about ten o'clock, he left the hotel. A pail of water, covered by a paper bag, was in his hand, and on his head a new straw hat of rakish weave. The plaza ornamented by the fountain was nearly deserted. A couple of sailors moved off as he approached and a respectable-looking elderly man hurried past. Taking as good a look around as the street light down the block permitted, Ditmars removed his hat and fanned himself with it. The gesture was not altogether idle: the thought of stealing the fish of a foreign municipality brought perspiration to his brow. He could see the unsuspecting creatures lying in little groups close to the bottom of the fountain's bowl. After a final glance about, Ditmars gently insinuated his new straw hat under them and made a quick swoop to the surface. Three silvery fish flopped within it. He transferred them to the pail and crossed to the other side of the fountain. After a couple more scoops he had about a dozen fish—and a hat reduced to a dissolving pulp. Abandoning it beside the fountain, he picked up his can of fish and, with as nonchalant an air as he could manage after such stress, strolled back to the hotel.

"Any luck?" inquired his wife.

"Sure. The fishing's fine," he answered, turning his catch into the bathtub and running water into it.

"Ray! Not the bathtub! What will we do for baths?"

"Just another sacrifice for science," he said firmly. "If I can jeopardize my liberty by stealing to keep this rare specimen alive, you can go bathless for it."

Meanwhile, the venomous snakes shipped from São Paulo had arrived. After much discussion with the management, Ditmars received permission to keep them in the laundry while carpenters built a couple of bureau-like contrivances, into which the flat boxes of snakes would fit like drawers. All laundry activities were ordered suspended by the manager until the crazy *Yanqui* took his snakes away.

The northbound ship on which the Ditmars troupe finally departed was captained by a man who wanted no nonsense. He assigned Ditmars' charges to an empty cabin, had all the furniture removed, the windows locked, and the two cases, with their sliding drawers full of snakes, bolted to floor and wall to prevent their upsetting and loosing incalculable terror among the passengers. Ditmars had to promise that he would do nothing more than slide open the drawers daily to water the serpents and remove dead specimens. The ship arrived in New York without alarm to the passengers. As for the curator, he was well satisfied: only one snake died *en route* and a valuable shipment reached the Bronx Zoo in excellent condition.

In 1926 came the inevitable announcement: Doctor Hornaday was retiring from the Zoological Park, having directed its development ever since it was just an idea in a few men's heads. Doctor Blair, the veterinarian, who had resumed his post at the zoo at the end of the war, became director, and Ditmars advanced from assistant curator to curator of mammals.

At the same time, Ditmars' educational work was broadening. He went to New Haven to hold discussions with Yale's science faculty about his films which were being used to teach zoology there. There were conferences with New York City teachers. He was appointed to the Committee of Visual Education in the New York City schools because of his zoological movies, which were generally recognized as a unique contribution to this type of teaching. His lectures took him all around the country, and brought him before tens of thousands of hearers.

Ditmars was fifty years old, and so busy he was breathless, and he wouldn't have exchanged his work with anyone on earth. All he needed to make him completely happy was to see the establishment of an antivenin laboratory in the United States—and to get another bushmaster.

TWENTY-SIX

THE LETTER FROM Doctor Thomas Barbour, one of the foremost herpetologists in the country, director of the Museum of Comparative Zoology at Harvard and a long-time friend of Ditmars', was encouraging. Doctor Afranio do Amaral, then lecturing at Harvard Medical School, would shortly arrive in New York, Doctor Barbour wrote, with good news for the curator of reptiles at the Zoological Park.

Ditmars had an idea what the good news was. For some months negotiations, in which Amaral was the moving spirit, had been afoot among the United Fruit Company, the Mulford Laboratories at Glenolden, Pennsylvania, and Harvard's Institute of Tropical Biology and Medicine. Representatives of the three organizations were discussing plans for the manufacture of antivenins, in this country, for North American snakes.

Doctor Amaral arrived, bearing gifts—some rare South American snakes never before exhibited in this country—and full of enthusiasm. Everything was settled. The United Fruit Company was going to establish a serpentarium at Tela, in Honduras. There snakes would be kept and venom extracted. The poison would be shipped to the Mulford Laboratories where antivenins would be prepared under Doctor Amaral's personal supervision. The Tropical Institute at Harvard was to be scientific adviser. The United Fruit Company, which needed considerable quantities of antivenin for the treatment of snake bite among its employees, was thus assured of a regular supply. Ditmars, authority on the incidence and mortality of snake bite accidents in North America, was to be technical consultant and director of the Institute's nearctic division.

"At last," Ditmars said, "we can stop imposing on our Brazilian friends for antivenins for our own reptiles."

Doctor Amaral protested. "It was no imposition. We were happy to prepare them for you. We regretted only that our own work prevented us from doing more."

"This is a development I've worked and waited twenty years to see." Ditmars was so excited he paced back and forth across his office.

"Until the serpentarium can be built and the reptiles assembled, we must count on local sources to provide us with the venoms to start our work."

"My dear doctor, you may certainly count on me! I'll fairly flood you with venoms!" Ditmars promised.

He kept his word. All the venomous reptiles in the New York Zoological Park's collection yielded their poison to the curator. Extracting venoms had always interested him, but he had never done it with such wholehearted pleasure as he did now, knowing they would be used right here in the United States to produce antivenins for bites of native reptiles.

A winter of lectures, film-making and educational work, in addition to his duties as curator, left Ditmars feeling tired. He prescribed a Mediterranean cruise for himself—and his family, of course—as a rest cure.

By the time the *S.S. Lapland* put in at Tangiers, Ditmars felt that he had been snakeless long enough. He even welcomed the chance to see a native snake charmer, and watched indulgently from the terrace of the hotel while the man went through his act ten yards away. His ragged, bearded assistant steadily beat a little drum the size of a nail keg, while the master charmer performed. The reptiles were harmless desert whipsnakes, the manipulations of the charmer were unspectacular. Ditmars enjoyed himself mildly until the man, holding a snake between his teeth by the tail, whirled around and around until the snake stood out straight and his nervous audience, fearing that the tail would be bitten through, begged him to stop.

There was no essential difference between the snake charming of this Moroccan and that of Mlle. Olga, of pleasant memory. Both were, simply, people who were unafraid of snakes, adroit in handling them, and quite devoid of any mysterious power over them. That, as Ditmars often pointed out, was precisely the kind of person he was, too.

In spite of all his experience with reptiles, he had no unusual influence over them, and was never able to tame or charm a venomous one, although, very cautiously, he had tried a few times. Always interested in snake charming, he had investigated it rather fully in the early days of the zoo. From Singapore he had obtained a snake charmer's outfit—basket and reedlike pipe—and had had records made of the music accompanying the performance. His efforts to charm the cobras at the zoo had come to exactly nothing. A cobra, to be sure, would rear up out of the basket and as Ditmars swayed back and forth in time to the music he was making on the pipe the snake would sway, too—not because it was dancing to the music, but because it was nervously and alertly trying to follow his movements. The performance amounted to no more than a good parlor trick with which anyone experienced in handling snakes could amuse his guests on an idle evening.

Ditmars observed then, however, that certain strains or notes of music had a strange effect on the cobras. They seemed to cause them to fall to the ground, and lie helpless for a moment. Never able to identify or recapture the sound that brought on the brief collapse, still he several times produced it in the course of experimenting with records and a sitar, the elongated, guitar-like instrument often used by snake charmers. Some scientific men have doubted that music affects snakes, but Ditmars' experimentation convinced him that, although they certainly do not react to music in any sense comparable to human beings, and probably do not hear it with their deeply imbedded, crude ears, they feel certain vibrations of strident and irritating pitch through their very sensitive scales and are rendered momentarily helpless by them. He believed, too, that real snake charmers knew how to produce those tones at will.

Skeptical about snake charming in his youth, he now believed in it—in rare instances. Aside from outright frauds and people who, like himself, handled snakes knowledgeably, there were also a very few who, as far as he could determine, had a real and inexplicable influence over venomous reptiles. They could, he had found, pick up a wild specimen of a deadly variety, and submissively the snake would allow itself to be handled. On a trip in the western United States, he had once met a man who could pick up rattlers barehanded with perfect impunity—rattlers that coiled and unmistakably prepared to strike when Ditmars, wearing heavy mitts, made a slow, gentle motion to touch them. The man, no freak at all, had no explanation for his curious ability; he just had it, and that was all he knew about it. It was just about all that Ditmars ever learned about it, too.

On this trip, too, he was lucky enough to meet another of these rare and authentic snake charmers. He was an itinerant charmer on his way from Algiers to Biskra where, he said, the air was better for his serpents. On his back, in an arrangement like a harness, he carried several kegs containing cobras of a species that lives in the region bordering the Sahara. He had only recently caught them, but he seemed to have perfect confidence in their docility.

Ditmars' blood momentarily chilled as the old fellow reached, with no precaution whatever, into a keg and pulled out three cobras which he dropped on the ground. They reared with their characteristic hiss. Through the interpreter the charmer explained that they knew their home; he placed the keg on the ground, and, sure enough, they glided toward it and fairly popped in. Pulling them out again, the old man invited Ditmars to approach. He did so, being careful to stay out of their striking range. Savagely and repeatedly they struck at him. Then, to the herpetologist's astonishment, the charmer quietly extended his bare hand, palm downward, over each angry snake in turn, and each contracted its hood, subsided to the ground and peaceably allowed itself to be returned to the keg. The last snake the charmer tapped gently on the nose with his forefinger, and the reptile, without resentment, opened its mouth slightly. There, as Ditmars could see, were its poison fangs. No cheating trick accounted for this old man's extraordinary performance. He had actually rendered serpents, of a kind deadly and savage, docile as garter snakes.

"It's almost unbelievable," Ditmars exclaimed, really impressed. "It's worth crossing the ocean to see this alone."

The old man pocketed the lavish tip and grinned. It was worth something to him, too.

There were other things, too, to engage the vacationing naturalist's attention—the weather, for instance. To one who merely submitted to it, it would have been no more than hot; to one who cared to study it, it was interesting. The sirocco was blowing.

Behind the town of Algiers were dusty hills, behind these, higher ridges. Even farther beyond, the sand began, the sand that edged the vast desert sweep of the Sahara from which the hot wind periodically blew. In the desert the air, heated between sun and sand, rushes upward, and, seeking traveling channels, expands in the direction of the coasts. Air pouring in to replace that which ascends forms sandstorms and whirlwinds in the desert, while the hot air of the sirocco, flowing seaward, blasts the coast and sometimes carries across the Mediterranean into Southern Europe.

After dinner one evening Ditmars hired a car driven by a silent, reckless, wonderfully skillful young Moslem, and with his wife and daughters and a young French officer, he drove into the hills to sample the desert wind as it topped the crests. They lounged and talked on grass as dry as a mat and under a huge red moon, while the sound of a softheaded drum, beaten in the open quadrangle of some house in the hills, reached them across the slopes. Exhilarated by the dry heat of the wind, they listened to the Frenchman's account of sandstorms, when whirlwinds, looking much like waterspouts at sea, march slowly and with an incessant roaring hiss across the desert, seeming to uphold the seething clouds of yellow sand above them; and desert-wise travelers unfurl their sheets or *habaiah* and, spreading them over man and beast or vehicle, patiently wait in their shelter until the fury is past.

The desert, far from being devoid of animal life, supports many creatures ingeniously adapted to withstand its rigors, and Ditmars and the young officer compared notes on the jerboa, the little desert rat with tiny forelimbs, strong back legs and long tail that the curator once used to carry in his vaudeville kit; the limbless lizard that "swims" in the sand; the desert viper that does not glide but, like the sidewinder rattler of the American desert, flattens its body and progresses by throwing its loops laterally.

Dawn was not far away when the little party drove down the hills toward the city. Ditmars and the French officer were still hard at it, delighted with each other's knowledge and conversation. The younger man was beginning to look a little red-eyed and haggard, but Ditmars seemed as fresh as when he got up in the morning.

Beatrice yawned and whispered to her mother, "Probably Papa's the only man in the world who's actually rested by staying up all night talking shop."

The Mediterranean cruise was such a success that they repeated it the next year, taking a side trip to Scotland as well. Old John Ditmars, had he lived to see Raymond touring foreign parts with all his family, might have marveled at how bad a well-meaning father's advice can be. Contrary to all his forebodings, his son had achieved both professional recognition and financial comfort.

Ditmars might now have begun to slack off his work a little, but he didn't. The reason was, simply, that he didn't want to. The problems that regularly occurred in connection with it were as interesting to him as ever. He made lecture tours, gave a series of talks to the New York Biology Teachers' Association, helped design a new and larger structure on the roof of the Washington Irving High School to house the specimens lent by the zoo, cajoled cranky and dangerous animals, advised humiliated ladies how to deal with parrots prone to coarse language. Big or little, all problems got his personal attention. He was intensely proud of the organization which had given him the ideal opportunity of his life, and to the reputation of which he had contributed so much, and he believed that it deserved his best efforts all the time.

In the early fall of 1927 Ditmars attended the meeting of the experts associated with the Antivenin Institute. Some of the best medical minds in the country were backing the project and among the doctors at the meeting were Hans Zinsser, Thomas Barbour, Colonel J. F. Siler of the Army Medical Corps, Johns Hopkins' celebrated Howard A. Kelly, and, of course, Afranio do Amaral. With such men won to the cause he had been advocating for twenty years, Ditmars knew it was bound to succeed. The serpent farm at Tela, already established and operating under the direction of Mr. Douglas March, was a token of its progress.

Seizing a breathing spell the next spring, Ditmars went down to Honduras himself, to see the snake farm, film fer-de-lances which were common in the country, augment his tropical collection, and, of course, look around for a bushmaster.

His desire to exhibit another of the big vipers was growing stronger the longer it was thwarted.

This was Ditmars' second trip well into the American tropics. The first, to Brazil, had given him little opportunity really to get away from populous places and into the wilds. After this one, a willing victim of tropical enchantments, he never cared to go anywhere else again. The smothering verdure of tropical forests, the star-spangled depth of tropical night skies, the profuse variety of tropical animal life, all lured him back, again and again.

Assigned to a carefully screened little house just outside the United Fruit Company's domain, he set up his headquarters and unlimbered his cameras. Douglas March showed him the officers' quarters, the offices, the commissary, the railroad yards, the research hospital, the serpentarium, and promised to accompany him on a junket into the interior. Narrow-gauge tracks, over which fruit was hauled, led into outlying regions that were a naturalist's paradise.

At three-thirty in the morning the tropical dark was still thick as velvet. The headlights of the Ford, which was equipped with railroad wheels to run on the tracks, shone on little creatures that scooted silently away into the jungle or banana plantations on either side of the track.

March cheerfully told his party stories of accidents that had occurred on similar runs: how a car had been derailed when it ran over a big boa constrictor stretched across the tracks; and how another had collided, at a brisk speed, with a large tapir, which somersaulted into it and clawed the riders.

"But the most interesting thing that's happened along here lately," he said, "was a death that we helped solve. One evening not very long ago two native workmen had a row in a *cantina*. They traded insults, and would have fought, but their friends separated them. Later, they started for home within a short time of each other, both still pretty angry. One of them never got there. The next day he was found dead on the tracks.

"Everybody knew about the quarrel the night before, so the other fellow was arrested on suspicion of murder. He insisted that he didn't know anything about the affair. Now, the funny thing about it was that the dead man didn't have any marks of violence on him—no wounds or bruises. There was a bloody froth on his lips which might have suggested strangulation, but there were no bruises on his throat. His extremities were swollen, too, and that didn't fit into a death-by-strangling picture.

"Well, to cut it short, the body was brought to the hospital and an autopsy performed. Two small puncture wounds were found on one leg, and blood of a bright rose color was found in the cerebrum, heart chambers and other organs. It was perfectly plain the poor fellow had been bitten by a snake, probably a fer-de-lance. He had died, very likely, in a few minutes. The suspect's innocence was established, of course, but the fer-de-lance came within an inch of getting two victims."

"I suppose he was going around barefooted, the dead man?" Ditmars inquired.

March sighed. "Both the men involved were going around barefooted. Many of the Honduranians persist in it. That's one of the things we have to overcome if we're going to reduce snake bite mortalities in Central America."

The Ford sped down the smooth track into the predawn darkness. Finally March switched it onto a siding. "Here we are," he said.

The little group, moving through waist-high mist in the gradually increasing light, went down to the river where a small powerboat was waiting to take them on the next leg of the excursion. The current was quick, the mosquitoes were negligible, and a few caymans, a kind of alligator, sprawling on logs were the only visible animal life. Most of the party dozed until they reached Sampana, where a train was to pick them up, but Ditmars was too interested to rest.

Barefooted Honduranians in cotton trousers lounged around the tiny station and commissary, talking amiably and sharpening their machetes to razor keenness. Deep, melancholy groans poured forth alarmingly from behind the commissary shed. His light-blue eyes narrowing, Ditmars glanced sharply at the cheerful, bronzed workmen whetting their saber-like knives and blandly ignoring the heart-rending moans. Braced for he knew not what scene of carnage, Ditmars stepped unobtrusively around the shed.

Behind it were two howler monkeys, tethered by cords knotted through a staple in the wall. They were young, and in excellent condition, and were carrying on what was, for howlers, a low-toned exchange. Looking at him with shrewd, startled expressions, they reminded Ditmars of the beloved Red that Gladyce had raised. Feeling self-conscious, he rejoined his party.

"My imagination's running riot," he confessed smilingly to March. "The tropics must be getting into my blood."

At San Pedro Sula, where the party established its base, they met a doctor formerly from Memphis, S. M. Waller, who accompanied them on their excursions into the wonderful valley full of monkeys, peccaries, jaguars, tapirs, birds and venomous snakes. Traveling sometimes in cars with huge tires, sometimes in big canoes hollowed from a single mahogany log, they covered miles of jungle on their collecting trips. Perennially hopeful, Ditmars maintained a lookout for a bushmaster, with the usual lack of success. He was getting used to disappointment.

The most memorable expedition was to the Ticamaya Lagoon, eighteen miles distant, over a trail so rough that only Fords could cover it. They started with the first light, in order to be back again before darkness and mosquito swarms took over the jungle. It would never have occurred to Ditmars that automobiles could go where the Honduranian drivers piloted their sturdy Fords that day. Coming to a river with a steep bank, they charged right over it, landed upright and with a tooth-loosening jolt, and zigzagged confidently along the bottom of the shallow stream. Ditmars was unashamedly relieved later when the lead car, in which he was riding, stuck in a mudhole and had to wait for the second one to help it out.

"This will give me an opportunity to get some good shots of this jungle background," he remarked. "And to get my breath back," he added to himself. He caught the eye of the driver who grinned at him knowingly, almost as though he had heard his thought.

Setting up his camera, Ditmars filmed the long roots of aerial vines, dangling like loose cables from branches of towering trees; handsome palms with big leaves; and a toucan, dingy black and the size of a crow, honking stridently through its grotesque, brilliant, banana-long beak, as it examined them from a branch.

Wandering to the other side of the mudhole, Ditmars came upon a procession of parasol ants and filmed it. Each carried a bit of leaf in its mouth, holding it over its head like a tiny umbrella. They were on their way to their nest where they would stack the leaves, interlarded with a fungus spore which when imbedded, develops the smooth, carefully rounded mound that serves as their food.

The mudhole provided not only the occasion for a recuperative rest but, a few minutes later, an anodyne, too. The driver, who had been following Ditmars about with interest, pointed to another parade of ants pouring purposefully over the ground. They were army ants. He shook his head.

"Bad!" he exclaimed.

Inquisitive, Ditmars stepped up to the edge of the stream of insects to see if they would alter their course. On the contrary, they swarmed up his legs. Their bites burned like tiny touches of fire. He sprang out of their path and, dancing up and down, tried to brush the fierce little insects off.

"Jump in the mud," yelled the driver. Ditmars did.

The other car drove up just as the bedraggled curator was struggling out of the sticky mud.

"What in the world are you doing there, Doctor?" demanded March.

"Oh, I've just learned something I didn't know before about ants," Ditmars told him.

After three hours of alternate driving and stalling, they passed through the bamboo brake bordering the lagoon and emerged on its bank. Iguanas, basilisks and lizards lounged on dead tree trunks sticking up out of the water. In their bare branches spoonbills and white egrets perched, and long-legged herons, intent on their fishing, waded knee-deep in the water. Diving birds plunged for fish, avoiding the spots where the caymans lurked. Until late afternoon the party paddled around the lagoon in a dugout canoe and hunted over the tiny islands for snakes.

With the morning's difficulties clearly in mind, they started back while they still had three hours of daylight. First the lead car dropped into a hole and ripped off a tire. The sun was low by the time repairs were made. Then the other car slid into a hole. Only the afterglow lit the sky by the time it was engineered out. Two-thirds of the way still remained to go when, in the failing light, one of the drivers struck a root and bent his steering-rod.

Mosquitoes, with a sinister reputation as fever carriers, began to swarm around their juicy victims, who protected themselves, and remarkably altered their appearance, by smearing automobile grease from the hub caps on faces and necks. Because nobody had expected to be out after dark, neither mosquito nets nor flashlights had been brought along. It was the last time that Ditmars ever went on even a short excursion in the tropics without those two pieces of equipment.

While the drivers worked on the sick car, Ditmars and Doctor Waller, lighting their way through the pitchy darkness with a gasoline-soaked torch, walked three miles up the road to the nearest habitation. It was a one-room house, the dwelling of a hospitable Honduranian, his wife, and their many bashful offspring. Two wicks, burning in saucers of palm oil, lit the bare interior and disclosed the children in various corners, peeping from behind the few pieces of furniture.

The host set before his tired visitors some native bread and a can of frankfurters of pale and repellent appearance. They made Ditmars think queasily of a horrid story he had heard somewhere about a man on a camping trip who opened a can of frankfurters and found a human finger among them. Gingerly taking one, he glanced at Doctor Waller, who was eating ravenously. Ditmars, half-starved, applied himself to them. In a few minutes not a scrap was left.

An hour later, after an exchange of presents—snakeskins from host to guests, several dollars from guests to host—the cars came grinding over the trail and picked up the two men. They settled into the back seat with weary sighs.

"Quite a day!" remarked Doctor Waller. "Full of hazards and adventures."

"You know," Ditmars said, "I rather think the most hazardous thing we did was eat those canned frankfurters."

In addition to a good collection of reptiles and some interesting films to show lecture audiences, Ditmars returned to the United States with a large amount of venoms, extracted at the serpentarium, for the use of the Antivenin Institute.

Showing the array of dried poisons to his wife, he remarked thoughtfully, "I guess my days of milking snakes are over now, Clara. It was fun while it lasted, but I'm certainly glad that the whole process of antivenin production is on a business-like basis at last."

"Yes, it's fine that it is, but I'll bet you anything you don't stop extracting venoms. You've always taken such interest in doing it that you'll seize on some excuse for keeping right on with it."

The Antivenin Institute's figures for 1928 proved, incidentally, the value of this enterprise that Ditmars had so long urged: in that year six hundred and seven cases of snake-bite poisoning were reported in the United States. Four hundred and thirty-three of the victims were treated with specific anti-venin. Of those treated, only thirteen, or three per cent, died. Four hundred and twenty lucky people lived, and some of the responsibility for their hastened recovery or survival was due to Ditmars.

TWENTY-SEVEN

Mrs. Ditmars was a good prophet; or rather, she knew her husband well. In no time he was extracting venom again. This time it was for the most interesting scientific work with which he had ever been associated.

Dr. Adolph Monaelesser, a prominent New York surgeon, came to call on him at his office one day. He wanted a large and steady supply of cobra venom. His reason was interesting. Years before, during the Spanish-American War, he had seen a leper who had been bitten by a tarantula. Strangely enough, the pain of the unfortunate man's malady had almost at once diminished. It was a curious, isolated fact that the doctor had stored in his memory. Now he was ready to do some experiments based on that old observation, and he wanted a venom which, like cobra, acts principally on the nerves.

"I'll need a very considerable quantity, you understand, Doctor Ditmars," the physician explained. "Several long series of test injections on animals will have to precede any treatment of human beings."

"Of course," Ditmars agreed. He did not tell Monaelesser that he would rather handle a dozen diamond-back rattlers or moccasins than one cobra. Although he had occasionally had to help one to shed or treat its sore mouth, he always felt as if he were precariously holding a live, flexible cable that might whip out of his grasp at any moment.

Now, as in his younger days, he was glad to co-operate in another man's scientific work, and to undertake the task, dangerous even to such an expert as he, of extracting venom from cobras. A bite, if the fang entered a vein, would probably be fatal even if antivenin was promptly administered. With the savage, comparatively intelligent cobra, there was more than the usual risk of accident. At the Oriental branch of the Pasteur Institute at Bangkok, he knew that cobras were chloroformed before they were milked. It was hard on the reptile, safe for the operator. There, however, cobras were readily obtainable and the loss of a few serpents was of no moment. At the Zoological Park, on the other hand, it was quite another matter: it usually took several months of correspondence to obtain even one specimen, and each was expensive.

When his caller had gone, Ditmars stood outside the cobra cages and looked at the splendid series he had assembled.

"No, I can't risk it," he decided aloud.

"Risk what, Doctor?" Toomey, overhearing him, asked.

"Risk chloroforming them to extract the venom. It's too hard on them. I'd rather take the chance myself."

Cobras have shorter poison fangs than viperine snakes and rattlers, so Ditmars used a somewhat different technique in extracting venom. Instead of making the reptile bite through a parchment covering a tumbler, he thrust a square of stout glass against the fangs, forcing the snake to deposit its venom directly on the glass. Thus none of the fluid was absorbed by the parchment and the six or eight drops of almost colorless poison could be dried and scraped into a test tube without waste.

Cobra poison, unlike viperine poisons which can be removed from the drying glass in flakes by several light taps, sticks almost like varnish, and has to be scraped away. Unlike many venoms, it can be absorbed through the mucous membranes. To prevent splinters from flying upward into his eyes, where even a minute amount might do serious damage, Ditmars wore goggles. As a further precaution, he scraped the venom-covered glass while holding it under a flat piece of glass placed on blocks, like a small table, on his desk. He realized how inadequate his precautions were after scraping the first dried batch.

He had transferred it into a test tube, put away his improvised glass table and was already occupied with other work when the first symptoms hit him. He felt a dull pain in his chest, a pain that quickly assumed unpleasant severity.

"I must have inhaled some of the stuff," he realized at once. Not without alarm, he watched his symptoms. The pain increased, and he felt a slight difficulty in breathing. He was moderately scared until, at the end of a half-hour, he noticed that he wasn't feeling any worse, and the pain seemed to be subsiding. In another hour, it was gone, leaving him with nothing more than a disagreeable sensation of restlessness. That was the closest that Raymond Ditmars ever came, in all his years of handling snakes, to being poisoned by a venomous one.

The next time he scraped cobra venom, he did it where a broad band of sunlight fell on the work. Then it was easy to see particles of the poison, rising in a fine dust as he scraped, curl like smoke into the air. Opening the door and the window slightly, he regulated the gentle draft to carry the drifting venom away from him.

The experience alarmed his wife, but he was undisturbed by it.

"Now I know something about cobra venom I didn't know before, Clara. I learned it the hard way, but that's all right—once in a while."

Now the herpetologist not only milked reptiles but held "poison parties" in his office. They were not social gatherings, but meetings of medical men interested in learning more about venoms. The poisons of different kinds of reptiles were extracted at these sessions and their relative potencies given various chemical tests. Experiments were run to check Doctor Monaelesser's theory that poisons of different chemical composition cracked, as they dried, in characteristic and identifiable ways. Ditmars would be on his feet two or three hours at a time in front of an intent circle of doctors, handling an assortment of angry reptiles and extracting, in one afternoon, enough poison to kill every man in the room. It was exacting work, allowing of no slips, no momentary relaxation. Ditmars was confident of his skill, but never fell into the error of over-confidence.

Charles Snyder, unhappily, had not learned that primary lesson as thoroughly as Ditmars. When a rattler just out of its hibernating den struck him one spring day in 1929, he examined the small wound and decided that the penetration of only one fang was not too serious. By the time he had walked three miles to the nearest help, he realized his mistake, but the harm done by the snake's venom, unusually potent because it had been stored unused in the poison glands all during the hibernating season, was already irremediable. Snyder's over-confidence cost him his life.

At the same time that he was milking cobras for Doctor Monaelesser's experimental work in cancer, Ditmars was supplying another New York doctor, Samuel M. Peck, with moccasin venom. This hemorrhagic poison, it had been discovered, when greatly diluted and injected into the blood stream, helped to control excessive bleeding.

Discoveries in medicine rarely are achieved in one *coup,* but come slowly through long testing and experimentation. Now a new one, therapeutic uses for venoms, was developing, and Ditmars was contributing to it. These terrible poisons, which for centuries had caused only harm to humanity, were now being put to work in its service.

The Zoological Society, recognizing thirty years of faithful service, presented Ditmars with a gold medal in the fall of 1929. Will Beebe, Elwin Sanborn, the zoo's staff photographer; John Toomey, and eight others, also received the same token for similar service at the ceremony held in the Administration Building on the thirtieth anniversary of the zoo's opening. Mrs. Ditmars was remembered with a big bouquet of red roses, and a graceful little speech.

Driving home afterward, her husband said, "I'm glad the Society recognized your years of hard service, too, Clara. Really, you're the one who deserves the gold medal for being so sympathetic and helpful to a husband with such queer tastes. I'll bet no other woman in the world would put up with me, not to mention my poisonous snakes."

Another honor was conferred on him shortly afterward. The Lincoln Memorial College in Tennessee, in 1930, at the same time that it made Doctor Monaelesser an honorary Doctor of Science, gave Ditmars an honorary degree of Doctor of Letters "in recognition of his reputation as a student and scholar . . . and particularly his recent humanitarian work concerning the habits and perils of poisonous serpents." The academic world for years had recognized his unique contribution to zoological knowledge and visual education through his lectures and films. Now this acknowledgment of his recent contributions to scientific work was particularly gratifying.

The National Zoological Park at Washington was planning to open a new reptile house and its director wanted to exhibit a king cobra. Cobras are not serpents that you can pick up in the animal market any day in the week. When Ditmars heard that some had arrived from Singapore and were resting from their trip at an animal farm in New Jersey, he investigated the rumor. It was true. In his car he drove to New Jersey and purchased two large king cobras, one for the National Zoological Park and the other for his own collection, and carried them back to New York. They were the largest king cobras he had ever seen, and he was quite proud of his acquisitions.

Both snakes were thin, and suffering from dried skins,

which they had been unable to shed, and bruised snouts, acquired in frantically striking against their teakwood cases. By the time the new reptile house in Washington was ready to open, winter had set in and their several months of care and recuperation at the Bronx Zoo had restored the two serpents to beautiful condition.

Winter is a poor time for shipping snakes, especially tropical snakes. Ditmars did not dare express the cobra to Washington. He could eliminate practically every chance of its escape by careful packing, but there was no way of eliminating the chance of its spending a few icy hours bouncing around Washington in a delivery van. If it were chilled, it would be all up with the handsome king cobra. Considerable money, and a great deal of truly loving care, would go for naught, and the director of the Washington zoo would be a bitterly disappointed man.

"I don't see anything to do but carry it with me in the sleeper when I go," Ditmars told his head keeper.

"Why not?" agreed Toomey. "It's the only way to make sure that a change of temperature won't get it. Take it in an ordinary suitcase, and nobody'll ever know the difference."

Toomey produced a stout cloth bag, and the snake was put in it. Ditmars typed a legend in capital letters stating that the bag contained a living cobra on its way to the National Zoological Park in Washington.

"Just in case somebody grabs the wrong bag on the train— just in case," he explained.

The bag, conspicuously labeled, was then put in a hardy sole-leather suitcase that had withstood the maltreatment of baggage-smashers all the way from Algiers to Rio. Ditmars, carrying a suitcase harboring a cobra in one hand, and one harboring a tuxedo in the other, boarded the train to Washington, and went to bed.

He woke up once in the night, feeling chilly, and spread his overcoat on top of his blanket. Realizing that the snake was probably cold, too, he lifted it, suitcase and all, into his berth and tucked it under the covers down at the foot of the bed. Then he went back to sleep.

When, the next morning, he delivered the cobra to the zoo, the director was filled with gratitude.

"And that was quite a bold stroke of yours, Doctor, carrying it with you in your berth," he commented.

"There was nothing to it. It was just another small piece of hand luggage."

The director laughed. "You must be sure to mention, in your talk this afternoon, how our star exhibit traveled. It's the kind of story audiences love."

The audience did love it, too, when Ditmars told it at an appropriate place in his commentary on the five-reel motion picture he had prepared for the occasion. Quite to his horror, the newspapers also loved the story and they printed it all over the country.

The only people who didn't care much for it were the officials of the sleeping car company. From one of its officers Ditmars received a stern rebuke for allegedly having exposed passengers and crew to a horrible peril and having undermined the traveling public's sense of security. The communication closed with a severe admonition *never* to do it again.

Ditmars was irritated. There had been no danger, because his precautions had eliminated it. He wrote a long, explanatory letter in defense of his action, and this exchange of letters came to the knowledge of one of the big airlines.

Glad to take a dig at an earthbound rival, to obtain a passenger whose movements were always attended with publicity, and, finally, to express confidence publicly in an eminent naturalist, its president hastened to inform Ditmars that the airline would be happy to have him travel its planes with any kind of baggage he chose, including king cobras.

TWENTY-EIGHT

AIRLINE PRESIDENTS might offer Ditmars *carte blanche,* but ship captains were a different matter. They were always stern about his live cargoes, particularly when they included insects. The skipper of the ship he took back from Panama in 1931 was a case in point.

When Ditmars went to Panama that summer, Doctor Monaelesser asked him to bring back some tarantulas, so that they could use their venom in the experimental work. While the fangs of a tarantula are as large as those of some rattlesnakes, the holes through which the poison is ejected, the poison glands and the amount of venom are all much smaller than a rattler's. This is just as well, since it is a much more toxic venom than a rattlesnake's. A tarantula's bite is rarely fatal but, if the spider could inject as large a dose of its peculiarly poisonous secretion as a rattler, death would probably follow very quickly. During his stay in Panama, Ditmars succeeded in capturing two dozen healthy tarantulas, enough to provide venom for experimentation. Mrs. Ditmars, having hobnobbed with all kinds of poisonous reptiles during her married life, had no hesitation in sharing a cabin with this collection.

Tarantulas like to eat insects; indeed, they like to eat each other. Ditmars caught grasshoppers enough before sailing from Cristobal to keep them supplied as far as Havana, and shut each tarantula in a separate box to prevent the indulgence of its cannibalistic appetite. To his confusion, some kind of epidemic broke out among the grasshoppers and killed them all.

"This is terrible!" Ditmars gloomily inspected the deceased insects. "And they're all shriveled up, too—not even a decent corpse to offer the tarantulas. I wonder if I can get any roaches in the galley."

"Why don't you ask the captain? It can't do any harm to try," Mrs. Ditmars suggested.

"I think I will." Ditmars went out to seek the captain. In half an hour he was back, looking discountenanced.

"So it can't do any harm to try!" he growled.

"Why, Ray! What happened?"

"The captain became practically glacial when I asked if I might look in the galley for roaches. He assigned an officer to take me to inspect it, just to prove that there weren't any. It simply glitters with cleanliness. My poor little tarantulas will have to fast to Havana."

"Never mind. They'll live," Mrs. Ditmars said unfeelingly. She didn't care much for the poor little tarantulas, and she knew, too, that the doctor would manage somehow.

In Havana, Doctor Ditmars' first visit was to Father Lanza, director of the weather observatory at Belén University. It was late afternoon when he finished his call on the Cuban priest and was free to attend to the catering problem of his tarantulas.

In search of an empty tin can in which to place the insects he hoped to catch, Ditmars visited a number of shops. None had empty cans. Finally he bought one full of baking powder and walked down to the ocean front, where there was meadow grass, and paused under the wall of the old fort. Crickets were singing cheerfully all around, without premonition of his design.

The naturalist pried off the top of the can and dumped its contents, which gave off a white cloud, at the foot of the wall. He had just captured his first cricket and popped it into the can, when a sharp command barked in Spanish brought him around with a start.

A dramatic-looking sentry, complete with gun, was addressing him. Only then did Ditmars recollect that Cuba was in the midst of a political upheaval incidental to the ousting of its president, Machado, and that, to the suspicious eye—which is the kind of eye sentries are supposed to have—a stranger dumping a can of white powder against the wall of a fortification must look queer indeed.

The sentry was assuming a ferocious expression when an officer appeared. He looked intelligent, and was, but he was not smart enough to make head or tail of Ditmars' story, couched in very limited and halting Spanish, about crickets and baking powder and starving tarantulas. He listened, stern and puzzled, then delivered a rapid, emphatic speech. Ditmars understood not a word of it.

He decided to take a chance. He didn't know whether he had been arrested, or asked for an explanation, or told to go on home; so he bowed, lifting his hat cordially, and walked away with all the haste consistent with dignity. It was not until he settled back safely in a taxi that he relaxed.

The tarantulas were still hungry. They were needed for experimental work, and Ditmars was determined that the progress of science should not be obstructed by the lack of a few insects to feed them. He asked the steward's advice. The steward, who had a low opinion of the port of Havana, told him that there wasn't a café along the entire water front that wasn't swarming with roaches.

That evening Ditmars presented himself at a large café, ordered refreshments and asked the proprietor if he could look about in back for a few roaches. The proprietor gave him an indignant stare and said no. Ditmars sighed. He hadn't thought that the owner of a water-front restaurant would be so touchy.

Ditmars was beginning to feel desperate. Maybe, after all, he would have to feed half the tarantulas to the other half, in order to save any for the service of science. Across the room he spotted his taxi driver of the afternoon. He had seemed a sensible, sympathetic fellow, and he spoke good English. Dit-mars sat down with him and explained his difficulty. The driver shouted with laughter.

"You did not hurt his feelings! You frightened him. Here we have political trouble. Police, soldiers, they swarm all over. And now you appear and want to search his premises, and on such an excuse! He does not believe you—naturally! But I will arrange everything."

The arranging took time and tipping, but half an hour before sailing time Ditmars boarded the ship with a can full of enormous roaches.

The captain, learning of the new passengers the next day, took a dark view of them, and warned that he would take an even darker one if any escaped. Ditmars had not been handling insects from boyhood on for nothing: none did.

Shortly before the ship made port, the captain applied to Ditmars for advice about a marmoset he was bringing to a friend. He had been offering it the most tempting bits of fruit available, but it refused food and moped dismally.

"No wonder," Ditmars told him. "They don't care much for fruit. He's probably pining for insects. Some nice fat roaches, for instance," he added, smiling.

"Oh, no!"

"Oh, yes. Wait a minute." Ditmars went to his cabin and returned with the can of roaches. The ravenous little monkey greedily bolted them.

Abashed and revolted, the skipper declared, "I'm off marmosets for life!"

Khartoum was not the oldest resident of the zoo, but he was certainly the biggest. He was the African elephant that had been purchased from Carl Hagenbeck in 1907. Animals that had been on exhibit longer than Khartoum still survived. There were old Mose, the alligator, who had attended the opening ceremonies back in 1899 and whom Ditmars had patched up when he had been badly torn in a fight years before; Pop, a hairy-eared bear of kindly nature, a gift from Carl Hagenbeck in 1899; Buster, a big Galapagos tortoise, acquired in 1902; the good-natured Indian elephant, Alice, who in a rare moment of pique had almost dismantled the Reptile House; and an Isabella bear that had arrived in 1901, a scared, hungry cub, so tiny that the young assistant curator of mammals had carried her to her cage in his derby. All these animals were celebrated veterans now, and so was Khartoum, but that was not the important thing about the five-ton elephant. The important thing was his size: he was about to pass the record of the immortal Jumbo.

Jumbo was the great African elephant brought to the United States in 1882 by the incomparable showman, P. T. Barnum. He was generally conceded to be the biggest pachyderm ever exhibited in this country. His fame was such that "jumbo" became a word synonymous with immensity. Anything jumbo size was huge indeed. When Doctor Hornaday, with the precise curiosity of a scientist, asked permission to measure Jumbo in 1883, the *lese majesty* was met with a glare, and a *"Measure Jumbo? In-deed!"*

It was not until some hours after his death, in a train accident in 1885, that Jumbo was finally subjected to measurement. His height, it was announced, was eleven feet four inches at the shoulder.

In 1912, Doctor Hornaday, whose curiosity about Jumbo's size had never faltered, came upon and published information that a pole-vaulter connected with the Barnum and Bailey circus had, on the quiet, measured the giant in life and found him ten feet nine inches tall at the shoulder. There is little doubt that a dead elephant, lying on its side, flattens after a few hours. This fact would account for the discrepancy between the two measurements.

At the time of Doctor Hornaday's revelation, it occurred to no one to look on Khartoum, then a bit over six feet tall.

as a rival to the kingly Jumbo. It was not until 1916, when he was nearing nine feet, that that idea dawned. From then on Khartoum's height was the subject of intense interest at the zoo. His measurement was taken frequently. His growth was erratic and exasperating. In one year he might grow four inches, in the following, only one. Finally, on the watched-pot-never-boils theory, it was decided to measure him only once a year. When he had been in residence for twenty years, Khartoum was ten and a half feet tall. Jumbo had topped him by only three inches. Everyone at the zoo was thoroughly tense about the record when, on December 30, 1930, it was found that Khartoum now stood ten feet eight and a half inches, just half an inch under Jumbo's magnificent height.

When a climax has been fifteen years in building, it is likely to be terrific. Ditmars was keyed up to the highest expectation. Old circus people, familiar with the great Jumbo, were coming to the elephant's cage and saying that Khartoum looked every bit as big as the late, legendary record-holder. The whole staff was holding its breath, waiting for the year's end, when Khartoum would again be measured.

Early on Sunday morning, October 25, 1931, the telephone rang in Ditmars' home. It was Richard Richards, the elephant-wise keeper in charge of Khartoum.

"Doctor," he reported, "Khartoum's down. He looks bad."

Ditmars hurried to the zoo, but there was not a thing that he or the veterinarian could do. Khartoum could not rise. The superb elephant, within a fraction of an inch of breaking Jumbo's record, died of heart disease.

When a climax has been fifteen years in building, the anti-climax, too, can be terrific. This was one of the keenest disappointments of Ditmars' career as curator of mammals.

"Dear Doctor Ditmars: I am fifteen years old. I want to be a scientist. How do you become a scientist?"

It was a rare month when the doctor didn't receive letters from youthful admirers asking some such question. Remembering his own boyhood, he always took them seriously and answered with good advice. If the writer seemed particularly keen or intelligent, he would add, "Drop in and see me sometime when you are in the park, and we can have a little talk about your problem."

When the bashful young writers appeared, Ditmars would find out their special interests and advise them on what course of study to follow. Sometimes his young callers would take up time he could ill spare, but he didn't begrudge it. He knew the value of a little well-placed encouragement.

Arthur Greenhall, big-eyed and nervous, had come to see the herpetologist, by one of these special invitations, one day in 1929, when he was about seventeen. He wanted to be a herpetologist, too, and the earnestness of his intention touched the older man as much as his alertness impressed him. The curator let the boy hang around the Reptile House watching him work; he suggested studies for him to take; and, when young Greenhall went to Cuba on collecting trips, during his vacations, he gave him lists of creatures that the Reptile House would like to exhibit, and in return received some interesting specimens.

In the summer of 1932, when Mrs. Ditmars and the girls were unable to accompany him to Panama, Ditmars took Greenhall, knowing he would be a congenial and helpful companion. Both of them had the same attitude toward expeditions: they preferred to pay their own way, to be accountable to no one for their catch, and to be at liberty to change the object of their search at will. It was fortunate that they were so perfectly in agreement, particularly on the last point: they started out looking for bushmasters, and came back with grasshoppers.

In the thirty-three years of its existence, the Zoological

Park had received only three bushmasters, the last of them from the indefatigable Mr. Mole of Trinidad, twenty-one years before. It was natural that Ditmars, like other herpetologists, should regard these vipers as rare. It was an increasingly cherished ambition of his to exhibit one and persuade it to eat. Suspecting that, if one could be caught without shock, it might eat voluntarily, he wanted to capture one himself to test the theory.

When word came from Doctor Herbert C. Clark, Director at the Gorgas Memorial Laboratory in Panama, that eighteen of the supposedly rare serpents had been killed in three months in the course of work on the Madden Dam, Ditmars had to investigate. He and his assistant both thought that nothing could be more fun than to explore the prowling grounds of the largest venomous snake of the American tropics during their vacation. The papers learned of their plans. Soon the reading public was amply informed that Doctor Ditmars was going to Panama in search of a bushmaster, and the era of the bushmaster's fame opened forthwith.

The Madden Dam, across the Chagres River, undertaken by United States engineers, had already been started. The valley on either side of the river bed had been explored for a considerable distance to detect channels through which backed-up water might get by. An interesting fact had been discovered. Beneath the rich soil from which the tangled forest sprang, were great layers of limestone that protruded from the earth as seamed ledges with cavelike openings. Water worked past these underground shelves, so on both sides of the dam borings had to be made through which cement and clay were pumped into the washed-out underground spaces. The condition was troublesome for engineers, congenial for bushmasters. It was during the surveys for borings, which extended some distance into the jungly river valley, that the bushmasters had been killed.

The heads of the reptiles were sent to the Gorgas Memorial Laboratory which had offered a bounty on all poisonous snakes, in an effort to learn which kinds prevailed in the Madden Dam region. At the laboratory, Doctor Clark showed them to his visiting colleague. Ditmars was frankly impressed.

"I never expected to see such an array of bushmasters, dead or alive. We're going to have to revise our notions about this creature. If eighteen have been killed around the dam in three months, it isn't as rare as we've supposed; and to judge from the size of these skulls and skins, eight feet, not twelve, is about their greatest length. I'm curious to see what kind of terrain they like, too."

"They like ledgy outcroppings and sheltering crevices, much like the timber rattler of the United States. The engineers at the dam can show you just the spot where each of these was killed," Doctor Clark told him.

"Given the prevalence of these things, and accurate knowledge of their haunts, it will be pure bad luck if we don't come back with a live bushmaster."

Pure bad luck was just what it was, too. From the engineers' camp up the river they set out daily to comb the jungle for bushmasters, under the guidance of a young engineer and a Panamanian who was a skilled woodsman. Rapid tropical growth was already reclaiming the trails where men and machines had gone to sink borings, and the jungle was much less disturbed by the operations than Ditmars had expected. But no bushmaster was to be found, in fact no snake of any kind.

The little company searched the same fissured limestone shelves where specimens had earlier been killed, and found not a trace of the reptiles. Every evening they returned to the clearing of the engineers' camp, where screened houses, showers, refrigerators and pure running water that could be drunk from the tap made an unexpected patch of civilization in the jungle, and discussed what they could do to change their luck. Nothing helped, even starting out at twilight and searching well into the night, with the aid of lanterns that made flickering, spooky shadows in the jungle and reflected, in red and green gleams, from the eyes of startled birds and rabbits. They found no bushmasters, no snakes at all.

An old hand at collecting, Ditmars took the disappointment philosophically. If he couldn't have a bushmaster, he would settle for what he could get. He got an interesting collection of grasshoppers, including one specimen five inches long with very heavy, spike-studded legs. The insect, improperly grasped, struck out with its legs and drew blood from its unwary captor's hand.

"Kicked by a grasshopper!" Ditmars exclaimed. "There's something for you to write home about, Arthur, even if we don't lay eyes on a bushmaster."

"Don't worry about my having something to write home about," the young assistant advised. "I'm having a great time."

A by-product of this bushmasterless excursion was important. It was Ditmars' interest in bats. Exploring a cavern at the base of a limestone ledge, the collectors stirred up some big bats. As elusive as shadows, they evaded all efforts to grab them.

The young engineer squinted at them. "These are carnivorous, but they're not vampires," he said. "The vampire bat is barely four inches long and has a wing spread of a foot or a bit more. Doctor Clark is doing some work on them at the laboratory. Infected ones spread a fatal blood organism among horses. They live in some of these caves."

Ditmars reviewed his recollections of bats. "It's my impression that no vampire has ever been exhibited in a zoological garden," he said. "That gives us something to try for."

The search for the vampire, however, had to wait until the next year. Their time in the dam region was up, and they went back to civilization, carrying a collection of grasshoppers and the tidings that the search for the bushmaster had been fruitless.

The footnote to the trip was ironic. The ship bearing the thwarted snake hunters, with their load of insects, had barely cast off when a nervous steward appeared at Ditmars' cabin with the announcement that the ship's doctor wanted to consult him at once.

Ditmars found the physician in his cabin, calmly smoking. "Somebody brought me a snake, and it got away," he explained, "and I don't know what it is. It's over there." He pointed toward the bookcase. Reclining on a row of medical volumes was a harmless baby boa constrictor.

Ditmars picked the little creature up and smilingly let it twine around his wrist. "I came down here for the one purpose of catching snakes, Doctor," he said, "and at last I've caught one."

TWENTY-NINE

THREE YEARS HAD PASSED since Doctor Monaelesser's first use
of modified cobra venom in the treatment of human cancer.
With Ditmars' help he had conducted a series of experiments
in New York, and in co-operation with Doctor Calmette and
other French physicians he had in that time injected one
hundred and fifteen cancer patients in various stages of the
disease at the famous Salpetrière Hospital in Paris. He in-
corporated the results of his work in a paper which was read by
one of his colleagues, Doctor André Gosset, before the Academy of Medicine in Paris. Monaelesser himself was prevented
from giving the paper by ill health traceable, in part, to the
accidental inhalation of dried venom. As Ditmars had similarly
learned, it was dangerous stuff even to handle.

The claims made for the new treatment were properly
cautious: it did not cure, but it gave relief from pain and, in
some instances, the disease appeared to be checked after its
use—whether *because* of it or not, it was too early to say. The
publication definitely established cobra venom as an agent
to be taken into account in cancer therapy. Papers all over
the country seized on the news and it was widely, and for the
most part, accurately reported. Ditmars' contribution, in fur-
nishing much of the venom, was appreciatively recognized.

It was a contribution which was, however, behind him now,
and he was occupied with other things. There was the usual
yearly lecture tour, marked by a scrapy throat that felt as if
it would never come back to normal, and highlighted, in
Baltimore, by a luncheon given him by the great Doctor Kelly,
his associate in the Antivenin Institute. He had written
Strange Animals I Have Known, his first popular book. and

Snakes of the World, in 1931. Now he was working on a revision of *Reptiles of the World*, and writing the only piece of fiction he ever undertook, *The Forest of Adventure*, a story based on his own tropical experiences. He was building, himself, a professionally equipped weather station in his home, full of elaborate electrical instruments, so that he could the more satisfactorily indulge his interest in the weather. Besides, there were all the usual duties, problems and crises at the zoo, with which he had learned to deal with an almost mechanical smoothness. And there was, finally, the provocative news that Douglas March, director of the serpentarium in Honduras, was the proud captor of a live bushmaster.

"I've never been so jealous in my life," Ditmars confessed to his wife. " 'Bushmaster or Bust!'—that's my slogan for this summer."

"Better play it safe, Ray—make it 'Bushmaster, or Bats, or Bust,' " she advised.

Before going back to Panama, Ditmars brushed up on bats. A search of the records of other zoos indicated that no vampire had ever been exhibited. Little was known about them, other than that they flew at night, darted like rats over cavern walls and into crevices, bit sleeping human beings and animals, apparently fed exclusively on fresh blood, and had teeth so developed that the wound they inflicted bled freely for a long time. All the natural history books Ditmars consulted said, too, that vampires sucked the blood from the cut they made.

When Ditmars and Greenhall arrived at the laboratory in Panama, Doctor Clark was able to give them additional information and lore. He and his associate, Doctor Lawrence H. Dunn, were making a study of vampire bats and demonstrating that they spread by their bites a certain parasitic blood organism fatal to horses. The two doctors had caught several vampires and had succeeded in keeping them alive on defibrinated blood—that is, blood so treated that the substance causing coagulation is removed. They advised the naturalists to begin their search in the Chilibrillo Caves, near the valley of the Chagres River.

Encamped again with the Madden Dam engineers, their hosts of the previous year, Ditmars and Greenhall set out to search for bats. The trail leading from the camp toward the Chilibrillo Caves was ankle deep in mud, and flanked by tick-infested vegetation and occasional native huts, most of whose inhabitants suffered from a severe form of malaria. Altogether, it was not a healthful walk that the hunters took and it was a long, hard one. Approaching the caves, the trail gradually ascended. and after covering a steep, densely forested slope the party came on the entrances. They looked rather like deserted mine shafts.

The exploration of the caves was an experience both fascinating and nightmarish. The floor of the first was slick with red mud and broken here and there with deep wells down which water roaringly cascaded. Side galleries, into which their lights penetrated vaguely and for a few feet, led off into blackness. Enormous roaches, straw-colored and three inches long, and spider-like insects whose legs could easily have spanned a plate, swarmed over the wet limestone walls. The air of the cave, hot, sweetish and soporific, was fanned to a breeze, as the upturned flashlights showed, by two streams of bats flying in opposite directions. Festooned like funeral decorations from the ceiling of a great chamber, hung thousands of bats of different species, each in a cluster of its own kind. Big carnivorous bats with a spear-shaped appendage on the snout and villainous-looking teeth dangled upside down in clumps off the main chamber. Ditmars and his aides, with short-handled nets, captured eighteen of these creatures and caged them.

It was not until they entered the third cave, however, that they saw vampires scuttle over the walls and into crevices.

Arthur and Ditmars, the only members of the party with enough energy left to traverse the difficult entrance, were too tired to explore further, or try to capture any.

The next morning, with a slender Panamanian boy, they came back. There were no bats now of any kind in the gallery where they had seen the vampires. A passage full of deep, loathsome-looking water led out of the gallery in one direction, in another a narrow tunnel through which a thin man might wriggle. Greenhall volunteered to squirm through the tunnel. With some apprehension Ditmars watched his assistant's light blot out as his shoulders filled the narrow passage, and saw the soles of his shoes disappear when he squirmed into it. His voice came back, in a few moments, hollowly.

"Vampires in here, all right, and there's no exit. Stand by with your net in case they get past me." Then there was a long silence. Ditmars waited uneasily.

"I've got one!" the disembodied voice finally croaked. "And another."

A loud splash followed, and silence.

"Arthur! Arthur! What's happened?"

Arthur sounded disgusted. "I'm in the water, and I can't seem to get out."

The Panamanian youth, at a word from Ditmars, writhed into the hole. Ditmars followed. The opening was almost too small for his shoulders, but he felt responsible for Arthur. The young man might be in serious trouble, and he had to get through to help him. His belt was torn from its moorings and his shirt was almost in shreds when he finally squeezed through the rough, slimy passage into the chamber beyond. The guide, straddling a water-filled crevasse, was hauling Greenhall back to the ledge from which he had slipped.

"All right, Arthur?" Ditmars, panting, wiped perspiration and the cave's ooze from his face.

"I am, but I'm not so sure about these." Greenhall handed a mesh cage with two captives in it to the doctor.

For the first time in his life Ditmars got a close look at vampire bats. One of them seemed to be half-drowned; the other leered at him like a miniature bulldog.

"What ugly, wonderful little creatures!" he said admiringly.

He still wanted a bushmaster. The search, radiating from the engineers' camp, was as futile this year as last. Ditmars was disappointed, but not downcast.

"It's a good thing I amended my motto," he remarked to Greenhall as they were packing to leave. "At least, we don't have to bust."

Supplied by Doctor Clark with defibrinated blood and good advice, Ditmars sailed for New York with his eighteen carnivorous bats and two vampires. All survived shipment except one of the vampires. The New York Zoological Park had the distinction of being the first zoo in this country, or, so far as Ditmars could learn, anywhere else, to exhibit a living vampire. Ditmars' travels and finds were perennially favorite topics for newspapermen in search of a good feature, and this story was no disappointment. The vampire provided copy for weeks in every corner of the country where people read papers.

To her custodian she was an absorbing object of study. He put her in the Reptile House where a congenial climate was artificially maintained throughout the year. At night, the dripping of the freshly watered palms and the songs of tropical insects and croaks of Panamanian frogs must have sounded much like home to the stranger. Ditmars' hours became irregular, as they always did when something of particular interest was occurring at the zoo. Every night after dark he placed a saucer of defibrinated blood, obtained in bulk from a slaughterhouse, in her cage and stood by, out of the circle of the dim light bulb, in the hope of seeing her eat. For two weeks she disappointed him. She peered anxiously at the dish, crawled down the wall a few steps and then crawled back to her favorite corner to resume hanging upside down by one leg. Disappointed but still hopeful, the patient curator would go home to a pick-up dinner from the refrigerator.

Then one night the vampire ate in his presence. He had put the dish of blood on the floor of her cage and had stepped back out of the light to watch. The strange creature, finally accustomed to him, deliberately and easily descended the composition board, roughened to simulate limestone, at the side of her cage and advanced toward the dish.

The wings of bats are forelimbs terminating in much elongated webbed "fingers." The "thumb" is a claw used in climbing. The vampire's thumb, however, is a long, fleshy member, tipped with the usual claw. It had long puzzled scientists.

Most bats, in walking, appear to grovel over the surface, but the vampire, reaching the floor, folded her wings so that they looked like slender forelimbs and thrust her back legs straight downward. With her body hunched and elevated two inches above the floor, she approached the saucer with a soft, stalking gait, looking like a huge spider. The long thumbs, pointed outward and forward, served as feet. So the puzzle was explained, and an unpublished habit of the vampire bat observed. This, the watcher realized, was probably how she prowled over the body of a victim, seeking a place to slash with razor-sharp teeth.

Her method of eating gave him another surprise. The vampire did not suck up the blood as all the natural history books said. Indeed, her lips did not approach it. Instead, she lapped it with a rapid, darting motion of the tongue. After twenty minutes, her dish was empty. Then, lightly and silently, she projected herself into the air with spread wings, and, hooking a hind claw in the top of her cage, hung head downward to digest her meal.

Tired, hungry, and well satisfied with his evening's observations, Ditmars went home, turning over in his mind plans for a motion picture of the rare captive and a paper on her habits.

Making the picture was tedious and exasperating, but Ditmars worked at it until he had good results. He knew from experience that the time to photograph a rare specimen is as soon as possible. Once or twice he had delayed filming an apparently healthy animal, only to find it unexpectedly dead.

The bat, had she shared all the curator's scientific zeal, could hardly have been more co-operative. She ate, flew, and stalked for his camera. Then, early in December, a few days less than three months after her capture, she had a baby.

In his thirty-four years at the zoo Ditmars could not remember a more exciting birth, or an infant that aroused wider interest. Stories serious and facetious ("Stork Drops in on Vampire") appeared on front pages everywhere. The telephone rang all day long, relaying solicitous inquiries. Editorials in metropolitan dailies congratulated the zoo, the curator, the mother. Almost the only dissident was *The New York Sun*. It quoted Ditmars as saying, "The thing is worth its weight in gold," made a complicated and perhaps witty reference to the lately abandoned gold standard, and grimly prophesied that the bats would breed, multiply, escape and become a scourge to the nation that had received them with open arms.

The Sun need not have worried. Twenty-four days later the mother vampire was found hanging from her customary position from the top of her cage, dead of some unfathomable cause. The baby, inspiring a wild flurry of hope in curator and keepers, survived four days, then followed its mother in death to the pickling jar. Ditmars had become attached to the queer little creatures. He felt very bad indeed.

All that remained was to prepare his article. No scientist with any regard for his own standing or the feelings of his colleagues lays claim to a new observation without searching the literature of the subject to determine if anyone else has beaten him to the discovery. Ditmars put Greenhall to work reading everything available on bats.

Although the natural history books described the vampire bat as a bloodsucker, the young man found that the observation of its eating habits which Ditmars had hopefully thought original had been remarked before: Doctor Dunn, in a 1932 issue of a medical magazine, had pointed out that vampires lapped, not sucked, blood. But the use of thumbs as walking feet, the bat's technique of launching itself into flight from the ground, and the observations on the baby were all new.

Altogether, the investigation had been eminently worth-while in contributing new knowledge of the natural history of an economic pest serious in tropical America. It had also produced a unique visual record of the creature. And it had been great fun for Ditmars.

"I'm going back next summer and catch more of these creatures," he told his wife, adding wistfully, "and maybe I'll be lucky enough to get a bushmaster, too."

"Great Britain's hagiography of the living, *Who's Who in 1934,*" announced *The New York Herald-Tribune* on December 29, 1933, "arrived . . . yesterday, bearing stark evidence of a year of change."

Some of the evidence: Josef Stalin, Mickey Mouse and Raymond Lee Ditmars made this compendium of the eminent for the first time.

THIRTY

OTHER CHANGES, important to Ditmars, but not meriting international notice, were taking place. Beatrice was married, and had a daughter. It was a shock to him to realize that he was a grandfather of several years' standing. His hair, which had early thinned and retreated to leave a deep fringe around his head, was white now. His light, cool eyes were unfaded, and his slim hands, from long practice in handling reptiles, were more muscular than in his youth.

When Pop, the hairy-eared bear whose residence at the Park dated from 1899, crawled into his den and unobtrusively died one November day in 1933, the curator was jolted and saddened. His distress was compounded a few months later when old Mose, the survivor of many a bloody fight and of young Ditmars' amateur surgery, was found floating limply, white belly up, in the alligator pool that he had so often turned into a battle site.

It took incidents such as these to make the doctor realize that, although his enthusiasm for his work and for living was unabated, the years were creeping up on him.

An outsider, observing him on his first trip to Trinidad, on the *Nerissa* in 1934, might well have taken him for a boy of incongruously elderly appearance. In the few hours ashore at the various ports, he hunted ants and lizards with an entomologist friend who was taking the cruise. In Antigua he investigated the depredations of the mongoose; in Dominica he bought, for a paltry two and a half dollars, a dozen frogs of a kind so rare as to cost five dollars apiece in the United States; and, on Martinique, admired the impressive, sterile cone of volcanic Mount Pelée which, thirty-two years earlier, had erupted and exterminated a city of thirty thousand people. This was supposed to be a vacation trip—all rest, no business. But Ditmars had never been able to tell the difference between the two, and he could no more help collecting and exploring than breathing.

Surrounded by his wife, daughters and granddaughter, he was completely happy. He was going to visit a new place, and get some vampires and a bushmaster (with luck) and other tropical creatures. He was making this annual tropical run, as he always tried to do, in late August at the height of the hurricane season; and if his luck was really superb, they might run into a hurricane and he would get some exciting use out of the barograph, aneroid barometer, hygrometer and other weather instruments with which his cabin was habitually jammed on his ocean trips.

He knew, of course, that due to the development of radio, there was little likelihood of a ship's being caught in a hurricane nowadays. In all his trips into the region of tropical storms, Ditmars brushed the edge of one only once. Then he hovered over his instruments, watched it develop from the deck for a few hours, and became slightly seasick from the heavy swell. He enjoyed himself heartily, and thought longingly how magnificent it must be toward the storm's center which the captain was wisely avoiding.

Arthur Greenhall and William Bridges, a reporter assigned by *The New York Sun* to cover the expedition, had gone down several weeks in advance of the Ditmars party to start collecting in Trinidad and British Guiana. Greenhall was to get, if he could, a fer-de-lance, constrictors, anacondas, a giant centipede, vampire bats—and a bushmaster. This might sound like a large order for one young naturalist aided, or rather covered, only by a newspaperman, but Arthur was undaunted. Ditmars had given him introductions to scientific men in each place, and he knew that many specimens, often the best, are acquired by letting local people know that you want certain creatures and will pay for them. In a region where, like Trinidad, bushmasters and fer-de-lances are killed not infrequently on plantations, such word passed by the owner among the workmen is likely to produce a live specimen in a few weeks. While this method of collecting may, to the untutored enthusiast, appear disappointingly tame, it is not. The collector who wants to can still take the field in circumstances as uncomfortable and dangerous as he pleases, and catch all he can himself. By getting other people on the job for him, he simply multiplies his chances of success.

As the *Nerissa* came into Port-of-Spain, Ditmars, putting the finishing touches on his luggage, was wondering aloud about Greenhall's success.

"I suppose it's too much to hope that Arthur will have got a bushmaster," he said.

"Oh, let's hope, anyway," Gladyce answered. "It's fun to hope."

With a rattling of chain, the *Nerissa* dropped anchor. A few minutes later a steward rapped on the door, to announce:

"Professor Urich has come aboard to meet you, sir."

Professor F. W. Urich, former government entomologist in Trinidad, was the man who knew probably more about the natural history of the island than any other living person. Ditmars had had considerable correspondence with him, and had given Greenhall a letter to him, but he had never met him.

Now he made his way up on deck and addressed the heavy-set, grizzled man with the lined, sun-browned face.

"Professor Urich?"

"Doctor Ditmars!"

They shook hands and exchanged pleasantries.

Gently, Professor Urich dropped his bomb:

"Well, we have a nice little bushmaster for you, Doctor."

The shock left Ditmars speechless for a moment. The quest

of twenty-three years terminated in a few quietly spoken words!

"No!" he exclaimed weakly. "How did you catch him?"

Urich smiled. "I didn't. He's a foundling. He was left on my doorstep. A Negro brought a box a couple of days ago while I was out and handed it to my cook with the warning that there was a bushmaster in it. He was scared to death, and fairly ran off, without any more explanation than that. I'll find out where it came from eventually, but it will probably take a little time."

"Well, that's collecting," Ditmars sighed. "For more than twenty years I've been trying to catch a bushmaster, and now somebody hands me one in a box."

The capture of the bushmaster was enough in itself to make the expedition an unqualified success, but there was much more than that to take back. There was a big fer-de-lance which Greenhall had snared, too full of water rat to offer any opposition, on the bank of a jungle pool; four giant Orinoco turtles, creatures so rare that none was on exhibit anywhere in the United States, which Greenhall had excitedly spotted and purchased for ten shillings each from their bored owner, who kept them in a little fountain in a Port-of-Spain yard; a crate of blue land crabs; a case of tarantulas; half a dozen big carnivorous bats; four vampires; ten boxes of snakes; a horrifying-looking centipede eight inches long, and a number of other good exhibition specimens. In addition, Bridges and Greenhall, in the most agonizingly insect-ridden night of their lives, had obtained what they believed to be the first picture ever taken of a vampire—the professor's captive vampire, Tommy—feeding on a live victim, a white goat.

The few days in Trinidad passed quickly. Ditmars and the professor were together most of the time, driving on the island and talking mostly about the vampire bat, known locally as "the surgeon." Here, as in Panama, it was a disease carrier, the disease being, in this case, paralytic rabies fatal to cattle and human beings. Knowing that his observations carried out on only one specimen were, scientifically, inadequate for final conclusions, Ditmars was interested to learn that Urich's observations, made in the course of a long study of the disease and its carrier, tallied with his own.

Urich also told him that the *Vampyrus spectrum*, a creature with a three-foot wingspread thought formerly to be *the* vampire bat, to which Ditmars had recently referred as a huge but harmless fruit eater, was in fact and contrary to popular impression a ferocious carnivore.

"There's my next summer's subject!" the doctor exclaimed. "*Vampyrus spectrum* has never been exhibited alive in the United States, I know."

"Fine!" Urich beamed. "Then we can look forward to having you back with us next year."

When Ditmars and his party steamed north in the *Nerissa* a few days later, they had with them the finest tropical collection that the Bronx Zoo had obtained in years. The public notice it got was almost overwhelming. It was proclaimed nationally that Ditmars' four vampires had traveled in his daughters' stateroom and annoyed them by splashing blood all over the tub as they lapped it; and the "fertile ants" (fer-de-lance) had been readily caught because "they" were lethargic from a recent meal of water rat (this curious statement brought Ditmars numerous inquiries from puzzled naturalists). As for the bushmaster, he was the climax, the hero, of every story. The press the viper got would have turned the head of any less self-sufficient celebrity.

The next summer it was Trinidad again, this time with Mrs. Ditmars and Gladyce. *Vampyrus spectrum,* and again the bushmaster, were the objects of search.

The file on the young bushmaster Ditmars had brought home the previous summer had been completed, and lamentably closed. Professor Urich had advised him that it had been captured by an intrepid American driller when it wandered into the engine house of an oil-drilling outfit in the wilds of Trinidad. Late one afternoon a short time after receiving this news, Ditmars had noticed that his prize exhibit seemed to be in distress. It was gasping and gaping as though it was having difficulty in breathing. The next morning it was dead, killed, as the autopsy revealed, by a heavy infestation of parasitic worms. It was a bad blow, but not irremediable; with the professor's help, Ditmars was confident that he could soon obtain another specimen.

This time he wanted a baby bushmaster—not because babies are cute, but because he thought there was more chance that a baby, captured without shock, would eat. There was only one record of a bushmaster's eating voluntarily in captivity: Mr. Mole had once had a specimen that took just one mouse before dying of an injury. Ditmars' own had been, with greatest care, force-fed—with greatest care, not only because a bushmaster is a highly dangerous reptile, but because the very fragile neck is likely to break when subjected to restraint. Young bushmasters are hard to find; where they go after hatching is a mystery. Professor Urich, however, hopefully passed the word around that Ditmars wanted a juvenile bushmaster.

When Ditmars' ship anchored in the Port-of-Spain harbor, Professor Urich again came aboard to meet him, and again, with the same calm, announced that he had a bushmaster— this one a baby, captured when newly hatched. And it had already eaten twenty-five mice since its capture!

"What wonderful news! How was it caught?"

"You'll be disappointed," Urich warned. "Early in February the wife of a consular official found it curled up in a palm leaf in her front yard. The leaf had a long, stiff stem, so she picked it up pretty much like a frying pan and slid the little snake into a hat box. It was as simple as that. For a while it looked as though it weren't going to eat, but after two months it took its first mouse, and it's eaten well ever since."

"I'm not disappointed. It's a dull story, and that's what's good about it. Nothing exciting happened, so the snake didn't sustain any shock."

"That's right. It's a beauty, too. I call her Cleo. The way she moves her head reminds me of an Egyptian dancer. The newspapers regard Cleo as Trinidad's leading citizen."

"She'll certainly be the leading citizen of the Zoological Park. All I need now to be entirely happy is some *Vampyrus*."

The capture of the first pair of *Vampyrus spectrum* bats was almost as easy as that of the bushmaster. The young Trinidadian who worked for the professor and served Ditmars as guide found them in a hollow tree by the roadside an hour's drive from town. Before an audience of goggling, bare-footed children and an immaculate, white-clad native police-man, Ditmars and his guide stepped into the big hollow at the base of the tree and snared the two creatures in nets. The capture of the second pair, the following day, was accomplished with only a little more excitement: the captors were bitten by "stingless" bees.

Again Ditmars returned to New York, able to present the zoo with another "first time exhibited" creature, the *Vampyrus spectrum* bat.

Going yearly to the tropics was a firmly established habit with the curator, and Trinidad became his favorite tropical hunting ground. The island, having a pitch lake with an inexhaustible supply of asphalt, has good roads extending even into its wilder regions, and travel on them greatly reduced the hardships of tropical collecting. Instead of slogging afoot through a wet, dense jungle, carrying a load of collecting equipment and cameras, Ditmars could put his gear in a car and drive wherever he wanted to go. Almost everything a naturalist's heart desired was to be found within a few hundred yards of a house or a road.

In 1934 Greenhall had found the rare Orinoco turtles in a fountain in the yard of a Port-of-Spain club. The following year, Ditmars had caught his first pair of *Vampyrus spectrum* bats in a hollow tree by the roadside, and the little bushmaster had been picked up in a front yard. Returning again, in 1936, in search of the rare and curious *Pseudis paradoxis*, the paradox frog that "grows up" by shrinking from a fourteen-inch tadpole to a two-inch adult, he found the prize in a pond within sight of a farmhouse. This kind of collecting produced rare and desirable specimens, and was often no more arduous than a drive in the country. Still an indefatigable naturalist as he entered his sixties, he was, however, willing to save himself time and needless exertion.

These "vacation" trips to the American tropics, regular features of the last few years of his life, were, in effect, variations on a theme, variations pleasantly recounted in his own books. Different members of his family accompanied him, and different creatures were the object of his interest, but each time he came back with new specimens and new data to add to the body of knowledge that makes up natural history.

His observations at the zoo on the behavior, breeding habits and longevity of his captives—vampire bats, bushmasters, paradox frogs, *Vampyrus spectrum* bats and the rest of the strange creatures—added further to it. His contributions gained rapid currency not only among scientists but, because of the popularity of his motion pictures, lectures and books, among the lay public whom he always thought it most important to reach.

With his happy flair for popular education, he designed his books both to amuse and inform. Adventures grave and comic were dropped into chapters describing the habits of animals or the proper way to approach a scientific problem.

The talent for urbane and entertaining writing, sharpened by use, was now employed with increasing effect in the final phase of his lifelong campaign to arouse popular sympathy toward all forms of animal life, including those usually thought repulsive. *Confessions of a Scientist* was published in 1934, and so was *The Book of Zoography,* suggested by the artist, Helene Carter, who illustrated it. She and Ditmars enjoyed working together, and the next year collaborated in *The Book of Prehistoric Animals.* In 1935, too, there was *Snake-Hunters' Holiday,* with William Bridges, by then the zoo's curator of publications. The next year *Reptiles of North America,* a revision of the old *Reptile Book,* appeared, and *The Book of Living Reptiles,* illustrated by Helene Carter. The year after that he brought out *The Making of a Scientist* and, again in collaboration with Bridges, *Wild Animal World.*

That his long campaign was having results was indicated by an editorial in the spring of 1937 in a metropolitan paper. Just thirty years after the publication of *The Reptile Book,* one purpose of which was to create sympathetic public interest in snakes, one of New York's leading dailies was able to hail the beginning of the snake-hunting season with the statement ". . . snake hunts are growing positively popular . . ." and to add that publishers were reporting that the word "snake" could now appear in the title of a book without insuring its prompt oblivion. Uncritical shudders at reptiles were giving place to intelligent interest in them. The day of the editor, once known to Ditmars, who had rejected the manuscript of a story about a snake by throwing it on the floor and jumping on it, was past. Now school children could hunt snakes as a matter of course and without being considered horrid little eccentrics. People were beginning to understand that most reptiles were harmless, interesting creatures and economically important, and that even the worst of them, the venomous ones, have valuable scientific uses. The changed attitude was traceable in very large part to the influence of Raymond Ditmars.

In spite of the pleasure the realization of this fact gave him, 1937 was still a bad year for the doctor. Two of his oldest associates, Doctor Hornaday and Madison Grant, president of the Zoological Society ever since its founding, died; so did Doctor Charles Noback, the young veterinarian who had taken Doctor Blair's place when he became director. Ditmars himself, suffering from an abdominal ailment, had little enjoyment out of his trips to Haiti and Panama that summer and, shortly after his return, had to go to the hospital for an operation. Daunted by the series of losses, everyone at the zoo was thoroughly apprehensive, and so was his family. Ditmars thought there was much ado about nothing, or successfully pretended to. The operation, however, was a complete success.

THIRTY-ONE

THE YEARS OF LECTURING had put a serious strain on the doctor's throat. He had addressed audiences in the best-equipped auditoriums in the country; he had also addressed them in halls where the acoustics were poor and where no microphones amplified the sound of his voice. Before or after a lecture he usually had to attend a reception by the sponsors of the occasion and talk some more. He would come home from his tours with his throat aching, his voice hoarse.

"I'm worried about you, Ray," Mrs. Ditmars finally told him. "Your throat goes back on you so easily these days."

"Easily!" he croaked. "After more than forty years of constant lecturing? Do you call that easily?"

"Hush. Don't argue. Just rest it."

"I'm not arguing!" he began, then smiled. "You're just teasing me, Chicky. You mustn't worry, though. It'll be all right again after a good rest in Trinidad this summer."

The trip to Trinidad in 1938 with the entire family, including his son-in-law and granddaughter, was fun and, in the main, successful. He brought back more paradox frogs and vampires, and a colony of parasol ants. The creatures that received the most attention from the press, however, were the giant frogs, not rare, but golden in color and showy exhibit specimens. The poor things never arrived: taken with a hankering for frogs' legs on the voyage back, Ditmars had every one of them cooked and served. He arrived in New York, unrepentantly smacking his lips, to greet reporters with the astounding news that he had eaten his trophies.

The only unsuccessful feature of the trip was that it didn't seem to do his voice much good, but in the busy and interesting months that followed, he paid little attention to the difficulty. For one thing, the presence of the first panda ever to be exhibited in a zoo was something to take the mind of any curator of mammals off a sore throat. For another, he was busy with insects. Long since having ceased to regard them with the jaundiced eye induced by mounting thousands of dead ones, he had recently collaborated with Helene Carter in *The Book of Insect Oddities*, and he now worked to establish the parasol ant colony. His success was complete: the interesting insects took to the specially designed cage he had built for them and were soon busily going about their affairs just as they did in their natural state. Another of his books appeared, *The Fight to Live*, and got the usual cordial reception. But the most memorable event of the year—indeed the most stupendous of many years—was the hurricane that struck the New England coast in September.

"I know it's going to hit, Clara!" Ditmars exclaimed after a session in his weather station.

"But don't they usually turn off before they get this far up the coast?" Mrs. Ditmars inquired.

"Not this one," he insisted, and bombarded her with instrument readings that she didn't understand. It did hit, too, with a ferocity that made the storm of 1893 seem just a breeze. Every possible minute of it Ditmars spent over his instruments or at the windows, marveling at the furious spectacle. When it was over he felt spent, just as he had as a child with the passing of a storm.

"That's the most impressive piece of weather I've seen in forty-five years," he sighed, lighting his pipe and wearily relaxing, "and I'll probably never see anything to equal it."

The lecture tours in fall and spring aggravated the condition of his throat, but he shrugged it off.

"It's a confounded nuisance. But even if I can't talk as much as I like, I can still write all I want to."

So he worked, with Lee Crandall, curator of birds, on *The*

Guide to the New York Zoological Park, and on his own
Field Book of North America Snakes, in which he employed
for the first time a new technique of reptile study he had
developed. For a number of years he had been preparing
sections of snakes with special care to preserve all details of
pattern and color. This collection he kept in special solutions
and in darkness to insure pliability and retard fading. He
used photographs of it, excellent because of their clearly
defined details and true colors, to illustrate the text of the
Field Book.

The New York World's Fair, opening in the spring, gave
him an opportunity to point a moral, in his unobtrusive and
good-humored way, to the assembled nations exhibiting: he
put on a display showing how unrelated animals live in amity
together. It also gave him the opportunity to indulge his old
passion for trains. In the railroad exhibit he spent hours
examining the lines of cars, hanging lovingly over the engines, exclaiming over every familiar, remembered detail,
until Gladyce, his usual companion, tottering with exhaus-
tion, would say:

"Pop, I'm about dead. I *have* to sit down a while."

He would look at his watch and exclaim, always with surprise, "No wonder, poor girl! It's way past lunchtime. We'll
look at something else this afternoon and come back here
tomorrow."

The usual trip to Trinidad in the late summer, productive
as it was of snakes, bats and insects, again failed to benefit
Ditmars' ailing throat as much as his family had hoped. Determined not to be hampered in his work, he insisted on making the customary lecture tour that fall. It was the last one
his doctor allowed.

"No more lecturing!" The throat specialist was emphatic.
"One of your vocal cords is seriously strained and enlarged. I
can treat it, but only you can give it the best treatment—
complete rest."

"How complete?"

"No lectures, no long discussions or conversations, no telephoning. Save all the words you can. Say 'yes' instead of 'yes indeed.' When you can make a nod do in place of 'yes,' nod."

"Great Scot! You do mean complete, don't you?"

"I do." The doctor looked at him doubtfully. "I don't suppose I could get you to go into seclusion for a year—entirely give up seeing people? It would mean leaving your work."

Ditmars shook his head, smiling. "No. I don't suppose you could. I'd as willingly go into a straitjacket for a year. But I'll follow to the letter any other orders you give me."

Gladyce began to go to the park with her father every day just as she had done when she was a little girl. Now she acted, as far as anyone could, as his voice. Familiar with the workings of the zoo and knowing a good deal of zoology, she handled his telephone calls, dealing with all the questions, important and trivial, that he had answered himself every day for forty-one years.

To a man accustomed all his life to expressing himself, having to refrain from ready speech was a strain. Ditmars felt it, betrayed it only occasionally by biting his pipestem with irritation. The disability was, he felt, a tiresome nuisance, but one to which he could, with some effort, adjust himself. It was not, after all, permanent, and he could speak when he wanted to.

"I'm afraid it's hard on you, though, Gladyce, getting up so early and spending all day in the office."

"I love it, Pop," she said truthfully.

In everything not involving the use of his voice, it was business as usual with Ditmars. He arrived at the park at his regular time, did the regular day's work, and, in the evenings, frequently spent a couple of hours in the motion picture studio, the weather room, or his study. Several batches of snakes had been hatched or born in the Reptile House, so he

247

was doing research into the feeding habits of young serpents. He was also preparing a new book, *Animal Kingdom*. Another problem that occupied him was the development of a department of insects. Ever since his connection with the zoo he had arranged frequent insect exhibits; now he wanted a full-fledged department.

One man, even a man with the energy of Raymond Ditmars, can get through only so much work. His new project took up so much time that, to devote himself more effectively to it, he resigned as curator of mammals in 1940 and became curator emeritus. As a rebellious boy he had dawdled over trays of dried insects at the American Museum of Natural History; now as a gray-haired man he was back to insects again. But there was a world of difference: these were alive. He had never been able to feel very much enthusiasm for dead things; it was studying and understanding the living creatures—insects, reptiles, mammals—that had always appealed to him. With all the zeal of his earlier years he applied himself to developing the department of insects.

The yearly trip to the tropics had to be omitted in 1940 because of the work and changes at the zoo incidental to a new administration. The one to Trinidad the next fall, however, produced a fine collection of insects as well as bats and paradox frogs. Eager, as always, to show his exhibits against backgrounds resembling their natural habitats, Ditmars had a plan for displaying the vampires in an artificial cave populated by all the insects that actually live in a real vampire cave.

Accompanied by Gladyce, he concentrated on vampires and the insects that went with them. United States Army troops were then stationed in Trinidad and, in an effort to eliminate paralytic rabies, the medical corps was waging a war of extermination against vampires, and waging it so successfully that, Ditmars estimated, vampires would be very rare in another two years. With the help of the congenial medical

248

officer directing the campaign, he obtained nineteen vampires to add to those already in residence at the zoo, and an array of insects for the cave.

Again he seined the only pond on the island where the paradox frog bred, and was rewarded by one specimen. He climbed a four-thousand-foot mountain to catch a dozen roaches as long as his finger, in a clear pool overhung with orchids; he collected tropical snakes, another colony of parasol ants. It was a grand vacation.

"Fifteen hundred specimens, altogether; that's a pretty good catch, isn't it, Gladyce?"

"Yes. It reminds me of those trips into New York State we used to take in the old Rambler when Beatrice and I were little. Remember how we'd all scramble up and down hills catching snakes and bugs, and come back with hundreds of them—and a leafy tree that made everybody gape at us as we drove down Broadway? What fun it was!"

"Indeed it was!" Ditmars tipped his hat over his forehead to shade his eyes from the glitter of the sun on the water and lounged comfortably back in his deck chair. "Everything we do together is fun to look back on. That's the nice thing about us as a family, don't you think? We enjoy the same things, and we've always taken our fun together—and our hard luck, what little there's been of it. Often I think we must be the luckiest family in the world."

"I'm sure we are."

"Now let me tell you what I've thought of for our trip next fall: you and Mama and Beatrice and her family and I . . ." he went on, outlining his plan for the coming vacation, while the cruise ship, churning through the blue Carribean, carried him northward for the last time.

Back at the zoo, he was busy again with his usual work, and with preparing a new book, *Twenty Little Pets*, with Helene Carter. Still under orders to use his weakened voice as little as possible, he let Gladyce do much of his talking for him, and faithfully refrained from speech wherever he could.

He was beginning to feel that there had been an improvement in the condition of his throat when, in February, 1942, he picked up the grippe and developed bronchitis. After being sick a few days he made up his mind.

"It'll be so much easier for everybody, Clara, if I just go to the hospital until I shake this thing," he told his wife. "Doctor Hunt's too busy to come all the way out to Scarsdale every day just to see me. I'll go to St. Luke's and he can look in on me without losing any time. And the household won't get all mixed up, the way it always does when it revolves around a sick person."

So, concerned only with being as little trouble as possible to anyone, Ditmars went to the hospital.

The hospital was, of course, the best place for him; still, he didn't get rid of his bronchitis. Instead, it dragged on for two months. Finally, bad coughing spells made his throat hemorrhagic, and pneumonia set in. His own determination and his doctors' skill, aided by the powerful sulfa drugs pulled him through the crisis.

Happy and hopeful after their bad scare, his family confidently expected his full recovery. It was a stunning shock when the relapse came. This time all the skill of the doctors, all the courage of the patient, all the potent miracles of modern pharmacy that went into the struggle for Raymond Ditmars' life were not enough. At eight o'clock on the morning of May 12 he died.

He died, but there remained the results of years of valuable work. In his modest and willing way, he had contributed to two important medical advances: the development of antivenins and the therapeutic uses of modified venoms. His patient, astute observations of some of the least-known of the earth's creatures had greatly extended the boundaries of our knowledge of natural history. His educational work, through motion pictures, lectures and writings popular and formal, had created, out of indifference and even distaste, a wide popular appreciation of the animal world he had so sympathetically championed.

And, what would have pleased him most, snakes had acquired a respectable status in that world. Little boys could hunt them in the springtime; school children could handle them as a matter of course in zoology courses; youthful students, sensing their curious fascination, could analyze them in learning their strange habits and their economic uses—all because, fifty years before, a young boy named Raymond Ditmars had decided that, above everything else on earth, he wanted to spend his life studying reptiles and justifying their ways.

INDEX

Date Due